THE COLOR OF OUR SHAME

The Color of Our Shame

RACE AND JUSTICE IN OUR TIME

Christopher J. Lebron

OXFORD
UNIVERSITY PRESS

OXFORD
UNIVERSITY PRESS

Oxford University Press is a department of the University of Oxford.
It furthers the University's objective of excellence in research, scholarship,
and education by publishing worldwide.

Oxford   New York
Auckland   Cape Town   Dar es Salaam   Hong Kong   Karachi
Kuala Lumpur   Madrid   Melbourne   Mexico City   Nairobi
New Delhi   Shanghai   Taipei   Toronto

With offices in
Argentina   Austria   Brazil   Chile   Czech Republic   France   Greece
Guatemala   Hungary   Italy   Japan   Poland   Portugal   Singapore
South Korea   Switzerland   Thailand   Turkey   Ukraine   Vietnam

Oxford is a registered trade mark of Oxford University Press
in the UK and certain other countries.

Published in the United States of America by
Oxford University Press
198 Madison Avenue, New York, NY 10016

© Oxford University Press 2013

First issued as an Oxford University Press paperback, 2015.

Library of Congress Cataloging-in-Publication Data
Lebron, Christopher J.
The color of our shame : race and justice in our time / Christopher J. Lebron.
pages cm.
Includes bibliographical references and index.
ISBN 978-0-19-993634-2 (hardback); 978-0-19-026467-3 (paperback)
1. African Americans—Social conditions— 21st century. 2. African Americans—Politics and
government—21st century. 3. Racism—Political aspects—United States. 4. Equality—
United States. 5. United States—Race relations. I. Title.
E185.615.L39 2013
305.896'073—dc23
2012047295

It seems to me that the real political task in a society such as ours is to criticize the workings of institutions, that appear to be both neutral and independent; to criticize them and attack them in such a manner that political violence [that] has always exercised itself obscurely through them will be unmasked, so that one may fight against them.

—MICHEL FOUCAULT *(debate with Noam Chomsky)*

Human nature being what we know it to be, there were, inevitably, examples of selfish fancies, feigned distractions, treacherous appeals to an all-too-easy sentimentality, deceptively seductive maneuverings, but there were also cases of admirable selflessness, of the kind that still allow us to believe that if we persevere in these and other such gestures worthy of abnegation we will, in the end, more than fulfill our small part in the monumental project of creation.

—JOSE SARAMAGO, *Seeing*

Contents

Preface

NOW WOULD BE a good time for us to become acquainted, for you are about to join me on a philosophical journey I began in 2005. I had entered the ranks of MIT's graduate program in Political Science the year before, after graduating from Baruch College, a part of the City University of New York—a low-cost, public university system. And all was not well. With all due respect to Baruch, a fine institution, MIT represented a significant departure and is in a rarefied league comprised of an elite community, from faculty all the way down to first-year undergraduates. From a strictly intellectual point of view, it felt a bit like stepping into an empty elevator shaft. Growing up where and how I did (lower class SES in the Lower East Side of Manhattan), I was ill-prepared for the intellectual and academic life demanded by MIT. But it is not strictly this part of the experience to which I am referring. Although I will return to the nature of the intellectual departure, the more immediately affecting departure was sociological.

When I entered MIT's program, my intention was to pursue applying John Rawls's work to the international arena because I had been fascinated for some time with the distinction between murder within a polity and the sanction to kill others in war so long as they were others, thus enemies. It is fair to say that this project reflected a personal fascination and I thought Rawls would be a good walking partner in exploring it.

But, personally, other matters became not merely interesting but urgent.

MIT has a dorm that is known as Chocolate City. Know why it's called that? Well, because of the relatively few brown folks who attend and have historically attended, that's where they tend to live. I would not have believed this story when I first heard it (I mean, it's the twenty-first century, right?) if it wasn't for the fact that one of my first interesting experiences on campus was that random brown folks were sure to greet me as if to say, "Hey, you're here too!" This was strange for me as I grew up in New York City where the first lesson is, greet no one unless you know that person. But, soon my own experiences would come to mirror the peculiar nature of this kind of phenomenon.

I am an introvert by nature but when I was accepted to the program, I made it a point to try to attend social events held by the department. On the very first day, I joined my cohort (me dressed in an urban sleeveless shirt, tattoos displayed, while everyone else was in polos or t-shirts with a rock band depicted on it and the like—so already the *picture* was off) and immediately began to realize that my expectations of readily fitting in might have been optimistically conceived. I was the only brown person in tow and everyone else already seemed to know each other. I couldn't figure out how this was possible, but as I paid attention to the flow and substance of the conversations surrounding me, I began to understand—they knew each other's life-world because they shared it. Stories went around of world travels alongside utterances like, "Did you know so and so while you were at Berkeley?" I was a kid who had lived a local life in the hood among others just like me, not them, and there was no one else like me there; and it began to become clear to me that I was meant to be like them—not like me. I sat, and though I am a person, I think, of strong presence, I felt fairly invisible. I had nothing to share—no one "knew" me; so I left and that marked the beginning of a categorically new experience.

I wish I could say that that experience was confined merely to the social, but I came to find out there was also a distinct intellectual world, the features of which bore an uncanny resemblance to my social experiences. I read the "classics" of theory, among which not a black author was assigned. Then I read the "great" contemporary thinkers, none of whom were black (few were even women) and very few of whom remarked upon racial injustice in an explicit fashion. Rather, attending to arguments that proceeded in the analytic tradition, I must be honest, I was never quite sure what these folks were talking about. Philosophers are trained to use examples to convey the substance of their arguments, and I was reading scholars who wanted to make a case for subsidizing fictional persons' ability to attend bullfights in Spain in order to satisfy the demands of justice. I read in wonderment—I could only think back upon the neighborhood I had left behind, filled with brown folks, home to many poor folks, drug addicts, and some homeless, and wonder to what world these philosophers meant to address their theories. It certainly was not my world and that was the one that needed what they ostensibly had to offer—a view of justice, which for them, could also represent a kind of hope.

Within a year I abandoned the work on Rawls and realized that it was a fancy that I no longer had any interest in indulging. At the risk of sounding inappropriately righteous, I felt that there was important work to be done, and if someone like me could get to MIT, then it was incumbent to try to make sense of the possibility for such an affecting sociological departure alongside that of such a puzzling intellectual disconnect between political moral theory and the politics responsible for that kind of sociological departure.

That is the book you hold in your hands. This is my attempt to systematically and philosophically explain the background sociopolitical circumstances that allowed my experiences to be possible for me, as well as to suggest a way for future generations of folks like myself to be able to pursue a plan of life in a manner indistinguishable from other Americans. Isn't that the American dream?

You will become familiar with the arguments of the book soon enough, so let us sit and chat just a bit more.

In the following pages, my main aim is to redescribe the problem of systemic racial inequality as that of social value—the notion that blacks hold a lower place in the scheme of normative value. This is a scholarly way of saying that racial inequality is basically about the way blacks are not really a part of our society in the deep way democracy presupposes, requires, nay demands. It is this basic observation that, for example, has fueled such outrage at the US government's failure to promptly, adequately, and continuously aid victims of Hurricane Katrina, a natural disaster that could have been mitigated by sufficient democratic care but which had an outsized harmful effect on blacks in New Orleans. That's a problem because such a failure, representative of the more general phenomenon of systemic racial inequality, violates the very mandate of liberal democracy—the thing we all take ourselves committed to upholding. It is on account of this disconnect between what we take ourselves to be committed to and the way things are that I suggest we should feel shame. For we consistently undermine our freedom as moral beings by being complicit in a system that systematically marginalizes brown people.

I know this sounds morally grim, so it would be unfair of me to have you accompany me on this leg of my journey if I didn't leave you somewhere that had space for a bit of optimism, so I will suggest a solution—our society needs to reimagine the measures entailed by achieving a democratic society we can reasonably describe as a good one, a society marked by racially relevant moral excellence. I won't yet divulge the details of that vision, but I can say that it is a vision born of the facts as I understand them.

So one reason for you to take the journey with me is to explore whether the facts strike you in a similar manner. That is the aim of philosophy. If they do, then we might agree. If they do not, then we might not agree—but I hope that by walking with me you will return to where you came from with a fresh perspective on that place and a desire to make sure it is a place all citizens are not merely entitled to inhabit, but can reasonably describe as just.

C.J.L.

THE COLOR OF OUR SHAME

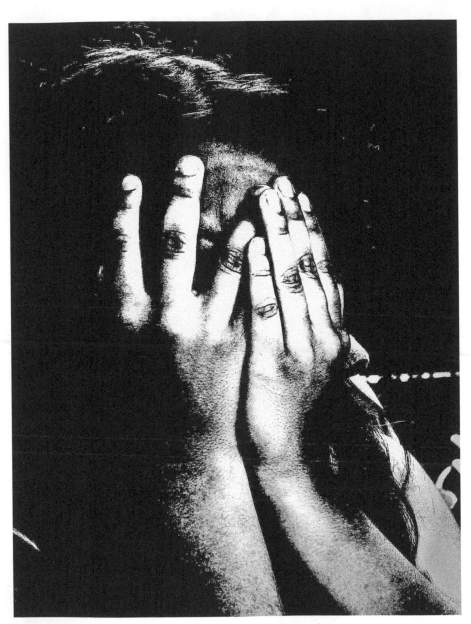

Shame © Kelsey McLaughlin

SHAME IS A powerful state of being. It can be self-admonishing, but importantly it can be redemptive as it alerts us to the potential to be better than we are. It can be deeply personal and directed toward the self, but it can also be public and expressed toward and on behalf of others who stand in some important relation to us. This photo portrays a black woman who is a current-day citizen of a democratic nation that remains marked by systemic racial injustice. Thus, our social, political, and economic practices leave her vulnerable to a moral vice whose roots reach into the seventeenth century. I invite you to imagine with me that she averts her gaze because she is deeply troubled by America's continual failure in the face of race to make good on its most basic ideals of equality. She is troubled that her counterparts have been unable to draw upon our basic and shared democratic commitment to equality and she wonders what role she can play in making America racially just. She wants better for herself, but she understands that this depends on her white counterparts being better co-travelers in the democratic project than they have been. She covers her face in shame over the facts of racial injustice and our collective failure to be better Americans on account of the values we daily affirm in the name of liberal democracy. But her reluctance to meet our gaze means that her shame should be shared—we ought to sit uncomfortably with ourselves as we acknowledge that we affirm better, know better, but fail to do better. Her shame invites our own, and we are thereby called to strive for the kind of democratic and moral excellence that would justify her uncovering her face and embracing her fellow citizens with the confidence that the cause of our shame in our time is being overcome; that her place as an equal is secure and that we—her fellow citizens—have taken up good democratic habits necessary for overcoming racial injustice, and that the institutions that help shape our democratic habits are free from the shackles of history.

Introduction

IN 1939, JAZZ vocalist Billie Holiday was compelled to musically document the peculiar and cruel treatment blacks continued to suffer more than fifty years after emancipation from slavery. The first verse of her beautifully eerie performance is thus:

Southern trees bear strange fruit,
Blood on the leaves and blood at the root,
Black bodies swinging in the southern breeze,
Strange fruit hanging from the poplar trees.

These lyrics haunt us aesthetically because the horror of human suffering is depicted in the form of a pastoral ode. Black death in the space normally occupied by verdant life. What is usually a scene of serenity instead depicts grotesque human suffering. But they haunt us in our time for another reason. Holiday released the song over fifty years after the Emancipation Proclamation yet blacks remained subject to cruel victimization as the slave master's whip seemed merely to be substituted by the common citizen's sense of license to dispose of black life. As horrendous as that treatment was, a contemporary observer could not have been surprised. America was nowhere near turning the corner on race. Reconstruction collapsed in the wake of Andrew Johnson's efforts to roll back a number of initiatives associated with the distribution of resources to former slaves while the Supreme Court proceeded to grant states more autonomy in deciding cases of rights violation. The era of Jim Crow was born signaling that the national character remained marred by racial evil. We sometimes like to think that the national character in our time is markedly different. Is it?

We might find it striking that of the many horrors resulting from the worst that humankind has to offer documented by Jonathan Glover in *Humanity: A Moral History of the Twentieth Century*, the problem of race in America fails to make the list. To be sure, the twentieth century was pocked with many injustices, but surely if environmental harms are worthy of notice, the continued systemic inequality that blacks[1] continue to suffer under—social strange fruit, if you will—is certainly worthy of our moral concern. Is persistent racial inequality evidence of continued racial evil? I think not, at least not in Holiday's sense. Is it evidence of flawed national character? I think so—and the relationship between character and racial justice is what I shall be concerned to address. How is it that forty years after the passage of the Civil Rights Act and relative disappearance of explicit racism can we account for the continued marginalization of blacks and black identity? In what follows, I hope to convince you that our country suffers from bad character, by which I understand a general pattern of attitudes and actions founded on a set or sets of beliefs having normative importance for our relations with others and our self-understanding as agents possessing the power to act morally or not.[2] While our character reveals important traces of historical continuity that we ought to find shameful, our nation's standing commitments nonetheless contain the resources for redemption. I think, for our time, the dual effort of reclaiming and living up to these commitments in the face of race is a matter of social justice. And I shall be concerned to articulate a theory of it. That is, I aim to articulate a philosophical account of the considerations that ought to inform and motivate that effort, as well as construct its prescriptive framework.

And what are we to make of Glover's omission of race as a worthy twentieth-century moral issue?[3] Since Ralph Ellison's publication of *The Invisible Man,* the linkage of race to invisibility has been regularly drawn. So it is disturbing that at such a moment as Glover's attempt to catalog injustice—writing in the twenty-first century thereby giving the author historical perspective—race in America seems invisible as a moral horror. Maybe Glover misses what Holiday captures because of the fact that black suffering has become much more difficult to catalog. It is one thing to witness a black corpse hanging from a tree; it is another for black suffering to become less overtly corporeal and increasingly economically, politically, and sociologically systemic. Yet, while we no longer publicly hang blacks by the neck, the fact of systemic racial inequality poses an existential threat all the same for it indicates America's lack of consistency to the ideal of moral equality, which has real costs for black lives. Stated succinctly, systemic inequality consistently and persistently diminishes the ability of blacks to conceive and/or pursue a good life. Thus, they remain strange fruit in the social sense since we, as a democratic society, do not express equal care and concern for their basic social and political well-being. The signal problem here is that we generally know better, but we rarely and inconsistently do better. The theory of racial justice I offer below sets out two main aims. First, I want to explicate exactly that formulation. That is, I want to specify the mechanics by which that statement seems to be true. Second, I then want to offer a prescriptive argument. These two moves turn on the idea that we ought to feel shame for being in possession of bad character, and, in light of that, it seems necessary for our society to embrace practices that cultivate moral excellence at both the level of institutions and persons.

What follows below is a work of political thought, not moral history, yet there is something to be said about invisibility in this domain as well—the domain responsible for imagining a world better than the one we have got. Since John Rawls's publication of *A Theory of Justice* in 1973, liberalism has become, I dare say, the dominant strand in normative political thought. Yet it is striking that a body of thought committed to the idea of moral equality has yet to offer a systematic response to the persistent problem of racial inequality. To be sure, normative theories of what counts as one's welfare, ask whether resources or opportunity are better distribuenda of justice, or suggest that the notion of well-being is the best fit for the idea of justice are in plentiful supply.[4] However, it is disappointing that so few liberal theorists have taken the time to think clearly about one or two actual cases of political injustice rather than dwelling in the conceptual stratosphere in the name of political thought.

Of course, philosophers who work specifically on race have attended to the subject matter's normative aspects. Some argue that liberalism's commitment to neutrality entails a commitment to color-blindness that cannot be sustained if we want to substantively engage race on its own terms. Others are concerned with the themes of responsibility promoted in liberal thought without consideration of the ways responsibility is framed under ideal conditions, in isolation from the way the circumstances of power interact with the agency of the disadvantaged. Yet others believe liberalism makes little space for the real experience of alienation for blacks living under a racial social scheme.[5] However, race theorists have been understandably weary of the project of "a theory of justice." Rawls's main and enduring innovations turn on a method of justification that denies history and situated social knowledge a place in normative reasoning, and anyone concerned with race will have a hard time turning a blind eye either to history or the social circumstances in which blacks continue to find themselves. So, these theorists have tended to relocate their concerns to that of description and in some cases explanation. How is race constructed? What are its implications for ideas of the self and for community? Should blacks be concerned with being "black" or would doing so merely reify an identity historically begotten by colonial relations? While I agree that Rawls's innovations present a series of obstacles for effectively engaging racial subordination, I believe the idea of a theory of justice remains significantly useful for addressing racial inequality. A thinker concerned with liberalism, race, and justice can indeed say something descriptively substantive, analytically coherent, and prescriptively insightful. This task, though, requires a journey through many conceptual lands. Before previewing the content of the chapters to follow, I want to lay out two central points of concern—one substantive, one methodological—that respectively underpin this book's focus and its approach.

First, substantively, how should we understand "racial inequality"? The notion has such an extended history and is used so casually, it can at times seem more of a catchphrase than a substantive descriptor. This probably is a main reason the term *systemic* is commonly attached to it, or is at least understood to be included in that concept. By racial inequality, we generally understand the basic phenomenon that blacks are not receiving as much of something as whites. That may be wealth or opportunity or resources broadly construed. Adding "systemic" does particular analytic work, for it unifies these many otherwise discrete instances under one problematic—that blacks are probabilistically at risk of having less of many things than whites have on account of being black. Maybe more importantly, the use of systemic removes intentionality from the picture, thus there can be racial abuse in the absence of racist intentions. This has been a useful development since overt racism is not the prevalent and dominant phenomenon it once was, yet blacks most certainly continue to have less of many things than whites. So, systemic racial inequality is a very effective term. But, it cannot do all the work we need it to do.

What systemic inequality helps bring into focus is the relationship between what Rawls terms the basic structure (the way major social, political, and economic institutions hang together in distributing society's benefits and burdens) and race in America. However, it cannot answer the question: What sustains the systemic nature of racial inequality at the level of institutional procedure and outcomes? Additionally, given that persons populate institutions, how is it that explicit racism can mostly be a thing of the past but that persons nonetheless seem to reason in racial ways? My response to both these questions is to argue that the problem of racial inequality is *the problem of social value*: the fact that blacks do not occupy an equal place in the scheme of normative attention and concern upon which our society depends in the first place to justify the distribution of benefits and burdens as well as to identify those who are deserving or appropriate recipients.

Now, the general conceptual sentiment embodied by social value is not my invention. Indeed, (particularly black) social theorists, since the time of Frederick Douglass and W. E. B. Du Bois have in one manner or another raised the challenging question to the broader polity: Why don't/won't/can't you *accept* us as your equals? More recently, Glenn Loury has offered a series of insights into the relationship between reason and rationality and the role stereotypes play in perpetuating racial stigma, highlighting how racial narratives work to substantiate racial attitudes and expectations.[6] Despite hewing to a familiar "economic man" view of persons that tacitly marginalizes the role of affect, sympathy, and shame (the same model used by analytic liberal philosophers in the Rawlsian tradition), Loury is right to look in the direction of norms as informing behavior. However, his view of what justice amounts to is mostly couched in negative terms. That is, he offers insightful criticisms of liberal individualism alongside liberals' commitments to procedural reform. Of course, the problem he signals is apparent. As denoted by my invocation of national character, we are all in this together, and as will be signaled by my own critical engagement with Rawls, a focus on distributive justice will subvert paying attention to the value we fail to accord black identity. While I will echo these criticisms in a more systematic fashion in what follows, we are still left to ask, what ought we to do in a more positive sense? That said, in fleshing out social value in the language of moral theory, it is used to motivate and inform a positive, systematic theory of racial justice. Thus, the contribution is twofold: I seek to articulate a systematic theory by relying on an idea that has not been used at the core of a systematic positive account of racial justice. Thus, social value serves as an analytic lynchpin for constructing explanation, giving content to description, and systematically justifying a distinct set of prescriptive moves.

What social value, as I shall map that idea, provides is a first-order normative explanation for racial inequality. Reasons for believing and reasons for action are essentially normative. If people are not explicitly racist—that is, they do not reflectively affirm a social framework in which blacks ought to be inferior—what motivates their implicit racial reasoning? My specification of social value suggests that institutions, themselves beholden to racial historical precedent, pass on bad moral lessons to the polity that inform which identity markers count as morally worthy. The resulting policies, actions, and dispositions evidence bad character at both the level of institutions and persons, so social value directs our attention to the ways our dispositions and actions can come undone from the moral democratic principles we tend to reflectively affirm in a manner that expresses less moral concern for black lives. As I shall argue below, that is grounds for shame.

This sets up the second, methodological, point of concern. As will be clear in the chapters below, my approach here, though sympathetic with the substance of liberal values, distances itself from the methodology employed by analytic liberals for more than three decades. Ideal theory "assumes strict compliance and works out the principles that characterize a well-ordered society under favorable circumstances. It develops the conception of a perfectly just basic structure and the corresponding duties and obligations of persons under the fixed constraints of human life."[7] Famously, Rawls argued that it is the only way to get a grasp on the more pressing issues of everyday experiences. I do not want to argue here whether this can *ever* be a sensible philosophical position. I do want to say, however, that it is a bad way to go for the person concerned with racial inequality. The mechanics of my criticisms are sketched below and worked out fully in the first chapter, so for now I simply want to say that there is a deep incongruence between understanding racial inequality as driven by historical relations of power and to at once deny the facts of those relations and that history a place in normative theory building right from the beginning. The larger problem is that ideal theory is largely where liberal theory has remained, hence my above complaint about its ignorance of race. For whatever the term is worth, this book is firmly located in the nonideal—my aim is to take the problem in view on its own terms and respond to it as the problem itself demands here and now. The conception of nonideal theory at work in this book can be stated as follows: (1) a mode of theory building responsive to reasonable interpretation of the (historical, social, economic, political) facts of injustice; (2) its response is attentive to ideal conceptions of goodness, rightness, and so on; (3) the application of those conceptions are moderated by the aforementioned reasonable interpretations of facts; finally, (4) this mode is given priority in responding directly to extant problems of injustice. This, to my mind, is what it means to do political thought. This, of course, means that it is entirely plausible that my own arguments and research can be shown as outmoded by changed circumstances at some point in the future, but I believe that is as it ought to be—a political philosophy that aims to be timeless is rarely timely.

This approach, however, comes with serious challenges. We can at least concede in Rawls's favor that it is certainly "neater" to work outside the bounds of real world problems. When we start in the middle, as nonideal theory insists we must, we are committed to reform from within political conditions and personal beliefs and preferences that have long been settled. As challenging as this may be, this set of conditions cannot deter us for we risk losing sight of the problem and suppressing the sense of urgency that initially impelled us to go down the harder road. What to do, then?

First, we must be clear on what we should expect from a theory of this kind. Briefly, I want to say that the best it can do is offer a comprehensive account of the problem; ideally, that account should shed more light, not merely a different light, on the problem than preceding accounts. Further, because it rejects the tabula rasa approach to conceiving of political society, we at best can expect justification for radical, yet reasonable reform, as well as some indication as to what that reform would look like. Second, we need to employ a bit of imagination as to how our recommendations will look when formulated in the light of knowledge about the society we already have. This seems daunting, for radical reform and realism are often uncomfortable bedfellows. Here we would do well to recall Otto Neurath's invocation of building a boat out at sea as a metaphor for the development of language needed to describe and theorize things in the world.[8] The metaphor conveys that we are almost always in the middle of developing processes fundamental to human experience, yet that experience simultaneously demands expansion and improvement of our capacities. Yet, precisely because we are in the middle of these processes—out at sea— we rely on what is already around us and beneath our feet, so the boat is improved upon while in motion with available material at hand. A tricky proposition, indeed.

For us, such a metaphor alerts us that democratic reform necessarily relies on the democratic institutions we already have. And while these come with vices, they also come with virtues, so we ought to use what resources we have at hand to continue refining a democratic project that is long underway. Further, and this will be particularly crucial, persons are already in possession of beliefs, preferences, and biases, but their affirmation of principles of racial justice are fundamental. Good persons must stand alongside good institutions for justice to take hold. On that view, we seek out ways to recover the basic moral fiber that is sympathetic with our cause and then locate nearby resources to bring that moral fiber into line with the requirements of racial justice. Of course, here I am speaking about the project of remaking the national character—urging normative reformation of our individual selves and of the polity as a collective in service to the good of racial equality. This is a perfectionist project of a certain kind that is entailed by the problem, but we will nonetheless have to take care in building our arguments for it. I now turn to the outline of the book to preview the structure of those arguments and indicate how they hang together.

My experiences as a brown person combined with extended reflection on the problem of race and discourses around it in the normative literature have convinced me that racial inequality demands an aggressive, yet simple, but highly nuanced response. During my first year in graduate school I was required to take a course in statistical analysis. I was the only person of color in the room (by which I mean, I was the only obviously brown person present, and a minority who had not come from a privileged background) when the teaching assistant saw fit to characterize the idea of conspicuous consumption as follows: "You know, the guys in the hood driving the cars with the big rims." Everyone had a good laugh at that one. Not me. Trading in easy racial stereotypes, the teaching assistant's unthoughtful remark only served to embarrass me. My access to a prestigious institution, at that moment, served to remind me that it was a socially unnatural fit for me. And it also indicated that it seemed perfectly natural for everyone else, and I had been given a glimpse as to what they thought about people "from the hood," an environment I called home. But, as embarrassed as I was, I think she ought to have been ashamed. Why? The answer is fundamentally illuminating in a way that matters for all that is to follow.

I became better acquainted with the person in question, and the person not only failed to prove to be a racist, but I got the strong sense that if I had recounted my experience of the comment, the person in question would have felt very bad about it precisely because of the realization that the utterance betrayed more deeply held principles—that all persons are due equal respect. But this person had fallen away from these affirmed ideals, and as the ancient Greeks have taught us, this is paradigmatically grounds for shame. The importance of shame for a theory responding to racial inequality as the problem of social value is that it cuts to the heart of the problem while respecting its complexity. Let me explain.

We occupy a unique period in history. It would be narrow-minded to deny that America has achieved a kind of racial progress. As an institutional fact, the Civil Rights Act of 1964 and the Voting Rights Act of 1965 both cemented in law equal rights for blacks. As a fact of American sociology and individual psychology, explicit racism is nowhere near as rampant as it was as recently as fifty years ago. Yet, for all that, systemic racial inequality is a robust feature of our society. Many of our institutions proceed in a way that frighteningly recalls a time past when strange fruit hung from the trees. Consider, for example, racial disparities in death sentencing. Other institutions may not operate so egregiously, but operate racially nonetheless, such as financial institutions that push otherwise creditworthy blacks into loans at subprime rates. On the other hand, an individual's rejecting bigotry would seem to forestall a discrepancy between commitments to principles and commitments to other-regardingness. However, implicit racism is a real phenomenon.[9] Thus, we, as a society, seem to know better, but not do better, hence, the appropriateness of shame.

I believe that the notion of shame is fit as a characterization of the state we ought to find ourselves upon reflection because the ideal of racial equality is not far in the distance—rather we are close to it because we already are committed to the principles that could make racial equality a live possibility for our social and political lives…but we lack the will in the face of these commitments to be racially egalitarian. Shame allows our moral sense to tune in to the beacon of goodness and justice. That is why the problem of race is the color of our shame—the color of a person's skin remains an obstacle in being the society we believe ourselves to value and hold true. Accordingly, this indicates what we might consider to be the political significance of character, for that idea signifies the seat of normative judgment, moral perception, and practical reasoning. In brief, one's character marks out the kind of person one is among others, and if we affirm democracy as a means of achieving the morally appropriate benefits of social cooperation, we need to have a way of not merely assessing the rules of the game, but the players as well—in our case, both persons and institutions. With respect to racial justice, it turns out that most of the necessary rules are in place, as well as a general affirmation of them. However, the players sometimes seem unwilling to play by the spirit of the rules; more often, we seem to have difficulties in remaining consistent with the spirit of the rules in the face of race. The theory of justice, then, should mark out a path to our moral improvement at all levels so that we can achieve the promise of our principles.

Indeed, one of my aims is to reclaim the language of "good character" as a progressive political esprit de corps for the purposes of racial justice. From the middle of the nineteenth century, with Ralph Waldo Emerson as an early exemplar, to the middle of the twentieth century with Martin Luther King, Jr. as one of the last, the notion of character was not merely considered helpful for marking out a vision of the best kind of polity America could come to embody, it was fundamental to articulating that vision. From Emerson to King, the notion of character was central to directly addressing the people of America, to exhort them to be the best citizens they could be in the face of commonly affirmed liberal democratic ideals. For example, King writes: "In their relations with Negroes, white people discovered that they had rejected the very center of their own ethical professions. They could not face the triumph of their lesser instincts and simultaneously have peace within."[10] And, in King's case, the notion was meant to elevate a nation on the cusp between realizing genuine racial equality and falling forever into the ways of white domination. He continues, "And so, to gain it, they rationalized—insisting that the unfortunate Negro, being less human, deserved and even enjoyed second-class status."[11] In the wake of King, America achieved some significant progress, but the Civil Rights victories were not enough and blacks began to languish yet again in the 1970s and 1980s. As the polity became less enthusiastic (if it ever truly was) about attending to racial inequality, Ronald Reagan became a key conservative actor who reappropriated the rhetoric of character to indicate the ways blacks were not keeping up their end of the social contract (à la the infamous reference to the black, Cadillac-driving welfare queen). But in some senses Reagan merely became the most public voice of a line of argument that grew out of the 1965 Moynihan Report excoriating black fathers for abandoning their families, thus being complicit in perpetuating racial disadvantage, thus being persons of bad character.

In a few moves, then, the notion of character became bound up with black deviance, rather than a lack of political will among Americans and the institutions that represent them—and once this language became thusly appropriated, social progressives distanced themselves from talk of character for fear of using language mobilized to blame victims of inequality, thereby denying themselves an idea that was rightly within their reach. On a parallel track, political thought appeared to close off the possibility of focusing on character and political ethics. The rise of Rawls's masterwork in the 1970s mobilized a cadre of future who became centrally preoccupied with institutional procedures, as if the people who make judgments within institutions are an insignificant part of the justice equation, and as if institutions themselves are not susceptible to character claims. This book is in part an attempt to show how we can invoke character and actually make critical claims of the polity and institutions without either reinforcing reasons for resentment among whites or stoking fears of blaming the victim among blacks while sensibly ascribing to institutions features of normative agency. It also, as has been remarked, calls upon political theory to once again focus on persons as important units of consideration with respect to justice while being more imaginative when reflecting on the moral nature of institutions. How is this achieved? In brief, by invoking the vision of basic democratic ideals to which few on either side of the racial divide would deny are fundamentally important and morally valuable: fairness, equality, and basic social, political, and civic reciprocity in a manner consistent with the spirit of the American charter while holding in view that institutions are not merely repositories for our preferences nor merely conduits for the outcome of voting procedures.[12] They are more than that—they precede and outlast generations precisely to lend America a sense of identity over time. And, it is worth noting, that the spirit of this invocation signals the use of shame alongside character not exclusively as a means for criticism and blame, but importantly for articulating an aspirational vision of the American polity and its institutions capable of generating wide consent and for which we can all reasonably feel enthusiastic, thus to which we may be persuaded to be active partners.

With this series of reflections and observations in hand, I dedicate the bulk of chapter 1 to an inquiry into the relationship between the method of normative theorizing and normative substance at the level of both description and prescription. Race must be dealt with on its own terms. Quite apart from whether or not there exists a theory of racial justice, my further argument is that we cannot simply plug race into an existing normative political theory. Many people have written on justice and many people have written about race—too many to meaningfully engage with respect to my larger aims. My inquiry into method and substance, thus, is framed as a confrontation between two of the most respected theorists in liberalism and race, respectively. John Rawls's conception, *justice as fairness*, remains the standard by which liberal theorists must test the mettle of their own arguments. Charles Mills has consistently championed the role of racially inflected power relations when thinking of racial injustice.[13]

Each of these theorists has something important to teach us about justice and race. Rawls attunes us to the centrality of the basic structure for distributing benefits and burdens and properly identifies society as a scheme of ongoing cooperation. Thus, he conceives justice as attending to realigning the working of the basic structure to support this scheme in a way that inherently respects persons as moral equals while providing background support to the pursuit of life plans. On the other hand, Mills insists that most aspects of our social existence, even the practice of doing philosophy, are burdened by the history and sociology of race. Mills's project is critical theory in the true sense in that, on his view, to think about race is to pull back the curtain of perceived reality and reveal white power as the enigmatic wizard responsible for racial inequality.

Yet, despite the potency and reach of each theorist's arguments, there remains much work to be done. On the one hand, as Rawls admits on his own view, his theory is one that theorizes justice, not one that responds to injustice. This is necessarily entailed by his commitment to ideal theory, yet he also insists that his theory is "political"—I think he is very confused about this, for on the view I put forth, a political theory is one that directly confronts the facts of political injustice and, moreover, begins from those facts. Thus, I seek to hold on to some of Rawls's key insights, namely the impact the basic structure has on our lives and on social justice, and move toward Mills's position in being sensitive to extant power relations that drive racial inequality. However, though Mills's basic intuitions about how deeply power runs in our society are fundamentally correct, I think the attribution of racial inequality to white power is overly simplistic and analytically empty. I argue that to think clearly about power is to theorize the ways early white dominance indeed became embedded in American institutional development, as well as the way it affects a very wide cross-section of persons under its influence. On my view, the descriptor "white power" distracts us from the increasing complexity of racial subordination.

In highlighting the strengths of each theorist while revealing key gaps or mistakes, I set the stage for developing a robust theory of power in chapter 2 that explains the mechanics of the problem of social value, or put another way, how it is we have come to have bad national character. This is a complex question and I have come to the conclusion that no one field of social inquiry exclusively holds the key to answering it. Thus, I synthesize views from sociology, political thought, and American political development to articulate a theory of power: *historically evolved, socially embedded power*.

Rawls argues that the basic structure has two defining qualities. First, it tends to replicate patterns that result in discrete outcomes for persons. This is an important claim but it requires analytic content. To that end, I mobilize the theory of path dependency (the theory of institutional mechanisms that result in either institutional inertia or very slow change over time) alongside the theory of social dominance (the theory of how dominant groups not only unilaterally construct valuational narratives, thus rendering some group or groups subordinate and unworthy, but also how they come to have early dominant access to institutions). The argument is, first, that we need to possess an understanding of how dominant groups become positioned to unilaterally develop narratives justifying their dominance over other groups. Second, there is the issue of how dominant groups come to not merely develop those narratives but are then able to make them something like widespread social doctrine. Finally, we need to understand how that doctrine becomes an operating logic for the basic structure. The result is a sketch of the mechanics of how a nation develops bad national character. The thought is that if we can understand the notion of bad national character, and reasonably believe shame is the appropriate response to the problem of social value, then we can develop a normative theory capable of overcoming racial inequality.

While I agree with other theorists that institutional design is fundamental in working toward a just society, I think it is a mistake to overlook an analysis of personal character—after all, we learn a good deal of our moral lessons under institutional tutelage. Further, we ultimately populate the institutions that matter for justice with those lessons in hand. This is Rawls's second major point—the basic structure has profound effects on our aims, desires, and plans. To shift the language a bit, a great deal of our moral character depends on the moral character of institutions. By understanding this mutual dependence, our prescriptive maneuvers secure the best chances for successfully responding to racial inequality. The articulation of the second half of the theory of power similarly depends on a synthesis. I revisit social dominance theory's argument about the effects narratives about groups have on persons to inform the view that institutionally sanctioned norms resulting in racial inequality affects those that benefit from group dominance, as well as those subordinated by it. Thus, my theory of power denies more extreme views of "white power."

However, that is not to say that all persons are affected in the same manner. Whites' advantaged position in the social scheme provides reasons and circumstances to deny the plight of blacks and in many instances hold negative beliefs and attitudes toward them even while they may not actually be racists. Racial injustice also affects blacks: their beliefs about themselves and/or the society around them and their rightful place in it. The argument I offer is not strictly psychological—it does not depend on notions like "damage imagery,"[14] but rather on philosophical conceptions of what it means to develop a self-conception under the influence of racial power. The two portions of the theory serve to explicate the mechanics upon which the development of bad national character depends. But that is not yet to understand the manner in which bad character has expressed itself, and this matters if we are to not merely identify the appropriate normative framework to respond to the problem of social value, but if we are also to be able to give content to that framework, as well as attempt to imagine the kinds of policies entailed by the arguments.

Our first engagement, then, is with institutional character. In what ways has institutional character developed over time and how has that character resulted in racial inequality? This is a difficult question to answer for the simple fact that racial inequality, as its systemic formulation suggests, is manifest in a constellation of practices that span the web of our social and political existence. Nonetheless, this does not necessarily prevent us from providing an account of the development of some of these practices over the course of our history.

Chapter 3 presents two policy case studies. Welfare and crime policy represent different kinds of social aims—the former ostensibly provides for those in need while the latter ostensibly pursues bona fide deviants. My goal is not to unearth new historical facts in providing a historical sketch of these two areas. Rather, turning to a rich array of secondary sources, I provide two analytic narratives meant to connect pieces of a large puzzle in order to present a streamlined account of how both welfare policy and crime policy developed into vehicles for the problem of social value. We emerge with a clearer understanding of what I mean to indicate by invoking the idea of bad institutional character. A recently influential argument offered by one scholar suggests that the muscular development of crime policy in the United States is more than merely temporally coincidental to the advent of racial civil rights. Indeed, the rapid growth of the carceral state was an act of political creativity by political elites concerned about the erosion of the racial status quo ante. Similarly, welfare policy, though an outgrowth of Roosevelt's New Deal, came to portray blacks as initially less deserving in the 1960s and 1970s, and then irresponsible and lazy from the 1980s to present. Welfare was thus stigmatized on account of being associated with blacks, and blacks on welfare were thus stigmatized because welfare came to symbolize a refuge for the lazy and irresponsible, thus as a handout for the undeserving. The problem of social value here underwrites a policy disposition (and a disposition toward that policy on the part of democratic citizens) shaped by beliefs and attitudes about blacks rather than primarily underwritten by the goodness of the policy for the polity in general. The failure of both policy areas to exhibit racial fairness crystallizes the appropriateness of national shame, for both institutions fell away from ideals they proclaim to embody—respectively, fairness in the name of the law and provision to the needy in the face of hardship.

While I believe it is important to acknowledge injustice in these two policy areas, I deploy these case studies as heuristics for understanding institutional bad character generally. This is important because institutional practices, such as those embodied in crime and welfare policy, not only limit or delimit opportunities, but they are engaged in a kind of normative education. They set the terms for social value. In turn, persons are influenced (if not compelled) to develop or not develop normative concern toward others and are themselves shaped by institutional lessons.

In chapter 4, I pursue a line of inquiry motivated by the notion of socially embedded power—the second component of the theory of power. Here, I am concerned with the effects social power has on our moral and ethical capacities. If it is the case that racial power affects whites and blacks differentially in a way that matters for character, how might we understand those effects?

As indicated earlier, I understand character to represent a general pattern of attitudes and actions founded on a set or sets of beliefs having normative importance for our relations with others and our self-understanding as agents possessing the power to act morally or not. Issues of character have implications for our moral and ethical make-up. Whites may become irrationally nervous when alone with a person of color in an elevator, or may unjustifiably refuse to consider a person with an Afro-centric name for an interview solely on the grounds of race despite their reflective rejection of attendant racial attitudes. Similarly, an urban youth might at the same time extol the virtues of success while simultaneously scorning education.

Now, one's character is often referred to as being a good or bad one, and as those work-ing in gender studies have discovered, goodness or badness of character is in part suscepti-ble to moral luck[15]—more specifically, it is susceptible to the environment and structures one is born into, as these are a significant source of our moral lessons. In this case, char-acter becomes an object of reflection that must be sensitive to the interplay between self and external power. I argue that the best way to conceive of this interplay is to understand whites as under the influence of moral disadvantage and blacks as under the influence of ethical disadvantage, respectively. By moral disadvantage I mean to indicate a state of affairs wherein whites would reflectively tend to disavow racial beliefs, but their place-ment in a scheme of power interposes burdens on the kind of moral agency that would allow that disavowal to more consistently inform practical deliberation. Similarly, by ethical disadvantage I mean to indicate a state of affairs wherein blacks would be better capable of conceiving the connection between preferred values (i.e., personal excellence) and good living (i.e., respecting the value and achievement of scholastic success).

In both cases—that of blacks and of whites—the linkage between deeply held beliefs and moral interests seem to be frayed in ways that impact moral reasoning (with clear implications for practical reasoning). That is why I conceive of these states of affairs as disadvantages. But there is a bright side to this story. To be a disadvantaged agent is not the same as being a determined agent. We retain the capacity to be better selves than we are. This is the value of mobilizing the idea of shame, for, as I noted earlier, it prompts reflection upon where we have gone wrong as moral agents and brings into view the prin-ciples we affirm but which we have violated. Shame, then, challenges us to display princi-pled consistency between beliefs and attitudes and actions. I imagine this being a deeply valuable tool for a society largely populated by morally and ethically disadvantaged agents, for it is a mechanism whereby persons can come to affirm the principles of justice in accordance with their own account of basic principles of rightness and goodness.

If racial justice depends on moral consistency—for persons to accommodate the prin-ciples of racial justice in accordance with their more deeply held principles—and if we take concerns over power and the forms of personal disadvantage seriously, we should readily recognize another way in which we shall have to depart from ideal theory: we cannot assume strict compliance. Further, the theory of justice requires confidence that its vision can be more than affirmed, but shared and motivational as well. We need to be prepared to actively, if not aggressively, encourage the amendment of bad moral habits. This is how I see the story of the search for racial justice ending, and its main political protagonist, so I shall argue, is democratic perfectionism.

Chapter 5 begins by assessing the agent-centered prerequisites for a morally excellent society (with respect to race) and accordingly offers a version of perfectionism I believe is pragmatically necessary and morally justifiable in light of how we will come to under-stand racial inequality. If we keep in mind that the problem of social value is one that flatly denies blacks the moral concern they are owed under our democratic practices, and if we think that the view of power I have put forth satisfactorily explains the development

and continued presence of the problem of social value, we will be committed to the position that persons cannot simply be left to assent to the principles of justice without significant guidance—if this were not necessary, I doubt we would have many concerns about
racial inequality forty years after the Civil Rights Act in the first place. But we do have
such concerns. However, that is not to say that should be accomplished by any means
necessary. Indeed, if we are to be consistent with salvaging the core principles of liberal
democratic practices, we cannot run roughshod over freedom and liberties. Thus we must
understand three things: What kind of perfectionism is most appropriate? What will
justify its being the guiding normative ideal? And, what will be its political vehicle?

First, I argue that of the kinds of agency-centered perfectionism available to us, the
kind concerned with moral excellence seems the most apt candidate—I term this moral-
agency perfectionism. This view seeks to elevate the character of all relevant agents by
achieving a level of moral excellence consistent with core principles that are already
affirmed. Second, this kind of perfectionism is politically justified—that is to say, when
we take a careful look at the nature of racial inequality and the way social value has infil-
trated major and minor aspects of institutional design, as well as personal character, we
are justified in offering a proportional response—that is, a response that can stand in the
arena with the problem in its full manifestation and come out a winner. What sets the
boundaries as to how aggressive or invasive my brand of perfectionism will be is that it
relegates itself to (1) addressing racial injustice (2) on account of basic democratic principles we all affirm. So, third, its proper vehicle will be democratic perfectionism—a
politically aware mode of institutional design that builds into its plans and procedures
ways to teach the proper moral lessons required by racial justice, as well as positioning
institutions themselves to consistently act upon appropriate moral lessons with respect to
race—the very lessons the core of which are encoded in the laws that established formal
racial equality, as well as the American charter.

So, that settles the conceptual framework of justice. I have yet to elucidate the principles or policies I think the investigation should yield. I imagine three principles of racial
justice: the "Real America" Re-education Act, the Just Trojan Horse, and the Boondocks
Institutions principles. The first of these principles argues for policies meant to augment
the epistemological resources of citizens, such that as citizens come to be more embedded
in civic matters, they carry with them a wider set of historical and social facts that serve
to suppress reliance on easy but offensive racial heuristics and help them to appropriately
value black identity. The Just Trojan Horse principle calls for a variety of policies wherein
the polity is nudged, or maybe in some instances, actively compelled to face the problem
of social value by being exposed to specially crafted public service announcements, or by
suppressing unfair news coverage in which blacks are overrepresented in crime segments,
for example. The final principle calls for sweeping reorganization of opportunities and
incentives for citizens to actively watch over and regulate the practices of institutions,
particularly those that have been most racially offensive, such as criminal justice. Doing
so requires systematically sanctioning (i.e., nationally and across all relevant institutions,

as embodied in distinct organizations) community advisory councils. Taken together these comprise democratic perfectionism as the political vehicle for the end-game—moral-agency perfectionism. I shall not further summarize these here—the business of addressing racial inequality presses us onward.

I offer a last remark. While this book was not conceived as principally contributing to the field of democratic theory, it has turned out, in retrospect to make a contribution to a view of democratic ethos. Throughout, I liberally use "democracy" and its cognates as a predicate meant to qualify a kind of concern, a kind of practice, a kind of attitude, a kind of policy, and so on. I will not proffer a definition of democracy but I should be forthright about my motivation for using the term as I do. In the end, we share in a kind of political organization for a reason. However much we may differ on defining democracy, we are a part of one because we think it is better for us as persons living a life; we think it provides a political system that despite its flaws and moments of deep error is the best hope for our respective and collective chances of securing lives worth respecting and that even if we fail, it is a system meant to engender proper respect and regard for us in any case. It should be clear that my use of the term 'social value' indicates my standing view that at the bases of social and political life are normative principles—principles that motivate and generate ethically important practical reasons in accordance with notions of rightness, goodness, and appropriateness. Thus, I deploy democracy in a sense very sympathetic with justice as a moral-theoretical construct that nonetheless has obvious import for everyday lives. That said, despite my liberal use of democracy, this work is one of a theory of justice for our democratic society, here and now. Thus, principles of justice ought to be good for one thing and mainly one thing—to demand a degree of moral integrity from us on account of the better treatment we owe others and even ourselves. Articulating the principles of justice, then, is never the final destination—the ship of liberal democracy as a shared political project has already cast off. Will we be prepared to improve it for the important journey upon which we have set out?

I

Shame and Method

ᴏN SEPTEMBER 2, 2005, Kanye West engaged in political moralizing that disturbed our understanding of a series of events that, on the face of it, appeared to be a national tragedy, but which in fact exposed persistent social and political continuities with America's troubled racial past. In front of an audience numbering 8.5 million television viewers he declared that George W. Bush did not care about black people.[1] What prompted such a scathing indictment? On August 29, 2005, the Gulf coast was battered by Hurricane Katrina, one of the worst storms in American history. New Orleans, a Deep South city bearing the legacy of segregation along two dimensions, was hardest hit. Residentially, it was and remains home to entire wards that are predominantly black. This dimension alone was not at issue, however. New Orleans is topographically diverse and it turns out that, as a result of a long racial history, blacks were located in New Orleans' low-lying lands. Katrina made short work of the coastal levees meant to prevent flooding, so it was not long before it devastated the low-lying wards, sections of New Orleans predominantly black and entirely poor.

To this day there remain questions as to why residents were not warned earlier, as there were indications that a natural disaster was imminent. But that failure was not West's motivation. Rather, it was a second failure of a much more fundamental kind—that of caring for citizens in the aftermath who mostly happened to be dark. The federal government took days to mobilize a response while people crowded into the Louisiana Superdome and proceeded to live in terror under conditions that deteriorated with alarming speed. Food and water were in short supply and people died in the absence of medical services. Where was the government? After all, as Spike Lee documents in his film *When the Levees Broke*, Canadian Mounties were on the scene before US federal agencies even figured out what to do. It seems their first concern was to simply help in a time of need.

Then there was a third failure—that of sympathy. West's complaints were not solely aimed at Bush. As the media covered the aftermath of the disaster, ugly images began to emerge of blacks entering stores and exiting with unpaid-for goods. Stories of looting began to proliferate, and they were accepted with ease because they depended on socio-historical tropes of black criminality. West was sure to not let this go unremarked. He further said, "They portray us in the media, when they see a black family they're looting; when they see a white family, it says, they're looking for food." In other words, two actions based on identical human needs nonetheless assigned different moral description. Although blacks were disproportionately suffering under conditions of severe neglect, they were nevertheless looked upon as pariahs. In less than one minute, West gave us a snapshot of how American society differentially values and assesses behavior along racial lines. But he also did something deeply political and engaged in a kind of moral discourse we tend to shy away from—he shamed us on account of displaying bad national character.

West was alternately maligned and praised for what almost all considered to be a public outburst. But much commentary focused on whether he had really meant to claim that Bush is a racist or whether he was accusing the media of unfair coverage. I think West was up to something much more sophisticated. Let's first take the statement: George Bush doesn't care about black people. This utterance makes reference to a person as the president and there is the target group, black people, and one way to read the relationship is that there is a group of people toward which George Bush does not seem motivated to show proper regard. But let's widen our interpretive lens. West had an audience of many millions, which is to say he had a significant audience comprised of his co-participants in the democratic social scheme. His utterance was not a political act merely because it registered a complaint, but it was a political act because it sought to speak directly to the public about a political failing with real social consequences. Seen in this light, West can be taken to say something else. Major American institutions—the president and his supporting apparatus—failed to express moral concern for a suffering subpopulation of the democratic body politic that happened to be mostly dark skinned. On this reading, West wants us to think about how and why we seem to care about some folks but not about others, although we are all formally equal members in the social scheme.

Let us now consider the other significant statement: When white people seek food, they're hungry; when blacks seek food, they're looting. Again, I believe his statement admits of more than one interpretation. Topically, he is simply saying that our judgments are in logical error: Either both are stealing or both are hungry, to suggest otherwise is to be confused about our use of descriptive terms. But, again, I think much more is happening. West is not only drawing our attention to a failure in logic but also problems of interpretation. It is important for him that the actions of whites are assumed to be reasonable, while the actions of blacks are prima facie deviant and criminal. The problem is that they are the same action taken for the same reasons. How can our judgment of the same action be so radically different on account of skin color? To be sure, he would want to say that a lot of it has to do with the media and how they frame racial images followed by critical commentary. However, I think he would want to say more. While his first indictment ostensibly targeted Bush, this second comment unsettles our self-understanding, for one reason the media proceeded as they did was because their interpretation of the relevant acts comfortably sat within a matrix of widely subscribed notions of black deviance. West's second comment is largely directed to us as members of a society bearing witness to an avoidable tragedy. In effect, the lesson is—the next time you consider what it means to have a need or pursue a reasonable course of action, be aware of how you corrupt your final judgment on account of your prior racial beliefs. Whites were stealing because they were hungry…and blacks get hungry, too.

In my view, West did something we need more of—he shamed us as a nation at two levels. In targeting Bush he also targeted what Rawls terms the basic structure: the major political, social, and economic arrangements responsible for distributing benefits and burdens. At the level of the basic structure, he meant to remark upon the way the US commitments to social welfare and equal regard for the value of each American life as equal seemed to simply collapse. Something between the commitment to valid principles of justice and institutional actions and dispositions was severed in the face of race. In targeting us, the audience, he was speaking to persons who play a role in the social scheme, for we populate these institutions by being employers, educators, service providers, municipal functionaries, judges, loan officers, politicians, and so on. However, particularly by way of calling attention to the different ways the stealing of food can be interpreted, he meant to draw our attention to fundamental inconsistencies in personal character—how our deeper and correct principle of the right to meet personal needs applied to whites while becoming corrupted in the face of black needs. West's second statement indicates a failure of other-regardingness upon which well-ordered democracies depend.

Shame is the moral response we should and tend to have when we fail to uphold principles we affirm on our own account in the face of conditions that cannot possibly be thought to justify that failure. The view of this book is that given the deeply complex nature of racial inequality over forty years after the ringing success of the Civil Rights Act, racial justice depends upon our being ashamed of a problem that both institutions and members of the polity ought to have already overcome.

In this chapter I give content to this claim as an initial step in developing a response to racial inequality. First, I provide an account of shame and the work it does in our sociomoral apparatus. What I mean to be doing in invoking shame is to orient the reader toward thinking of justice in a more capacious manner than has been typical in contemporary political thought. Shame does not indicate a fault in rules or laws or expectations, but a failure, as a society, both institutionally and personally, to consistently align actions and dispositions with a commitment to those rules, laws, and expectations. It indicates a failure of national character. So that is my complaint against contemporary political thought—it needs to re-envision what it means to think about justice and race in the face of the appropriateness of shame.

Thus, my second aim is to do the preparatory work of the normative political thinker and offer a critical engagement of two perspectives I take to represent the core of the philosophical intersection of race and justice. I turn to the two leading thinkers of those respective fields: John Rawls and Charles Mills. Each has developed important tools in thinking about their respective areas of concern, but there is a way in which they each fall into error or confusion that seriously hinders the project of racial justice. As I shall argue, while Rawls justifiably focuses on the basic structure as the primary subject of justice, he has an importantly incomplete view of what is "political" about a political theory. And while Mills is right to direct our attention to relations of power and concerns over social epistemology, he relies on overly blunt analytic devices, such as "white supremacy"; further his recent embrace of reparations is a puzzling solution to a problem that is not fundamentally rooted in problems of distribution. As Mills seems to acknowledge (though in different terms), and as I shall argue in more precise terms in chapter 2, the problem of racial inequality is that of social value. That is to say, blacks do not occupy an equal place in the scheme of normative attention and concern upon which our society depends in the first place to justify the distribution of benefits and burdens, as well as to identify those who are deserving or appropriate recipients. If I am right about this, we will have to move beyond Rawls and Mills onto new ground in understanding racial inequality. Shame sets us up to reconceive that ground. George W. Bush might or might not care about black people, but he is not alone in being subject to that descriptive ambiguity, and that is certainly shameful.

THE COLOR OF OUR SHAME

The Idea of Shame

Racial inequality is a peculiar kind of a moral problem for our society. Typically, political debates surrounding moral problems begin from disagreement about whether one side or another of an issue is the right one. For example, consider the battle over reproductive rights. One side believes that morality requires the decision over abortion to be left within the domain of a woman's choice. On this view, you try to construct the most persuasive argument that settles the viewpoint of a woman's choice as the right perspective—if that can be accomplished one imagines there is a clear way to embody reproductive rights in law. However, the other side of the argument denies that a woman's choice is paramount because it is believed that a life, even at such an early stage, is (morally on religious grounds) sacred thus abortion offends against certain fundamental values. Similarly this view believes it has the right approach to the question, and if it can establish its standpoint as the most appropriate one, a rather clear way forward presents itself. This exercise can be repeated with respect to many other morally inflected issues. Consider the death penalty. As with abortion, there are two sides that think there is a clear right and wrong answer to the question, is the death penalty a morally acceptable way for a society to deal with severe deviance? However, there is such little overlap between the opposing views in both the above cases that they seem destined to clash for the foreseeable future, thus we are without a shared public normative standpoint on these and similar questions.

What makes the problem of racial inequality peculiar is that there is almost no disagreement that inequality on account of one's race is morally acceptable. Only the strident racist accepts the rightness of blacks being denied an opportunity to conceive and pursue a good life on account of their racial heritage. There is a reliable normative consensus on this question that is absent in most others. Interestingly enough, however, the possibility of coherence from consensus to solution runs in the opposite direction from the cases of abortion or the death penalty. As soon and as readily as we can agree on the moral status of racial inequality, possible solutions become elusive. One main reason for this, as indicated in chapter 2 and explored further in chapter 3, has to do with the sheer number of practices that exhibit racial bias and unfairness. But another more basic reason for the ensuing confusion is likely grounded in our being perplexed over why something so obviously wrong can be so clearly persistent. We affirm better, but we rarely do better, so over forty years after the success of the Civil Rights Movement, racial inequality remains a distinctive feature of American society. And, for this reason, the problem of racial inequality ought to be a source of great shame. But why should it be a source of shame rather than, say, moral outrage?

Consider the recent environmental disaster in the American gulf. Due to a number of questionable decisions, BP Amoco's operations resulted in one of the worst oil spills in American history.[2] Although it will take time to fully assess the damage it has wrought, there was and is an immediate response that is entirely appropriate: moral outrage. As citizens, we place a good deal of trust in institutions, organizations, and companies. However, it sometimes turns out that they behave badly. Many are morally outraged over the spill because it is clear that it was in part a result of corporate greed that ultimately marginalized considerations over environmental prudence and responsibility. In short, it seems BP was committed to the wrong kinds of principles (i.e., profit at the expense of environmental sustainability or public accountability). We are therefore morally angered because we think, given the nature of and risks inherent to the oil industry, BP should have reflected upon what it means for it to take on such incredible responsibility in pursuing profit. Because it (or, maybe better put, its management) did not do so, we are eager to hold it responsible for it is fairly easy to identify where things went wrong.

The problem of racial inequality surely recommends an urgent response but moral outrage seems an incomplete response, maybe even one that risks confusing the issue. The reason is that people generally affirm the right principles with respect to basic moral equality, so we cannot say that there is confusion about race's appropriate moral status. In contrast to BP, people are generally very clear about the principle of basic moral equality (even if they do not put it in those same words). But yet, persons and institutions act badly. Both kinds of actors often exhibit a morally important failure due to a rupture between deeply held or publicly affirmed beliefs and the practices they respectively employ in dealing with blacks. So while the rupture is morally important—after all, it subordinates blacks—the outrage appropriately expressed toward BP seems incommensurate with respect to racial inequality.[3]

Shame, however, does seems appropriate with respect to racial inequality. Shame is commonly understood as a moral reaction of a certain kind. It is one in which a person becomes aware of a discrepancy between the person one takes oneself to be and the person one is at a given moment. As some have argued, shame is likely to arise "where there is a contrast...between [one's] unselfconscious state, what [one] thought or hoped or unthinkingly assumed [one] was, or was doing, and what [one] has now under the observer-description turned out to be."[4] The reaction of shame is one of disappointment and dismay over a perceived failing or a falling away from one's ideals.[5]

Now, it is clear that the notion of ideals can make trouble for us. If I have an ideal to be the laziest person I can be though others have always recognized in me a certain talent for art, it would be highly peculiar for me to rightfully feel shame, for few think that being lazy is the right kind of ideal for anyone, much less a person with distinct productive capabilities.

Thus, while it is certainly important for shame that one recognize that one is coming up short on account of one's own standards, judgment requires perspective. Anthony O'Hear writes, "Logically, there is obviously a connexion between one's judgments and those of others."[6] Thus, the basis for our judgment is partially grounded in sources located outside of our independent moral apparatus. That is to say, our judgments are not freestanding. Rather, as morally capable beings situated within social and political practices, we come to learn rules of the game—the game of interest to us is democratic life, the rules are embodied in the ideal of moral equality. However, this need not commit us to the notion that shame always requires a distinct other. Rather, shame minimally requires a shift in our perspective such that we become our own audience. Even though moral learning is partly a function of socialization, we come to independently identify with particular principles in such a way that our sense of self is bound up with them. Shame, then, is an important notion for moral assessment because it opens the way for each of us to be active participants in holding ourselves accountable. Further, it allows us to be sensitive to the fact that sometimes our morally questionable attitudes and behavior are psychologically complex, but nevertheless are ours, thus we also own responsibility for bringing our way of being into line with our more deeply held principles. We are at once owners and agents of our normative commitments, as well as observers of our successes and failures in living up to them. Moreover, this feature of the self is situated within a wider community that plays a role in teaching us our moral lessons, as well as accepting or rejecting us on account of our successes and failures.

The relationship between shame indicating a failure in achieving morally relevant excellence, responsibility for responding to that failure, as well as our situatedness within a broader community indicates the place and role of perfectionism in the final chapter. Taken as the view that others may be justified in urging, even compelling us, to be better selves, perfectionism is a moral doctrine that attends to human fallibility and limitations while respecting human possibility and potential. Perfectionists generally hold that the value of genuine freedom underwrites and justifies the actions of external agents to redeem fallibility by way of realizing potential. As I shall later sketch it, perfectionism can play a powerful role, then, in correcting that which causes us shame (in this case, by prompting amendments to character), thus being an effective partner in responding to racial inequality.

Shame and Politics?

The preceding comments suggest three distinctive features of shame. First, we are each an active participant in our own moral judgment because we care about our standards. Our standards provide a sense of personal integrity, and when we fail to meet them we come to recognize a disparity between what we affirm, as well as what we thought we were like as persons in light of our affirmations and what we actually turn out to be like on any given occasion. This disjuncture demands our attention and we call ourselves to account. This is in fact a remarkable feature when compared to guilt, wherein we tend to feel bad over something we have done or felt (or, maybe only imagined doing or feeling, i.e., the child who out of anger wishes his parents would go away or come to harm) but without that feeling necessarily having substantive correspondence to our respective principles. Think of the locution, "I did it because you made me feel guilty for backing out." I do not want to make too much of a comparison between shame and guilt save to say that shame is important on account that it readily implicates us in coming up short on our own account, on account of principles and standards for which we have expressed a prior standing preference: "What is important here is precisely the idea that in the experience of shame there is a sense in which the individual concerned is playing two roles, judger and judged."[7] And, as judger of oneself, one has a particular and particularly important connection to the moral apparatus in question. Thus, when we observe a falling away, we also perceive failure to be a whole and good self—a person of integrity in a manner demanded by principles of right and virtue we readily recognize as worth abiding by.

We sometimes fall away from our ideals because of basic confusion or a failure to connect the morally important dots between virtue and practical reasoning, but these instances themselves can sometimes be explained by moments wherein we are beset by cognitive-affective blindness. Consider a situation wherein you pick up your child from school to find her in the company of a classmate whose parents are not alarmingly late, but late enough to warrant concern—not for the parents, but the well-being of the child. As you reach for your child, she asks if you can give her friend a ride—after all, it is on the way home. You decline muttering that her parents should learn to pick up their own children on time and that finding their child on the curb outside the school should set them straight. That evening as you recount the event to your partner, you find that you are met with deep disapproval—how can one justify making a child pay for the shortcomings of an adult? And rather than defend your decision, you immediately know you did the wrong thing. Moreover, you feel shame precisely because you so easily recognize this error. Why is the error easily recognizable as such? It will partially be on account of you possibly flouting a rule of reciprocity you have affirmed in the past to assist your child's friends when possible as a member of a community of local parents. However, it will also be because you will wonder how you let trivial resentment trump your typically operative ethic of care and concern for those unable to care for themselves. Here, we see shame's second important feature—shame illuminates the temporary dark spots in our cognitive-affective capacities, and while this often happens after the relevant moment, such moments position us to "see" better next time.

One reason we care about our ideals and the possibility of falling away from them is that they are instrumental, if not intrinsically valuable, for our flourishing. In light of this, the final feature of shame is that it serves as a kind of harbinger of our failure to flourish. Here we should note that precisely because notions such as shame and character are most comfortable in the company of virtue ethics, this view depends in part on a view of the virtues. That the virtues are crucial for flourishing is a fairly standard view, articulated by Aristotle and further elucidated by scholars since.[8] The interesting point to be pressed here is that even the person who is typically virtuous can be in error, substituting virtues for vices (i.e., not being sufficiently courageous to chastise a friend for making a racist comment), thus the virtuous can fall away from their own ideals. This does not endanger the possibility of reclaiming virtue, but in those moments where confusion is involved, we may need to rely upon a number of mechanisms to prompt reflection and to be confident that it is the kind of reflection where our falling away can be understood in its proper light thus adequately addressed. In this sense, shame can be deeply important for realizing a flourishing life.

But there is another aspect of flourishing that comes with significant politically important goods. A flourishing life on the standard account of virtue ethics is not an egoistic endeavor. Rather, to truly be virtuous, thus to flourish, we must attend to the circumstances necessary for others' flourishing, and the most immediate circumstances for which we can reasonably be held accountable are the ways in which we treat others. A clear example is that of justice, which is fundamentally a matter of giving to one what one is owed. Importantly, what one is owed can depend on a number of criteria not least of which is being owed something on account of sharing a life in common by dint of citizenship, as a partner in the stability and rightness of the polity. As Nancy Sherman notes: "Virtuous agents conceive of their well-being as including the well-being of others. It is not simply that they benefit each other, though to do so is both morally appropriate and especially fine. It is that in addition, they design together a common good...the ends of life become shared, and similarly the resources for promoting it."[9] Thus, extending the view of shame as that in which it serves as an important reflective mechanism, it is clear that in those moments when it operates fully and best, it also represents a foundational feature of our normative apparatus wherein the work of acting on behalf of others, particularly where it concerns justice, is strongly supported. I want to indicate, then, that beyond the role of shame as a means for critical self-reflection, thus raising concerns, on the one hand, of prompting persons to turn away from the critical gaze, while, on the other hand, prompting insurmountable resentment, shame can be important for aspirational politics. On this view, the critical self-assessment unleashed by shame is meant to operate in the light of achieving a better life on our own, as well as with and among others; thus, it can be embraced as a resource for positive change rather than merely stirring within us a sense of shortcoming. Let's further consider shame's political significance to better appreciate its role as instrumental to an aspirational view of achieving the good and right.

In engaging Plato's *The Gorgias*, Christina Tarnapolsky finds that Socrates, and Plato in a more refined manner, holds a view of shame as both respectful and public. Socrates's dialectic approach relied upon lulling people into fallacies if he perceived weaknesses in an argument. For him, the strategy was not to embarrass people by showing they lacked philosophical skill, but in a manner consistent with how we have been proceeding, show that they could not be committed to some initial principle and ultimately be committed to a conclusion that fundamentally undercut the initial principle. It was also presumed that such inconsistency could have detrimental affects on shared democratic life. She writes: "Socrates and Plato felt there was something salutary for moral and political reflection and deliberation within the occurrent experience of shame and that this experience could have both intra-psychic and inter-psychic consequences. This is precisely why they tried to shame others."[10] For Tarnapolsky, it is important for democratic politics that Socrates and Plato offer a vision of respectful shame—respectful because it takes persons where they stand but also aims to help them hold themselves accountable on their own view of appropriate principles and ideals. "In the Gorgias, itself, the moment of recognition is vividly illustrated by Socrates' ability to shame each of his interlocutors into contradicting one of their deeply held beliefs."[11]

So what Socrates sees as potentially salutary about the moment of recognition is that it can reveal a common truth between the self and the 'other' about the fact of our human vulnerabilities....the 'other' can be the repository of a realistic and yet still wholly new and admirable image of human life. Furthermore the person shamed and the person doing the shaming can both come to recognize this in the shame situation. Thus, Socrates felt that discomfort and perplexity don't necessarily lead the person who is shamed to hide or withdraw from a debate or discussion. Instead they may lead the person to transform themselves in accordance with new or old 'others' and/or to contest new or old 'others'.[12]

Tarnapolsky senses the political utility of shame on the grounds that (1) it is not necessarily demeaning to the person being shamed, and (2) it can be particularly valuable for a democratic society that depends on clear and consistent arguments that shape the terms of our shared association.

I think Tarnapolsky is right to make this move. Moreover, it is a move that is especially useful for racial inequality, for as has already been noted, it is a form of mistreatment that few would reflectively endorse but in which the polity is largely complicit. The US founding charter embodies a principle of fundamental human equality—this is a good moral principle. Moreover it is affirmed in the widest possible sense. It is on account of this affirmation that I think there is a third way in which shame is politically useful, as well as normatively valuable. Precisely because fundamental human equality is affirmed in the first place, shame carries with it significant aspirational ambitions. The notion of being in error has been used many times for a particular reason: Error is a different kind of thing from stubborn refusal or dogmatic shortsightedness. To revisit an earlier example, we may disagree as to whether federal taxation promotes or suppresses freedom, but we do not disagree that freedom itself is a core, nonnegotiable value for democratic life. Indeed, our disagreement is important because we feel the need to be clear so as to best secure it. Being in error does not undercut the goal of making certain ideals manifest, nor does it offend against the possibility of being capable of achieving those ideals, thus reaping the attendant goods. Needless to say, we cannot achieve those ideals if we are in error or confused, save by the grace of fortune. Because we think justice is something we can do rather than receive as a result of fortune, it also indicates our common aspiration to be better, more good, and more upstanding. To the extent that we can fall short of these ambitions on account of error or confusion, and to the extent that shame can be instrumental in setting us straight, we should conceive of shame as something more than a means of criticism or prompting feelings of failure or guilt. Shame on this view can support our best aspirations in a manner beyond helping make our vision for a better way clearer; indeed, it can help bring our deliberations and actions into coherence with our prior affirmed ideals.

Before moving on—a word on the relationship between the idea of shame and the nature of institutions. Racial inequality has often been characterized as structural or institutional inequality. Further, I said above that persons and institutions sometimes act badly, thus I drew a distinction between kinds of actors. This raises the question as to whether shame applies to institutions as well. A major argument of this book is that, following Rawls, the idea of institutions is important for conceiving of justice. He says that justice is the first virtue of institutions because they are responsible for distributing society's benefits and burdens. I think this is right given, as I shall argue, that the dynamics driving racial inequality have become deeply embedded in institutional development. Moreover, institutional practices beget the reproduction of racial disadvantage. However, because shame is often considered an emotion, thus expressing an affective capacity, and institutions are not agents in the way persons are, it may seem out of place to speak about shame as extending beyond the scope of personal morality.

The above position is not inherently unreasonable since institutions do not have emotions. But so far as shame is also a particular kind of moral idea, I think there is a way in which it makes sense to speak of shame with respect to institutions. Consider that institutions have, just as persons, ideals that give shape to their being. As Rawls argues, a basic ideal is fairness, but these may get more specific with respect to various institutions (i.e., the legal system would also be committed to the ideals of neutrality and consistency). Just as institutions can be committed to ideals, they can fall away from them. There is a rich literature describing the many ways the legal system, for example, fails with respect to blacks and that this failure is on account of race[13]—it is not coincidental or merely unfortunate. While I acknowledge that this discussion reaches into complex phenomenological and ontological territory, I simply want to flag that there is nothing incoherent about the idea of us ascribing to institutions, as actors, for the purposes of moral assessment, the notion of shame. We easily and coherently make statements such as, "Congress should be ashamed for failing to pass educational reform." We do so because an entity—Congress—has definitively failed to uphold an ideal we all know it to affirm on its own account. This is what is most important about the idea of shame from the more general point of view of moral assessment.[14]

Race and Shame

Racial inequality and inappropriate racial treatment persist contrary to our better judgment. Shame, then, is a fundamentally important moral notion when reflecting on racial injustice for it simultaneously holds in view the fact that we are already positioned in principle to overcome racial inequality, but despite that fact, we have not and seem to not be doing so. More precisely, the idea of shame helps us develop a view of racial justice in three respects. First, it settles the general moral nature of a social wrong in which we all play a part. Second, in doing so, it helps specify the direction a broad inquiry and response to racial inequality must take. Last, it indicates and frames the central aims of that response, especially from a political perspective.

In what way does shame help settle the moral nature of racial inequality as a social wrong? To begin, let's keep in view the differences between the example of a racially unjust society and that of the clearly culpable oil company. I said above that what justifies moral outrage in the latter example is that the company was fundamentally committed to the wrong principles in the first place; whereas in the former, the moral problem enters later when a rupture between affirmed principles and attitudes or actions is exhibited. An important feature of this example is that in the case of a racial society, the question of responsibility becomes very complex—how responsible is a person for her moral failings when she has grown up in a community where there are no blacks, but yet plenty of stereotypes abound, thereby significantly shaping her racial views? This person may find herself acting in ways that, reflectively, she would disavow, thus causing shame. How so? At base, there is an inconsistency between a principle of equal respect and attitudes or acts reflecting groundless differential normative consideration. More importantly, the person in question is likely to not merely acknowledge some failing, but is likely to experience consternation and dismay over this failing exactly because she is not the person she took herself to be—she has fallen away from an ideal she has set herself.

This indicates why shame is important for settling the moral nature of racial inequality as a social and political problem. We tend to fall away from our ideals when blacks come into view. This indicates that, first, we can be made aware of where we go wrong; further, it introduces nuance into notions of responsibility for it allows more complex explanations of moral wrongdoing, especially in light of race's social and historical nature (see below discussion); last, it opens the way for redemption for it simultaneously acknowledges that we retain the power to reflect on our shortcomings and thus empowers us to try to do better when next we are faced with a kind of situation that we felt shame over in the first place.

This in turn sets the direction for a broader inquiry into and response to racial inequality. Moral wrongs typically result in blame or assignment of responsibility wherein the actor must first, own his or her wrongdoing, and second, must in some ways make amends. A distinct line connects agent, act, and outcome. However, racial inequality resists this usual way of thinking about moral responsibility. As I shall argue in the section below and chapter 2, the fundamental problem underlying racial inequality is complex because of its long historical lineage, its many manifestations in a wide array of social, economic, and political practices, and last, because explicit racism is not an explanation for its persistence. The fact that we ought to feel shame means that when we do find ourselves holding racial beliefs or disrespecting ourselves on account of our race, we betray the principles with which we identify and those represent ways of being and of comporting oneself to others and ourselves as having inherent moral worth. Importantly, they are principles within which racial justice can find a home in. This means that a general inquiry must accomplish a number of things.

In the first instance, it must appropriately specify the nature of racial inequality. It is clear that we cannot simply say that racial inequality is a matter of blacks not getting as many goods or receiving as many opportunities as others. This much is patently obvious, but it explains nothing. However, that we ought to feel shame begins to indicate that some other ideas and beliefs are playing a role in our practical judgments (i.e., that many blacks are poor because they prefer handouts to working hard), making our failing a more common social occurrence than it ought to be. Second, once the right conception of racial inequality is specified, we will have to settle on a general explanatory framework for the problem over which we ought to feel shame—the problem of social value. This conception of racial inequality states that racial inequality is fundamentally a function of blacks holding a lower place in our normative scheme from the perspective of social, economic, and political arrangements—what this means more precisely is explored in chapter 2.

Finally, the appropriateness of shame indicates what the content of a response to racial inequality ought to take as central and fundamentally appropriate given the nature of the problem. In the final chapter, I shall offer a perfectionist argument for institutional design in the pursuit of helping align democratic citizens' actions and dispositions with important moral lessons with which we already identify. In brief, democratic perfectionism holds that we can be nudged or directed to become persons of better character, not on account of some elite or independent conception of what makes a person good, but on account of what we tend to rationally affirm yet fail to accomplish. The fit with shame is immediate—a society committed to guiding its citizens in being the kinds of persons they already affirm and desire to be is one in which our falling away from racial ideals can be redeemed, and importantly, preempted on future occasions. Of course, this is a position that requires more justification than merely saying it is a good fit with the appropriateness of our shame—a fuller argument is offered in the final chapter. However, I want to flag that a basic concept like shame can drastically reorient our assessment of a moral problem we would all prefer to live without. Its stubborn persistence in our social, economic, and political arrangements forty years after the Civil Rights Movement suggests that it may be time to take a fresh look at racial inequality, for we are often lulled into the simplicity of our observations even though those sometimes fail to adequately describe the moral nature of the problem in view.

The question we now face, and must answer with precision, is the following: Where does political thought, in the scheme of intellectual division of labor, stand with respect to the problem of racial inequality? What resources are available to us and to what degree and in what ways will we have to re-imagine the theory of justice with race in mind? My view is that political thought has significantly failed to come close to properly addressing racial inequality on its own terms, yet it does provide resources for doing so, as I will highlight in the next section. Rescuing these resources requires a shift in method, as well as a concession to basic facts of American sociology. An engagement with Rawls and Mills will be particularly helpful in giving content to these admittedly vague comments. This in turn pivots us toward focusing solely on the social and political problem of race rather than academic debates over it or justice generally.

EXPLORING THE FUNDAMENTALS OF A THEORY OF RACIAL JUSTICE

Rawls, Justice, and the Political

Rawls was not one for making assertions, so it is of some moment that *A Theory of Justice* begins: "Justice is the first virtue of social institutions, as truth is of systems of thought."[15] Although an assertion, it is one worth accepting with respect to racial justice, for institutions are central to the idea of systemic racial inequality as they systematically distribute benefits and burdens along racial lines. However, while Rawls offers important guidance in thinking about the role of the basic structure, the potential efficacy of his theory for addressing cases of injustice hinges on it being political in the right way. This matters because first, Rawls's work has become a dominant force in political thought, and second, because he himself claims the theory is political, not metaphysical. That claim suggests that the theory is a ready friend to those who wish to address extant matters of socio-political concerns relevant for justice. In what follows, then, I am not so much interested in contesting the general goodness or moral desirability of the principles he articulates as I am in making sense of what it means for a normative theory to be a "political" one. Rawls's theory is often accepted as political, thus is often, to the consternation of race and gender scholars, taken to be robust enough to settle what counts as a just society, regardless of the facts or nuances of actual inequalities. I think this is wrong. To ultimately move toward a more appropriate position, I begin by elucidating some compelling aspects of Rawls's philosophy that theorists concerned with race can and ought to appreciate.

To begin, Rawls's theory of justice is intended to regulate a society imagined as possessing a fundamentally important feature—it is a scheme of ongoing cooperation among moral equals. The idea of moral equality is meant to ground a principled commitment that each person is owed fair treatment without qualification. Thus, the main enemy of justice is moral arbitrariness coupled with institutional practices. How does this relationship affect each of us, thus raise questions of social justice? First, we are each endowed with varying skills and attributes that may or may not be to our instrumental benefit. In either the better or worse case, these are undeserved but inevitably play a role in our ability to achieve lives of our choosing. Second, we are born into societies that already value certain pursuits and abilities. For example, regardless of how intuitively invaluable the education of young children may be, our society chooses to pay many millions of dollars to bankers for moving other people's money around compared to the barely working-wage provided many schoolteachers. Both these observations suggest that much of what we can hope to achieve in life is shaped prior to our birth by the nature and shape of major institutions: They distribute the benefits and burdens that we will experience over the course of a complete life. Thus, the basic structure is the primary subject of justice on Rawls's account—the principles of justice apply to them in the first instance so as to appropriately guide their distributive practices.[16]

Rawls's next move is to devise a bargaining situation that models perfect rationality by imposing radical epistemic constraints on those behind what he terms the veil of ignorance, thus placing them in the original position—a device that denies participants any situated knowledge of themselves (i.e., whether they are currently rich or poor) as well as of their society (i.e., whether it is currently a very rich one or not). But they are allowed to know basic facts, such as those pertaining to economic laws of supply and demand. Rawls argues that imposing such conditions guarantees fair deliberation as it represents a morally appropriate initial status quo.[17] The implication is that building fairness into the deliberative scheme ensures fair principles of justice, thus a fair society. Of course,

Rawls is looking to eliminate the greater or lesser advantages gained through moral arbitrariness, so behind the veil of ignorance we contract for principles of justice that will necessarily be fair, since we cannot know ahead of time what our own position in the resulting society will be. Rawls's innovations are attractive on account of the fact that they seem to reflect the substance of serious concerns over the way social and political structures greatly influence the way our lives turn out; further, the placement behind the veil of ignorance seems to reflect a common sense intuition that pure fairness is necessarily hindered by the facts of what we stand to gain or lose when we bargain.

This last move, however, is controversial for those concerned about cases of systemic inequality because while the original position is an epistemically minimal environment for deciding, choosing, and preferring, thus seemingly effective at securing fairness at one level, it eliminates whole histories of sociopolitical subordination from consideration, thus endangering fairness from a different moral and practical perspective. As Rawls writes, ideal theory "assumes strict compliance and works out the principles that characterize a well-ordered society under favorable circumstances. It develops the conception of a perfectly just basic structure and the corresponding duties and obligations of persons under the fixed constraints of human life."[18] From another perspective, then, Rawls appears deeply confused about the proper nature of *political* theory because his method effectively marginalizes the relationship between injustice and justice, and the history and practices that have shaped that relationship.[19] On this view, a political theory ought to be in part genealogical. Its main guiding question should be: How did we, as a society, get to this point? Further, it ought to be attentive to the experiences of those subject to injustice and the claims those experiences give rise to. Is this the right way to think about a "political" theory?

To answer that question we need to first be clear as to what Rawls understands by the idea of the political and the extent to which it is taken to settle the political relevance of the theory. On the view Rawls advances, justice as fairness is rightly considered a political conception because (1) its subject is the basic structure and (2) it is a public conception in that it depends on widely accepted reasons among competing political views once out from behind the veil of ignorance (what later in Rawls's corpus comes to be termed an "overlapping consensus"[20]). I will take each of these in turn and show that while the first criteria does some work in holding off Rawls's critics, the second introduces deep problems that strain the idea of Rawls's theory being political in the sense demanded by racial inequality.

As mentioned above, the principles of justice are to apply in the first instance to the basic structure, which is defined as "society's main political, social, and economic institutions, and how they fit together into one unified system of social cooperation."[21] In one sense, a focus on the basic structure is understood to qualify justice as fairness as a political conception precisely because major institutions structure opportunities thus impact our plans of life. But the story here is deeper in a way that very much matters for race and justice.

In *Theory*, Rawls offers two arguments for making the basic structure the primary subject of justice. First, is what I call the historical contingency premise. Rawls says that agreements which are initially fair may aggregate in such a way that "together with social trends and historical contingencies are likely in the course of time to alter citizens' relationships and opportunities so that the conditions for free and fair agreements no longer hold."[22] Institutions can be informed by the arc of history in such a way that the circumstances supporting fair agreements at one time can change to undermine justice at a later time. Second, Rawls justifies the focus on the basic structure on the grounds of social psychology. Rawls writes, "A theory of justice must take into account how the aims and aspirations of people are formed; and doing this belong to the wider framework of thought in the light of which a conception of justice is to be explained."[23] Thus, the basic structure is taken as the primary subject in part because it plays a nontrivial role in determining the kind of persons we ultimately become—it affects the sense of self. The basic structure limits persons' hopes and ambitions "for they will with reason view themselves in part according to their position in it and take account of the means and opportunities they can realistically expect," as well as provide support for the proper development of respectful and supportive attitudes of other free and equal persons who share in the benefits of a scheme of ongoing cooperation.[24] Thus, the basic structure has a nonnegligible impact on our sense of self, internal deliberations, attitudes, and belief formation. It seems to me, then, that justice as fairness is political because it focuses on a site of political development that has pervasive effects for each of our lives. To this point, Rawls is on solid ground—his theory does seem political in a way sympathetic to concerns over race and racial inequality.

The second aspect of justice as fairness that Rawls argues makes it a political conception is that it can be agreed upon from within a diversity of what he terms comprehensive doctrines. The mechanism that makes this possible is the original position, a state of reflective deliberation that Rawls imagines we can enter and exit at will. We will recall that the original position models perfect rationality insofar as it imposes radical epistemic constraints upon us. From within the original position, influences on judgment that may stem from religion, for example, are redirected so that they may be reformulated in widely acceptable reasonable terms. Rawls writes, "We introduce an idea like the original position because there is no better way to elaborate a *political* conception of justice for the basic structure from the fundamental intuitive idea of society as a fair system of cooperation between citizens as free and equal persons."[25] And this is so because "Society's main institutions and how they fit together into one scheme of social cooperation can be examined on the same basis by each citizen, whatever that citizen's social position or more particular interests."[26]

However, I believe Rawls is involved in a serious muddle—a muddle that did not hinder the argument for the primacy of the basic structure in justice as fairness. Indeed, I believe that his justifications for making the basic structure primary help inform why he seems confused about the original position serving to qualify justice as fairness as a political conception. Let me explain.

The first step is to appreciate the impact the imposed radical epistemic constraints have on deliberating agents in the original position. I take it that it is fairly uncontroversial that in the most general sense, justice importantly depends upon giving one what one is properly owed, and liberal justice ultimately depends on moral reasons for doing so. But the epistemic constraints imposed by the veil of ignorance strip the possibility of history informing the idea of owing; and, one might think, absent that information, moral reasons became significantly and, on my view, problematically pulled apart from our actual status, here and now, as moral beings. Thus, it is very difficult to imagine how one can identify and demand what one is owed if one is not allowed to invoke a narrative of past transgressions which are the grounds for moral and morally relevant reasons—transgressions grounded in social positions sanctioned by the political process.[27] Thus, while the original position certainly provides a moment wherein discord can give way to consensus, it comes at the price of important historical, sociological, and political truths that limit the kinds of justice claims one would have reason to press.

The second step is to get a hold on the idea of the reasonable. Persons eventually "emerge" from behind the veil of ignorance, and once out, they will face the more prickly questions of how to implement the principles of justice. Reasonableness is the criteria for taking for granted the kinds of seemingly absurd demands for which we assume people simply will not make a case. Thus, for Rawls, something being reasonable depends in large part on certain propositions that we can take for granted as having obvious moral force. For instance, "slavery is rejected as inherently unjust, and however much the aftermath of slavery may persist in social practices and unavowed attitudes, no one is willing to defend it.... We can regard these convictions as provisional fixed points which any conception of justice must account for if it is to be *reasonable* for us."[28] But notice what Rawls has done here. What seems to settle matters for him is that "no one is willing to defend it." However, a theorist concerned with racial inequality as it actually stands in the lives of blacks would focus on the following portion of the statement as embodying unreasonableness: "however much the aftermath of slavery may persist in social practices and unavowed attitudes." And this would be unreasonable precisely because almost no one in the twenty-first century would defend the proposition that blacks are inherently inferior or less worthy. (The reader will notice that this formulation indicates the preconditions for shame.) Thus, Rawls's reliance on reasonableness is likely to lead to racially uncertain outcomes, since he merely requires that no one will defend slavery, rather than being attentive to the unreasonable fact that the aftermath of slavery persists even though no one will defend that practice. I said above that Rawls's premises for making the basic structure the primary subject of justice actually tell against this second argument for how his conception qualifies as political. The preceding comments suggest the basis for this line of criticism.

The historical contingency premise indicates that practices of asymmetrical power can insinuate themselves in the workings of institutions, and importantly, that the patterns begotten by asymmetrical power can over time undermine fair agreements reached at some earlier point. Thus, in thinking about justice, we would need to know the extent and robustness of the relevant patterns of power over the relevant periods in history. Further, the sociopsychological premise tells us that our position in the social scheme has a profound impact on becoming the persons we ultimately develop into. Now, if a society is home to systemic racial inequality, it is not surprising that its members will not defend slavery and nevertheless be populated by agents with unavowed racial attitudes. This is captured by the idea of implicit racism: a sociopsychological disposition wherein people might consciously and wholeheartedly disavow racist doctrine yet find themselves holding racial beliefs (i.e., that black employees are not to be equally trusted). The crucial point about implicit racism is that, on the one hand, it need not overtly and explicitly invoke racial reasons during the deliberative process. However, on the other, it will nevertheless lead some to draw conclusions consistent with racially motivated reasoning. On this view, it seems the fact that no one will defend slavery or racism cannot do the work of providing the platform for sociopolitical reasonableness. And the reason is very important—as we shall see in the next chapter, a hallmark of American race relations in our time has been a certain tragic consistency between holding a view denying the appropriateness of slavery and a set of normatively relevant attitudes that nonetheless arbitrarily and systematically deny blacks a place of normative worth in American society. Just as we sometimes say that one man's terrorist is another's freedom fighter, one theorist's view of the reasonable is an oppressed person's experience of marginalization. The major critical point here, then, is that if we depend on the original position, we give up too much knowledge about the world, and if we depend on what Rawls considers reasonable, what we do know about the world is reshaped in ways that denies the issue appropriate moral urgency. In either case, the political is suppressed or it is ignored.

The conclusion we are working toward, then, is that a political conception of justice must take a view and stand located in the relevant temporally aware social position rather than a view from no particular social position at all. This is to say, it must be attentive to the way political history interacts with institutional practices, which have implications for persons' sense of self and others depending on their place in the social scheme. Ruth Frankenburg, in writing on her experiences in the field of whiteness studies says: "There is a link between where one stands in society and what one perceives. In addition, this epistemological stance made another, stronger claim: that the oppressed can see with the greatest clarity not only their own position but also that of the oppressor/privileged, and indeed the shape of the social system as a whole."[29] Frankenburg's observation suggests that the experience of racial inequality keeps us honest about the content of reasonableness and related normative devices and their scope within the theory of justice. More generally, it helps us bring the formal nature of moral principles into coherence with the actual mechanisms of injustice, allowing us to give robust content to our principles thereby allowing them to be political in the right way—they will take the problem of racial inequality on its own terms as informed by political reality.

Now I suspect a defender of Rawls may yet try to salvage the applicability, thus political value of Rawls's theory by saying that all the needs of racial inequality could be handled in what Rawls terms the four-stage sequence.[30] Here, Rawls refers to a process in which the veil of ignorance is gradually lifted at increasingly more applied stages of institutional design, and at each stage we have more empirical evidence, as well as judgmental latitude, in attending to instances of injustice. Thus, the defender would say, we can simply adjust policies and laws to reflect the facts of racial inequality across all relevant social, economic, and political practices.

This response seems to pose a serious challenge at first glance—but only at first glance. The defender would have to distinguish between two ways of understanding racial inequality. First, she might believe that racial inequality is merely blacks not being paid equal wages in some cases and in other discrete cases young blacks are denied quality education and in yet other cases have difficulty acquiring quality housing. That is to say, she would have to believe that racial inequality is merely a collection of discrete instances of inequality wherein the disadvantaged party is black. If this were all racial inequality consisted in, the two principles would almost be sufficient under the purview of the four-stage sequence. But if, second, she instead understood the idea of *systemic* racial inequality as not linking discrete instances of racial disadvantage but rather indicating substantive failures in the underlying public racial norms that serve to undergird the various policies, procedures, etc. that produce racial inequality she would consequently understand race as fundamental to the way politics works. That is to say, by the time we reach the later stages where full knowledge is brought to bear, we would be poorly positioned to reflect on how race pervades everyday lived experience in a myriad of ways, some of which are not susceptible to legal action or reform. A final related point: the four-stage sequence nevertheless treats matters of injustice as matters of institutional reform or response wherein the appropriate attendant civic ethos necessary for justice is a byproduct of rightly ordered institutions. In principle I have no complaint to raise against an ethos being a byproduct of institutional practices, but given the deeply embedded nature of racial norms in the polity, we ought to desire from the four-stage sequence a more secure way of directly addressing our co-participants' ethical shortcoming in forwarding the interests of a scheme of ongoing cooperation among moral equals.

We may yet think that despite issues of methodology, we ought to nevertheless fall back to the substance of Rawls's theory as embodied in his two principles of justice Rawls's two principles of justice. The two principles are general guidelines that (1) guarantee basic rights, and (2) mandate equality of opportunity while ensuring a material minimum for the least advantaged. However, it is difficult to see how they might yet redeem the shortcomings of Rawls's method with respect to systemic racial inequality. Consider that our society already affirms and legally guarantees equal rights and equal opportunity; further, consider that what we call a social minimum today, welfare, has become a hotly contested policy domain on account of race and our racial past.[31] I mean to indicate here that the political nature of racial inequality casts a shadow over our ability to merely rely on formal principles, particularly ones focusing on distributive justice, no matter their soundness. Put another way, that no one will defend slavery is little help in the face of an aftermath that replicates not merely the outcomes of racial disadvantage, but the underlying normative status of blacks that gives rise to that disadvantage. So, our response to the four-stage sequence objection should be, even if we want to accompany Rawls all the way to the four-stage sequence, at some point, probably early in the second stage (the constitutional convention stage), we will need some other resources to begin dealing with cases of injustice—resources that help us assess the normative substance of those cases, as well as justify more muscular specific responses that move us beyond the procedures and transactions Rawls's theory makes central. Indeed, we would need to question the state of our national character. So nothing in the defender's response embarrasses the project of a theory of racial justice as distinctly necessary, if not preferable. If anything, it further calls attention to the limits of Rawls's theory—limits that Rawls himself acknowledges.[32]

A political theory of racial justice will rightly focus on the basic structure but must be positioned to assess the ways a society is actually unjust—this is what it means to be political in the right way. From this perspective, the nuances of systemic racial inequality become much more distinct, since we are now sensitive to the ways our political history begat racial norms that in turn burden personal judgment and interfere with institutional fairness. This is what the idea of social value will do for us in supplementing the idea of systemic racial inequality as we move toward a positive account of racial justice. However, once we expand our view of the political, we are further committed to understanding the forces that shape the political processes that in turn give rise to racial inequality.[33] In a word, we must be attentive to power. Here, Mills makes an important contribution to thinking about race and justice that must be acknowledged even if we ultimately believe it to be crucially flawed in other respects.

Mills on Race and Justice

Characterizing racial inequality as systemic implicates relations of power in shaping social, economic, and political arrangements in a racially disadvantageous manner. While Rawls's focus on the basic structure provides (an unexploited) opportunity for reflecting on the ways in which racial power operates, Mills, in contrast, takes considerations of power to be central to an inquiry into racial injustice. Mills's approach to power and race depends on two propositions. First, racial inequality is the result of a particular system of power: white supremacy. Second, Mills identifies what I consider to be a problem of experientially informed perspective—white supremacy is (mostly) only visible to either its colored victims or the genuinely morally attuned.

I want to first show that Mills's general description of the various facets of racial inequality is spot-on. Indeed, Mills is to be applauded for seeking to bring matters of power and social epistemology to the theoretical fore. In doing so, he invites us to embrace a more capacious and immediate understanding of the political. Yet, there is a two-prong flaw in his work that demands our attention. First, Mills underspecifies the mechanics of racial power, proceeding as if defining various dimensions of the problem using the predicate "white" (i.e., white supremacy, white privilege) settles our understanding of what drives and sustains systemic racial inequality. However, this is a radically incomplete specification of systemic racial inequality—simply indicating background processes and describing those as "white" or beneficial to whites is of marginal analytic usefulness. Mills might respond that all he means by "white supremacy" is that it describes the beneficiaries who perpetuate racial inequality by accepting its benefits. This is fine save that it fails to specify the mechanics by which racial inequality evolves and reproduces itself.[34] It also fails to analyze the distinctive nature of race in the twenty-first century as compared to the nineteenth century, for example. Second, Mills's recent foray into prescriptive theory mobilizing a modified original position and distributive justice to argue for reparations is inconsistent with the substance of his own arguments regarding the moral utility and critical force of a situated perspective. Surely, if a virtue of Mills's work is his call to be attentive to the facts of the experience of race, we should be puzzled at an attempt to sharply qualify its inclusion in a normative theory. Let's take up these two critical points in turn.

In working toward the first critical point regarding Mills's approach to racial power, we need to be clear on what he means when he relies on the idea of "white supremacy." I perceive two components to Mills's understanding of the notion. First, it is coextensive with what Mills refers to as *Herrenvolk* ethics and is intended to address the sociology of knowledge in political thought.[35] When Mills invokes this term, he means to bring a charge against the social contract tradition that undergirds contemporary liberal theory. On his view, the social contract did not achieve, and was not intended to achieve, universal validity. Upon analyzing Immanuel Kant's wider racist beliefs and citing John Locke's support for racist practices in North Carolina alongside considering the abstraction introduced by the social contract, Mills claims that one of the most important ideas in Western political thought was produced by whites in service to whites. The social contract, so Mills argues, is a vehicle for a set of values that are antithetical to racial egalitarianism.

The second component, more concerned with social conditions outside the academy, is that whites are simply in a position of power not readily or easily available to blacks (though Mills would argue that this power disparity indeed has shaped the academy's sociology of knowledge). Mills tells us that white supremacy is "a *system* run by, and in the interests of whites."[36] When pressed for further specification, Mills draws upon the work of Frances Lee Ansley: "[White supremacy is] a political, economic, and cultural system in which whites overwhelmingly control power and material resources, conscious and unconscious ideas of white superiority and entitlement are widespread, and relations of white supremacy and non-white subordination are daily reenacted across a broad array of institutions and social settings."[37] So, on the one hand, there is the issue of asymmetrical access to the levers of power. On the other, there is a psychological component in which explicit and implicit racism are in play.

Although I will ultimately disavow Mills's deployment of white supremacy, I want to first highlight what is analytically useful about the term. The idea of white supremacy forces us to reflect on the past and to accept that it has implications for the present. By this I mean that historically it is absolutely true that whites (white men, more precisely) unilaterally wielded power in America and unilaterally enslaved blacks and rendered them something less than human. On this first cut, we simply acknowledge that racial inequality would not be a live problem if it were not for the brutal history of black mistreatment. On a second cut, white supremacy has the virtue of drawing our attention to the continuing relevance of race in twenty-first-century America. The comedian Chris Rock offers an anecdotal lesson when he informs us that only a handful of blacks live in his neighborhood, one of America's most exclusive. Each of his black neighbors has attained wealth by being nearly the best at what they do in their respective professions (i.e., acting or singing) thereby earning them fame. Meanwhile, and here is the punch-line, his white neighbor is merely a dentist—not a world-famous dentist, just a dentist. (*Kill The Messenger*. Perf. Chris Rock. 2008. DVD. HBO Home Video. 2009.) By this, Rock means to tell us that while it is true that blacks can get rich and even buy their way into traditionally white bastions of advantage and prestige, it seems that the bar for having that privilege is inordinately high and that its height is set by race. Mills's approach, then, is appropriately political.

The idea of white supremacy is somewhat useful as a reminder that blacks are often social, political, and economic losers in the social scheme or can be winners at great cost thus inviting us to be suspicious of commonly deployed narratives of Americans who pull themselves up by their bootstraps, whose wealth and mansions are purely a result of dedicated labor, thus available to anyone with the right amount of get-up-and-go. White supremacy, then, serves a partly evaluative function in that it replaces a purportedly neutral causal explanation for racial inequality with one that allows history to inform our current observations about disparities of power.

However, as true as the historical thesis of white supremacy might be, we need something that is both more robust and more nuanced to address racial inequality in our time. If we turn back to Mills's precedent framing of white supremacy, we notice an aspect of its definition that even the most racially suspicious of us ought to accept in only a qualified sense: a system run by whites in the interests of whites. There is a strong and weak sense in which this may be true. On the strong view, whites widely coordinate activities to co-opt and subordinate blacks. I do not need to say much for this notion's exaggerated thesis to disqualify itself. Let me be clear—there are racists in American society, and there are even instances where some may get together to deny benefits with respect to race, but all the evidence we have suggests that widespread explicit racism is not the phenomenon it once was. Additionally, although racial inequality is a fact, it would take coordination (nay, conspiracy) of the first order to multiply racial outcomes across all the domains in which race plays a part. So, this clearly cannot be what Mills means.

We are then left with a weak view: that it is true whites disproportionately occupy positions of power and it is true that blacks are systematically at risk of not being able to pursue and achieve a good life in equal measure as their white co-citizens. This weak view admits empirical descriptors of racial inequality yet remains non-committal with respect to intentional causality. Yet, when we deny the stronger view and acknowledge that explicit racism is no longer a significant explanatory variable, it now seems that white advantage is nearly epiphenomenal—this is why it is a weak view. That it is weak signals the important ways in which we need to move beyond Mills to best understand racial inequality. Let's work through this point carefully.

Institutions and political structures position persons within a scheme of advantage and disadvantage. The effect of this positioning is that it works to create kinds of persons. John Gaventa has found that some structures of power create quiescent subjects while Michel Foucault argues that they create pliant subjects.[38,39] Nonetheless, in addition to structuring opportunity, the basic structure becomes a purveyor of norms that citizens orient themselves toward and are very likely to adopt in various ways such that the persons they are reflect broader norms, expectations, and values—this is in large part shaped by one's place in the racial scheme.

Now, my charge against Mills is not that he is unaware of this, for he writes:

> In a sense, it all comes down to the "ontological."…the dismantling of white supremacy will require an ontological leveling, ontological equality, the end of differentiation, once overt and de jure, now hidden and de facto, between persons and subpersons.…dismantling of the supports of whiteness.…is not to be directly legislated into existence or rather nonexistence, rather it will be the cumulative result of social change, the eradication of the multiple social structures that underpin the social ontology of hierarchy.[40]

It seems to me that Mills's diagnosis is correct and farther reaching than he might imagine. Racial power is robust and operates widely, thus, it helps make all citizens in certain ways, namely either sensitive to their disadvantage as blacks, for example, or unappreciative that more than mere hard work brings benefits to whites. This is a natural entailment of the ontological argument in the face of political and social reality, but the nuance it allows plays a minor role, if any, in Mills's understanding of racial power. Describing the workings of power as "white" and linking it to white interests analytically distracts us from closely inquiring into "the multiple social structures that *underpin* the social ontology of hierarchy." On the view I put forth in chapter 2, racial justice requires precisely that we unpack the mechanisms that allow for the social ontology of hierarchy to be underpinned by multiple social structures. There, the idea of white supremacy can be implied in the genealogical aspects of the argument, but that is where the implication remains—as society has changed over time, we will find that the causal link between distinct white interests and distinct cases of black disadvantage becomes less clear-cut. However, Mills's invocation of the ontological concern is not without its merits. This gives way to my second complaint against Mills.

If we accommodate the weak view of white supremacy (as informed by the ontological argument), then we also must be committed to a conception of justice that can be sufficiently responsive to the deep nuance the weak view of white supremacy presents us—justice must reach down into the practices of race, informed by the perspective of subordination. At base, this requires attention to (conceptual) detail. Consider that one of Mills's major complaints, and the one pressed in "Repairing the Racial Contract," is that ideal theory is far too abstract to grant us purchase on the complexities of racial inequality. He writes, "The issue of racial justice is, by definition, a matter of *non-ideal theory*, since it presupposes corrective measures to remedy the legacy and ongoing practices of racial oppression."[41] This informs his criticism of contemporary liberalism as being inattentive to the facts of racial subordination and the power dynamics that make it a social and political reality. This conclusion is supported by my above analysis of justice as fairness and the criticism of it as insufficiently political. We also just saw that Mills believes racial ontology to be a fundamental problem of racial inequality. So two of Mills's moves in that essay are particularly confusing.

Mills's first move is to argue for a veil of ignorance "thinner" than that in Rawls's theory. In his amended original position persons still lack all information about their own place in society, as well as their own attributes, but they are provided information on extant and historical injustices (i.e., racial inequality against the backdrop of slavery). Mills's basic argument is that holding Rawls's application of the rules of rational choice constant, it is easy to justify and articulate principles of racial reparation (you might affirm the rightness of reparations on the chance that you are black upon exiting the original position).

However, the first move would only be sensible if Mills were to endorse a basic premise of Rawls's method—that ideal theory gives us the best grasp on nonideal cases, thus we must begin our normative deliberations under racial epistemic constraints. But, as indicated in the above cited passage, Mills's corpus has been (rightly) built upon rejecting that premise. A major component of Mills's work hinges on the problem of racial perspective and the deep value of subjective experience under a regime of racial disadvantage—this largely drives his criticism of the social contract tradition as beholden to *Herrenvolk* ethics. To have such a perspective is the first step toward being a genuinely free agent under oppressive circumstances; it is also the first important step toward attaining the kind of critical awareness crucial for whites' participation in seeing racial inequality for what it is. This is in part what makes his view appropriately political on my view. I have always understood Mills to hold his position precisely because the experiential aspect of racial injustice provides epistemic resources to speak truth to power, thus to deny *Herrenvolk* ethics primacy in our structure of normative reflections. For example, with respect to what Mills terms alternative epistemologies, he writes:

> The sentiment tends to be that [the status quo] framework needs to be transcended and that the standard, hallowed array of "problems" in the field should itself be seen as problematic. Thus a destructive genealogical inquiry underpins part of their rec- ommended reconceptualization, the suggestion being that certain issues have been seen as problems in the first place only because of the privileged universalization of the experience and outlook of a very limited (particularistic) sector of humanity— largely white, male, and propertied.[42]

The deployment of a thin veil of ignorance, then, is consistent with the aim of justi- fying reparations but precisely because persons still work under epistemic constraints, other approaches to racial injustice informed by the experience of social subordination will be marginalized. (This unfortunately seems to make Mills complicit in develop- ing a theory that retains what he himself might consider a colonial tinge embodied in historically European conceptions of property and individualism.) On this view, then, the original position should remain, on Mills's own account, an enemy of racial equality in the deepest sense—it denies us the weapons of the weak. Consequently there seems to be a significant asymmetry between Mills's demands that we directly confront racial power and an approach that discounts exactly that principle. I want to say, then, that Mills's concerns about power, even on a weaker view of white supremacy, appear to fall to the wayside for one cannot speak truth to power of any sort without knowledge of it in its deepest sense.

Second, Mills's presentation of the arguments in the amended original position is intended to yield justification for reparations, which he conceives as a distributive solu- tion.[43] Mills's failure to look beyond reparations is puzzling, and it is not difficult to see why. He argues that the problem of ontology is fundamental to the problem of racial inequality, so it is difficult to grasp how an argument for reparations from behind a thick or thin veil of ignorance can do the necessary work. Consider that the title of Mills's 2003 volume is *From Class to Race*—many of the essays in this volume are intended to lay the groundwork for understanding the idea of domination as more comprehensive than that captured by Marxist critiques of social power indexed to property (material) relations. This reveals an inconsistency in Mills's commitment to approaching justice as motivated by a desire to undermine racial power since an argument for reparations sug- gests that material distribution morally and analytically tracks a history of disrespect, as well as being able to address the power dynamics underpinning the social ontology of hierarchy—indeed Mills says this is what it all comes down to. On Mills's own critical views, responding to race requires directly confronting the problem of the status of blacks as begot by power—not the deployment of a device such as the original position that is bankrupt of epistemic utility, and certainly not by writing a check in response to being socially marginalized.

I submit, then, that in Mills's move to argue for a material solution to racial equality—a solution generated from behind the veil of ignorance no less—he has lost sight of what a transformative theory of racial justice would entail. In effect, he has succumbed to the same errors he often accuses Rawls of making in offering a normative political theory. While the theory of racial justice must be sufficiently nuanced to diagnose the problem of race in our time, as well as stay true to the principle of addressing the way power makes race a problem for our social scheme, it must resist understanding racial inequality as equivalent to white supremacy. It must stay true in speaking experientially informed truth to power, as well as continuing to resist distributive frameworks that necessarily fail to address questions of moral status. Mills opens the space for us to think of racial inequality in very political ways but precisely because the political is complex, we must address racial inequality in a manner that more accurately reflects a deep understanding of what it consists in—we must be able to address racial inequality as it is in our time.

CONCLUSION

Academic orthodoxy tells us that Kanye West is a long way from John Rawls and Charles Mills. After all, these are "elite" thinkers "trained" to "analyze" social phenomena and think "clearly" about the problems therein. Is that right? If there is such a distance, how is it that in West's two utterances we have been given a more urgent and, because more urgent, more relevant analysis of the state of race in America than either Rawls or Mills has provided. Of course, West does not have a theory of institutional design nor does he have a theory of social epistemology. However, he has the conviction of an intuition situated as a concerned observer of political processes—the intuition is that something is so fundamentally flawed in our national character that before we can talk about what blacks should have, we should examine our shared understanding of what blacks are worth as members of the social scheme. That is to say, how is it possible to say that we do not care about them as persons yet simultaneously claim to be participants in a fair democratic social scheme? We affirm those principles but they fail us in the face of race. That is why shame is appropriate—we are not generally morally corrupt people but we are in moral error of a most significant kind. But, our engagement with Rawls and Mills may yet be be profitable for it helps us to better understand the role of institutions in both reproducing racial inequality and the potential they have in eradicating it so long as we remain aware of the power relations that underwrite racial subordination.

Thus, racial inequality is a truly complex phenomenon for if studied closely, it indicates the interaction between a lack of affective concern and moral care alongside formal institutional processes to result in offenses that span a wide range of social, political, and economic practices. But, it is susceptible of a rigorous response if we approach it from the right perspective and are willing to depart from commonly relied upon theoretical frameworks. In the first instance, we need to recognize that racial inequality does not represent a moral problem for which we do not possess ready resources. In principle, it requires affirmation of moral equality, and it then requires that that principle be made the guiding light for personal attitudes and behaviors, as well as institutional policy and development. It is precisely because we already have some of the appropriate resources in hand—namely, affirmation of moral equality—that racial injustice should be a cause of shame. Our most deeply held principles seem to come apart—we seem to fall away from our ideals as individuals and as a society—in the face of race. That shame is the proper response to invoke does double duty—it prompts earnest moral assessment of our failings but also motivates us to be better than we are, in just the ways our own affirmation of moral equality obligates us.

And this is why racial inequality is peculiar. Why is it that we fall away from our ideals in the face of race? I argue in the next chapter that the answer is as simple as it is morally problematic—blacks hold a lower position in the normative valuational scheme from the point of view of social, economic, and political arrangements. This is the problem of social value, and on my view of it, it drives all forms of racial inequality on account that racial inequality is racial. The problem of social value is fundamental to understanding racial inequality. As elegant as this conception may be in providing a comprehensive explanation of the persistence and reproduction of racial inequality, it actually presents us with a set of challenges from the point of view of normative thought. I would like to briefly set these out to prepare the way for the remaining series of arguments.

If we refuse to give "white power" a role in explaining the persistence of racial inequality, what ought to take its place and how shall we specify it? My response in the next chapter is a conception of power: historically evolved socially embedded power. It is a conception that takes the historical thesis of white supremacy seriously and deciphers its more nuanced remnants in terms appropriate for dealing with racial inequality in our time. The conception is pivotal for explaining the persistence of racial practices both institutionally and personally and thereby serves as the grounds for assessing racial inequality as problematically tied to bad national character. If we use the term "character," we need to have a clear understanding how we make character claims of a whole nation at both the aforementioned levels. Additionally, what makes that character a bad one? The first step taken by the chapter is to specify the problem of racial inequality as one of social value: Blacks do not hold an equal place as whites do in the nation's normative framework, thus our character is one that marginalizes black interests and well-being.

2

The Problem of Social Value

A 2008 UNITED for a Fair Economy report reveals disturbing trends in real estate practices prior to and during the 2007 US economic meltdown.[1] It is commonly assumed that home loan interest rates vary by an applicant's creditworthiness. They also impact a person's or family's remaining economic resources. It is one reason the typical American strives to have good credit—it not only determines access to capital but its cost as well. During the time leading up to the collapse of the real estate market in 2007, access to capital was easy to come by but its cost varied. Ostensibly, the variations should have tracked the only variable that is supposed to matter: creditworthiness. The disturbing trend to which I alluded unsurprisingly refers to a matter of racial inequality. Specifically, it turns out that lower income blacks were more than twice as likely to be targeted for subprime loans as lower income whites, while middle and upper-income blacks were nearly three times more likely to be pushed into a loan with a subprime rate as compared to whites with similar income standing. More troubling is that this was not an isolated practice within one company but was more or less a national phenomenon. These facts are particularly illuminating as a commnon objection to the idea of racial inequality is that poor blacks comprise the racially disadvantaged, thus the problem is really one of class. But this is obviously wrong—here, racial disadvantage is simply, racial.

Discounting Mills's view of white supremacy, as we did in the previous chapter, how can we explain something so plainly racial but clearly uncoordinated? The problem has two components. On the one hand, we might think that this kind of inequality is possible given the logic of financial institutions. When we think about other aspects of the financial crisis we note, for example, risk became an institutionally accepted modus operandi so there were few protections in place to prevent rogue instances of inappropriate betting at the table of global finance. However, the idea of risk is integral to finance, so it is unsurprising when the business cycle moves through moments of ebullience followed by humbling lows. Race is another story—no MBA in the twenty-first century is taught that race is a structurally given determinative variable in loan rate calculations. On this view, then, there are practices embedded deeply within the working of major institutions that somehow allow noneconomic reasons to bear on economic decisions.

On the other hand, real estate agents engage clients, show them homes, counsel them on their options, make recommendations, and process paperwork. That means actual persons deploy judgments. In this example, a number of people taking (uncoordinated) action seem to have made judgments that resulted in ostensibly racist activities. However, we would do well to keep in mind the marked reduction in explicit overt racism. Even if some of these agents were genuine racists, it is implausible that all of them were. Rather, on the view of implicit racism, it is much more likely that if any of these agents were pressed to give an account of their racial views, many would be genuinely upset to learn their judgments were unmistakably racially motivated.

We now seem to be facing a real difficulty. How do we account for the persistence of these kinds of institutional practices? Additionally, what do we make of behavior at the individual level? This chapter begins by specifying a term that represents a first-order normative principle crucial for answering these questions: the problem of social value. The idea of social value is meant to denote the way narratives, power, and values coalesce around racial identity thereby serving to justify blacks' lower normative standing— they are not accorded equal concern, respect, or civic consideration. The argument below is that conceiving of racial inequality as the problem of social value resolves the above puzzle in a rather straightforward yet theoretically robust manner. On the view of social value, the social construction of race comes with the baggage of past explicit racial bias; in our time, as argued against Mills, racial bias is present but modified and finds a home in institutional processes, which in turn have implications for belief and attitude formation at the level of individuals. Put another way: Institutions display bad character that underwrites the development of bad character traits among members of the polity. This view is sympathetic to that offered by critical theorists, such as Charles Mills but we require a systematic way of understanding the mechanics of this phenomenon. Further, I do not think we can do the work of justice without first understanding how a nation can come to possess bad character. My position in the final chapter will be that racial justice fundamentally amounts to reforming and redeeming our national character. To that end, I specify the problem of social value in the first section of this chapter. That is followed by an account of power meant to sketch the mechanics of how the problem of social value translates into persistent racial inequality that reproduces itself over time.

I develop a two-prong conception of power, *historically evolved/socially embedded power*, that maps onto Rawls's two premises justifying the position the basic structure occupies in his theory as the primary subject of justice. We will recall they are the histori-cal contingency premise and the sociopsychological premise. My conception of power acknowledges the compelling features of this particular claim in Rawls's work, as well as the useful features of Mills's own concerns about racial power relations. I position the explanatory role of the conception as fundamental for specifying the prescriptive aspects of the theory of racial justice. It states:

> *Historically evolved power is the phenomenon of historically patterned group domi-nance founded upon racism embodied in path-dependent institutions resulting in robust contemporary inequality that no longer depends on explicit racism; socially embedded power is the ability for extant racial asymmetries to affect our sense of self and others such that those better positioned tend to hold beliefs and attitudes that motivate a lack of normative concern for the systemically disadvantaged, while those worse positioned are burdened in developing a full sense of being an equal democratic self.*[2]

The basic notion embodied by this conception of power is that there exists a certain sym-biotic nature between the way institutions make racial power manifest in practice and the way persons comport themselves to that power with respect to their standing in the social scheme.

As I indicated in chapter 1, this relationship evidences bad national character and because it betrays principles we already affirm, it is a cause of shame. The theory of power offered below following a specification of the problem of social value provides an explan-atory framework for how we have come to possess bad national character and sets the stage for the democratic perfectionist argument in chapter 5. Revisiting the example at the beginning of this chapter: It seems that both agents and institutions deployed bad judgment that may or may not have been consistently informed by intentional racist motives. Indeed, I have suggested that the relevant actions were not informed by such motives. If so, then, amidst basic democratic commitments, such biased behavior indi-cates a failure not of ideal judgment (knowing the difference between right and wrong) but of practical judgment (applying reasonable conceptions if right and wrong to action). Here, both persons and institutions are in error about the best and most consistent way to connect notions of right and wrong in democratic society the moment race comes into the picture. Here, perfectionism aims to repair the connection between basic notions of right and wrong under democratic norms and racial responses. I ultimately argue that a perfectionist stance is our best hope for achieving racial justice. In specifying the nature of racial power, I open up space for what is to follow in chapters 3 and 4, where I explore the nature of certain institutional practices that clearly exhibit racial reasoning, thus bad institutional character, and more closely examine the problem of bad personal character, respectively.

RACE AND THE PROBLEM OF SOCIAL VALUE

Social Value

The idea of systemic inequality is often mobilized to capture a truly important social, economic, and political phenomenon—the empirical fact that blacks are highly likely to be economically poorer,[3] encounter the criminal justice system,[4] face difficulties in fairly securing employment,[5] and be in poorer health,[6] just to name a few categories of disadvantage. The term unifies a wide array of injustices under a heuristic. To say that racial inequality is systemic is to indicate the variety of practices that result in one category of inequality—racial. It serves a further purpose in linking inequality to systematicity by directing our attention to ways in which race can be operative in the background of institutional practices yet produce results in the foreground. Certainly, the idea is important for responding to those who deny the role race plays in inequality. Such a response is typically motivated by noting the victories of 1964 (the Civil Rights Act) and 1965 (the Voting Rights Act) and further claiming that something else must be the problem, but whatever it is, it is not race. Thus, the notion of systemic inequality is helpful because it rejects the implied thesis that racial inequality depends on overt subordination, a feature of racial power that has faded over time. However, the notion of systemic inequality becomes less useful when we try to further specify it for the purposes of normative theory because it directs our attentions to the outcomes of a racialized system, but not what drives it. As the point was pressed against Mills, looking at end-states distracts us from effectively studying causes and mechanisms.

We need a conception of racial inequality's first-order cause—a principle that gives contemporary racial inequality its texture and shape and keeps it alive and adaptable for our time. Institutional processes and individual actions and attitudes are driven by reasons, and reasons are normative in nature—they direct action in ways that we affirm as being appropriate according to some aim or a plan. So, what is the normative framework that serves to justify and motivate the actions and dispositions that result in systemic inequality? I want to suggest that the fundamental move necessary to undermine racial inequality in the deepest sense is to understand it as the *problem of social value*—the fact that blacks do not occupy an equal place in the scheme of normative attention and concern upon which our society depends in the first place to justify the distribution of benefits and burdens, as well as to identify those who are deserving or appropriate recipients. In other words, we either altogether lack or otherwise possess distorted reasons for the ways we treat blacks qua them being black.

The view of racial inequality as the problem of social value is intended to be an explanatory analytic device relevant for normative theory rather than a social scientific one capable of generating empirical hypotheses. By this I mean, that while occurrences of racial injustice are certainly to be accounted for by my conception, I am seeking to draw attention to what I understand as being a normative framework that serves to justify and motivate the actions and dispositions that produce racially distinct outcomes.[7] This is what I mean when I say that we ought to seek a first-order cause. The conception claims that social value is explanatory in that it defines the terms of normative consideration that are withheld from blacks. If it is the case that blacks are consistently on the receiving end of bad treatment, this tells us something about the motivating reasons and beliefs that generate mistreatment. To help settle our notions, consider possibilities for understanding the phenomenon of systemic racial inequality.

Along one dimension, we might simply consider the sheer number of practices that, when taken together, produce racial inequality. Systemic racial inequality can be understood as the systematically diminished probability that a person of color will be able to achieve or pursue a satisfying plan of life as compared to other members of society. Merely being born black is a reliable predictor of one's future life prospects.

This definition implicates a number of economic, political, and social practices. The difficulty blacks face across income categories to secure employment on a fair basis is a racial injustice. The inferior quality of inner city public schools is a racial injustice. The inability of inner city residents to easily purchase fruits and vegetables, thus live healthy lives, without having to take a twenty-minute bus ride to the nearest green grocer, yet are able to purchase liquor within a block or two of their residence is a racial injustice. These three examples begin to indicate the remarkable diversity of practices that result in racial inequality. The implication is quite clear: When a problem falling under a single descriptive category is in reality one that straddles numerous practical categories that ostensibly operate under distinct logics, there is no immediately clear way to simultaneously address them all under the guidance of that one descriptive category. However, I believe there is a way forward, and as I shall argue below, part of the problem in addressing racial inequality consists in the tendency to engage the various practices with race in mind, rather than to engage race with the practices in the background. I shall explain below exactly what I mean by this.

Along another dimension, racial inequality is a significant problem because of the very idea of race. The notion that race is a social construct has become commonplace. That it is a social construct means we are depending upon a concept of dubious analytic worth to do a lot of analytic work for us with respect to assessing human behavior. Further, regardless of race's constructed nature, it has always been and continues to remain a loaded concept. From our contemporary perspective, the idea of race recalls a morally offensive and deeply embarrassing stretch of American history that bore witness to human rights violations of the worst kind—instances of those abuses prompted Billie Holiday to sing of blacks hanging from trees as "strange fruit." Moreover, because we live in a post-Civil Rights Era, we sometimes believe we live in a "post-racial" era. In reality, we have no good evidence to support, thus no good reason to believe, that race is less important for the purposes of social analysis. Although a catalog of illustrations could be provided, we may simply consider not only the marked racial disparity in the suffering of Katrina victims (the Lower 9th Ward was predominantly black) but also the racial disparity in people's willingness to give aid to Katrina victims of one race rather than another.[8] Moments like these make clear that for all our desire to move past race, doing so may actually be a morally dangerous proposition—we give up a concept that still has a significant role in determining the social and political order. Thus, "race" matters.

That is why I said above that we need to engage race with practices of inequality in the background for race is the prominent social and political feature that unifies the wide variety of kinds of racial disadvantage. This may seem obvious and mundane to the point of being of minimal analytic use. That conclusion is a mistake. When I say we ought to focus on race with practices in the background, I mean to convey a strategy that has the virtue of simplicity, yet can yield significant normative conclusions. To say that race is a social construct is to say that race is an invention of social relations in which a constellation of practices over the course of history positions members of some groups advantageously or disadvantageously vis-à-vis members of other groups. I want to say, then, that this ordinal positioning is underwritten by a social scheme that assigns groups and their members differential normative status—it mandates who is worth what and why.

Two points are fundamental to the conception of racial inequality as the problem of social value. First, it presupposes a rather rudimentary but I think uncontroversial model of motivation: that reasons and beliefs are responsible for dispositions and actions. Second, and important for my engagement with Rawls, institutions play an important role in giving sanction to certain norms through their commitments and actions, thus having a significant impact on our own beliefs and reasons (thus, on our dispositions and actions). When a person of color comes into view for an agent, social value holds that at that moment a constellation of normatively diminishing judgments are likely to be triggered on account of the socially and politically marginalized value of blackness.

I want to highlight a benefit that will matter for building a positive normative theory— the conception diagnoses a moral malaise but does not overdetermine the outcome. The idea of social value satisfies an important condition for avoiding being overdeterministic: it is at once very general but acknowledges that reasons and beliefs can be amended upon deep and careful reflection. That is to say, that the problem of social value straddles the divide between agency and social construction by at once being sensitive to the way social power impacts beliefs and attitudes but denies that it does so in a manner that rejects the possibility of agency, thus agents can still be held accountable for their racial beliefs and actions after they have been made aware of how they offend against racially egalitarian principles. This is deeply important for the perfectionist argument presented in the final chapter, for the preceding indicates the appropriateness of prompting persons to attend to the incoherence between deeply held principles and the reasons and beliefs that result in racially inflected actions, utterances, attitudes, and so on.

Why Social Value?

Now, some are likely to remain unconvinced by my conception of racial inequality. It might be said that it is plausible but maybe too abstract to generate precise hypotheses that can inform social policy. I think there are two particular views one might find more desirable with respect to affecting social and political change: (1) the culture of poverty explanation; and (2) the goods beget other goods explanation. A brief engagement with each shows that both are better accommodated by my conception without either having to abandon its basic propositions. However, the alternative views ultimately leave untouched an inquiry into what motivates and justifies the processes they take as central to empirical investigation, thereby undercutting their own concerns over specifying effective policy responses. My position, then, is that social value provides a brighter guiding light for the theory of racial justice.

First, the culture of poverty thesis. This is an argument the conceptual roots of which are often attributed to Patrick Moynihan's report on the relationship between black disadvantage and family structure.[9] Its basic argument is that blacks are the cause of their disproportionate inequality because they have developed a culture that not merely embraces disadvantage but uses it as a wedge to blame society for their ills when in fact, their embrace of disadvantage has perpetrated a culture or shared way of life among blacks that justifies poor social, economic, and political choices.[10] For example, if blacks do not want to get a proper education, then of course they will not be gainfully employed, and if they are not gainfully employed, then of course they will be on welfare. The further implication is that since their reliance on welfare is really a result of a lack of industriousness, then their being deemed lazy is simply a response to that feature of their life choices. Thus, if they would simply "get their act together," they could solve the race problem themselves. On this view, one acknowledges that blacks have been horrendously treated in the past, but holds that it is also true that at some point blacks bought into their misfortune and have themselves reproduced it through irresponsible acts.

The content of the judgment, "irresponsible," is informed and motivated by a viewpoint that is signally ignorant of the way deep disadvantage and agency can intersect. If we acknowledge the empirical fact that black lives are systematically disadvantaged, is it reasonable to suppose that blacks are systematically irresponsible as the culture of poverty thesis implies? That is to say, are we to suppose that their powers of judgment are so damaged that all or a great deal of their misfortune is really a function of their choices and little else? I find this to be a dubious claim. Why? For example, condsider the difficulties that meet the exercise of 'responsible' free agency when small business loans are unavailable or when one's local job market is marked by double-digit unemployment rates after an urban neighborhood is decimated by a flight of capital. In examples like these, reasonable conceptions of responsible action face the obstacle of structural features that in fact preempt the possibility of responsible action. Of course, a defender could claim the culture of poverty thesis is not meant to be so sweeping—rather, it ought to be employed to evaluate crucial life choices, such as investing vs. not investing one's energies in pursuing an education, and these kinds of choices, conceived as within the range of black responsibility, perpetuate racial inequality. Let us take this view seriously.

As I stated above, attitudes and actions are motivated by beliefs and reasons. If we take the weaker version of the culture of poverty thesis into account this is what we are left with: Blacks hold beliefs and reasons about the good of their lives that are counterproductive to achieving a truly good life. Now one route to take in response to this weaker view would be along the lines of Tommie Shelby's diagnosis of ghetto deviance and concede that unfortunate decisions are made by blacks, but further argue that they are *rational* decisions in the face of radical institutional unfairness.[11] Moreover, such decisions are not unethical, since the basic structure of society is fundamentally unjust with respect to race thus suspending the principle of reciprocity that social justice typically depends upon. Another route to take would be the one given by the social value conception—to the extent that blacks make bad decisions, it will be because their social position, which could not possibly be their fault in the first place, confirms some notions of what it means to *be* a person living on the margins of an otherwise well-ordered society.[12] Marginalization concretizes racial norms that operate at a general social level by defining and shaping the life conditions blacks find themselves born into. The important distinction here is that on the more rationalistic model of "ghetto deviance" persons seem to merely make reasonable choices given their circumstances. On the view of social value, persons' choices may be reasonable, but the choices are significantly informed by the social lessons learned about the status, worth, and social place of black identity that further impacts the sense of the self beyond the purview of rational choice theory. Notice that this also accommodates Shelby's response to the person holding the culture of poverty view, but further stipulates that even if a black person's judgment is structurally rational, it is formed on the basis of self-understanding coupled with social observation. And what social observation suggests to a rational person in that position is that blacks must not be worth much. Thus, social value suggests itself as being the underlying causal principle in any case.

Second, there is the goods beget goods conception of racial inequality. On this view, racial inequality is a fact of life because the majority of blacks do not have access to wealth, resources, and opportunity.[13] Give them these goods and they are provided the most important means of eradicating racial disadvantage. Now, no one can deny that a lack of resources explains a good deal of the disadvantages that, for example, black children face, i.e. substandard school buildings and learning materials. Also, no one can deny that access to resource-rich schools would help improve their future opportunities. But we ought to be wary of the supposed scope of this explanation. We can easily appreciate that value must be at work here by considering an entirely plausible example of a Mercedes-Benz-driving black man being groundlessly profiled by state highway patrol personnel. We might also refer to studies showing racial discrimination in interviewing equally qualified job candidates whose only distinguishing feature is race.[14] We can also recall the case of racially disadvantageous home loans with which this chapter began. It is clear that the goods beget goods explanation would fall short in cases where access to resources, wealth, or opportunity are not in question. But race does remain in effect in these and other cases since relatively well-off blacks are nevertheless mistreated based on wrongful judgments of character or competence regardless of their prior access to elite institutions or prior proven experience of productive employment. On my view, then, social value remains the most effective and comprehensive conception of racial inequality.

Moving Forward with Social Value

Conceiving of the problem of race as that of social value, then, is both more robust and more elegant than competing conceptions, since it does not seek to undermine them—rather it does a better job at supporting some of those conceptions' analysis of racial inequality. Social value, then, is pivotal as it completes the constellation of concepts that informs our diagnosis of racial inequality, as well as a positive response. It turns out that social value is a particularly good fit with the notions of shame and character. How so? The core of the idea of shame, as shown in the previous chapter, is captured in the slogan: we often know better, but fail to do better. And with respect to race, this amounts to the typical American citizen and institution affirming the basic idea of moral equality but failing to consistently act from that affirmation in the face of race. That is, when that basic affirmation is necessary for showing black equal regard and their needs equal concern, we often fail to do so. And it is significant that this is not due to supposedly prudential interests, such as competition for limited resources. Rather, time and again, it is shown to be due simply to race. Social value takes this basic failure as being fundamental to understanding racial inequality by positing persons as reasons-dependent and further understanding that reasons are essentially normative: they tell us what we ought to do, what we ought to believe, and why. The puzzle here is that we affirm basic moral equality generally for good reasons, but fail to uphold that affirmation in the face of race for bad reasons. This leads to the basic but underutilized conclusion that there is something we think, feel, believe, desire, wish, fear, and so on about blacks qua being blacks that interferes with acting as well as we otherwise know we should.

The preceding also indicates where character fits into the theoretical picture. As indicated in the introduction, and expressed more completely in chapter 4, character represents the seat of judgment. It is not too analytically "plain," I think, to say that character represents the kinds of persons we are, the quality and texture of our personhood. It essentially represents the seat of our judgments toward others and ourselves, and we engage in character talk insofar as those judgments show us to be ethically consistent, upright, virtuous, villainous, a scoundrel, and so on. Now a theory of racial justice is not properly concerned with the kinds of persons we are and the kinds of institutions we rely upon, in all senses. Rather it is concerned with the kinds of persons we are and institutions we rely upon as relevant to matters concerning race. The way then to understand how people can come to be properly ashamed is when their racial values are in direct conflict with more basic normative principles for bad reasons; and, further, their apparatus of judgment seems to fail them from their failure to resolve that conflict.

But, of course, the above raises the basic question as to how such a rescue is effected if we respectively seem ill-equipped or insufficiently motivated or possessing flawed moral vision necessary to resolve conflict. To further preview, this marks the place of perfectionism in an effective account of racial justice. It is crucial that our racial failings are largely accounted for not by intentional desires to belittle or marginalize blacks, but rather a failure to resolve a conflict that does not really have a desired place in our judgmental apparatus. Rather, it amounts to a moral and ethical burden which we must be aided in relieving—others must help us be free of it, since we often lack the full schedule of capacities necessary to do it ourselves. And be free of it we must if we are to eliminate the cause of our shame, begotten by color as it is.

So that settles mapping the fit between social value and shame and character, and how they inform a perfectionist approach to justice. Social value also has another virtue. It imparts three lessons that correct important confusions in Rawls's and Mills's projects.

First, social value alerts us to the political nature of racial inequality. On the one hand, racial inequality is born of political history—for centuries, black oppression was inscribed in law, as well as social norms. Indeed, the two interacted to form an unfortunate alliance wherein the formative years of American institutional design was deeply influenced by racism. And, as we shall see, institutional practices have implications for personal beliefs. On the other, racial inequality is a lived experience under actual democratic institutions—we, as political agents, live under unjust circumstances that purport to carry a degree of legitimacy. On this view, a theory is appropriately political for the needs of racial inequality when it takes seriously the importance of history, its implications for institutional development that are always a result of politics and which in turn impact the political process, and, last, the interplay between institutional development and moral learning at a personal level.

Second, the theory must acknowledge not only that explicit racism has been on a steep decline for some time but also that on the above view of institutions' role in personal belief formation, blunt notions like "white domination" distract us from the more pressing work of determining the ways the characterological makeup of members of the polity is shaped under the influence of racial power. In the absence of this kind of nuance, we easily lapse into racial finger-pointing without understanding that social value affects all persons. However, it is important to recognize that we are impacted differentially on account of our place in the social scheme. Michael Dawson, for example, finds substantial gaps in racial perceptions of the meaning of the Katrina disaster and what ought to be done in its wake. Consider that 90 percent of blacks as compared to 38 percent of whites believe that the disaster showed that racial inequality remains a problem for America. Consider further that 79 percent of blacks felt that the government should spend whatever is necessary to restore New Orleans as compared to 33 percent of whites.[15] What explains these significant gaps? Dawson invokes the idea of "life-worlds" in order to describe how blacks experience a political reality that is at odds with whites' assessment of political reality (and vice versa). On this view, blacks and whites do not share "a basis for consensus, communicative action, shared comprehension, and therefore, social integration and reproduction."[16] Thus, distinct life-worlds entail divergent explanations for social problems. And, as seems clear in Dawson's finding, distinct life-worlds seem to make possible, if not necessarily entail, distinct social valuational schemes.

Last, conceiving of race as the problem of social value has implications for a theory of racial justice in a positive sense. The conception indicates that the theory must take seriously the role of ideas and norms in our attitudes and actions, thus be willing to consider that old norms must be refashioned to overcome how we typically value black lives and interests. On this view, we have to broaden the toolbox of a theory of justice by realizing that persons do not merely disagree about what they are owed or what shape society's major institutions should take simply or merely based on prudential interests as informed by rational choice. Rather, racial justice must have something to say about the character of persons and institutions as developed within current patterns of racial power and against the full backdrop of our racial history. Doing so will clearly shift our prescriptive tactics from attending to matters of distribution to matters of individual and shared attitudes and beliefs about blacks—the theory will make central attention to a kind of democratic ethos fundamental to a good democratic society marked by race. Put differently, it attends to American soulcrafting.

RACE AND THE THEORY OF POWER IN TWO PARTS

Part I. Historically Evolved Power

Institutions: Their Possessing Character and How

Rawls conceives of the basic structure as "the way in which the main political and social institutions of society fit together into one system of social cooperation, and the way they assign basic rights and duties and regulate the division of advantages that arises from social cooperation over time."[17] Importantly, "the basic structure is the all-inclusive system that determines background justice."[18] This definition treats the basic structure holistically and in a somewhat explanatory manner—there is something about how institutions cohere and act in combination with individuals' collective actions, with regard to the relevant distributions, that deserves to be the primary subject of justice.

By major social institutions, which are constitutive of the basic structure, Rawls understands "the political constitution and the principal economic and social arrangements. Thus the legal protection of freedom of thought and liberty of conscience, competitive markets, private property in the means of production, and the monogamous family are examples of major social institutions."[19] Now, in a sense, what is meant here by "institution" is straightforward. An institution is a significant regulative force that sets the parameters for some form of social, political, economic transaction or private association. When we refer to an institution, it is clear that there is a sense that institutions are what Douglas North calls "rules of the game," by which he means, "the humanly devised constraints that shape human interaction"; further, "they structure incentives in human exchange" politically, socially, and economically.[20] But it is clear that institutions are more than that. Rawls stipulates that the principles of justice apply to the basic structure in the first instance because institutions do more than constrain—they produce. Further, while they certainly structure incentives, they also moderate normative aspects of human interaction that depend on ethical commitments that may or may not have a relationship to the idea of incentives. On Rawls's account institutions articulate the nature and content of rights, as well as determine each person's level of advantage, which affects the ability to pursue a life of one's choosing. However, there is more to the story. On the one hand, the things institutions do are couched in more than the idea of rules, but also in the idea of norms and social narratives revolving around worth and which are informed by bias. On the other, the fact that institutions are conduits for norms and values means they also impart lessons on what (kinds of) persons occupy which places in the social scheme, and why they do; and these lessons affect how we comport ourselves toward others in the social scheme, as well as our self-conception as agents who occupy various places in that scheme. And because institutions do these things and can do them well or badly, morally or immorally, they are subject to character assessment. Let's spend a bit of time getting clear on the relationship between institutions and character claims.

We will recall that Rawls relies on two premises meant to substantiate the claim that the basic structure ought to be the primary subject of justice. The first—the *historical contingency* premise—holds that even when fair rules are developed for institutions, they may still succumb to historical patterns of unfairness. This premise seems right but presents us with a significant problem. If institutions are rightly conceived as being the primary subject of justice but can fail to abide by principles of justice, then we possibly face an unfortunate paradox: Our most potent resource for realizing justice may not be particularly reliable. This is concerning, but not deeply so, if we appreciate that the first premise in its current form is vague. The theory of power must accomplish two goals. First, it must illuminate the true nature of what is concerning about the paradox. That is, it must explain the substantial scope of how institutions have been shaped and in turn shape race relations without collapsing into a determinist account of that process. Second, in specifying the nuances of the premise, and taking the warning seriously, it should provide resources for escaping what seems at this point to be a paradox. I propose that we move in two steps. First, if we buy the argument for social value, we should want to know how it comes to shape institutions. That is, how do institutions come to possess bad character? Second, we need a clearer sense as to how institutions reproduce offensive practices and outcomes even in an era of formal equality.

In chapter 1, I argued that shame is a sensible analytic term when applied to institutions on account of the fact that they affirm principles that they nevertheless can fall away from. And their failures are ones that could have been avoided if only their moral compass was consistently aligned in the direction their commitments point. By extension, I take it that the notion of character is likewise suitably applicable. In the Introduction

I gestured toward a definition of character: a general pattern of attitudes and actions founded on a set or sets of beliefs having normative importance for our relations with others and our understanding of ourselves as agents possessing the power to act morally or not. Clearly, this is a definition formed with persons in mind—agents in possession of affective and rational capacities. Obviously it would be peculiar to attempt to make a one-to-one comparison in applying this definition to institutions—they certainly do not possess attitudes in the way persons do. Yet, I maintain that the notion of character is intelligible when applied to institutions all the same. They may not have attitudes, but they do have a relevantly close equivalent in dispositions (i.e., being disposed to aid the poor). Here we mean to ask whether the relevant institutions are egalitarian in nature or not. If they are, they are so disposed—if not, then not. Further, they may not have "self-understanding" in the way that persons do, but they do have institutional identity. The banking system, for example, is not in the business of philanthropy—that is not what it advertises as its purpose and function so it does not engage in that practice (as its main way of operating in the world).

As I offer these arguments and employ utterances indicating something like a "self" with respect to institutions, I suspect the reader nonetheless understands my meaning. Moreover, he or she understands it not merely as a metaphor but as analytically significant such that should the banking system tomorrow "decide" to dedicate a major portion of its efforts toward philanthropy, the reader him or herself is likely to say something to the effect, "what a peculiar strategy to adopt." At that moment, we would find it intelligible and coherent to pass judgments on the nature of an institution's behavior in a manner we think is susceptible to explanation on account of that institution's choices and practices. Though we may at one level deny that institutions "choose," at another level we depend on the idea that their actions are neither accidental nor merely an emergent property of a collectivity of individuals' decisions. What I mean to indicate here is that we often take institutions and the organizations that may comprise them as agents in some sense, and that is all I require to deploy the term "character" in a manner consistent with its general intent (as referring to agents capable of, and culpable for moral and immoral actions and dispositions), as well as consistent with the needs of this argument (agents that have engaged in culpable immoral actions and held offensive dispositions). When we think of institutions as something more than a mere repository for human preferences or patterns of preferences, they can and ought to be assessed as agents that do some things rather than other things and as agents that promote certain values or ends over other values or ends. And, if they can do these things, that means they can do them well or badly, virtuously or immorally. That they "can" do these things in these various, normatively relevant qualitative ways is a hallmark of what it means to judge an agent as possessing better or worse, good or bad character.

Precisely because of these significant features, it is important to recall that institutions are, historically speaking, in the first instance creations of intentional human social practices, assent, and compliance—nothing in the above is an argument that institutions owe nothing to the effects of human agency. Although they are not reducible to being understood in terms of discrete human actions, that is not to deny that they are created by people and susceptible to being shaped by human agency. This indicates that they ought not be taken as de facto justified, for the important questions are twofold. First, what is the moral nature of those intentional actions? And, second, who has historically been able to assent to their creation thus find reason to comply with their strictures? An approach to these two questions should begin at the beginning—what are the antecedent social dynamics as institutions come into being?

Institutions are initially created and subsequently populated by people, and a basic feature of social organization is that societies are consistently marked by hierarchical group relations. While hierarchy is often taken in a pejorative sense, it is not intrinsically offensive. At base, it simply indicates an order of accountability in the relations of agents to each other and is a reliable way of organizing persons to achieve ends from which everyone can benefit. This is the underlying principle of corporations, for example, where leadership is essential to accomplishing major goals and realizing core visions. But let's now imagine a scenario wherein, as an employee, I am not merely accountable to my boss, but my being is defined on his terms. He thinks, for example, that what marks him as a leader is something about him that makes him and others "like him" more valuable than people "like me." (Notice, at this point, the content of the values is not of central importance. The simple fact that value judgments based on something other than measurable performance as per my function indicates that the frame of value is significantly different in a moral sense that is worth attending to.) In this scenario my value to the corporation is no longer measured by my role and performance but by arbitrary norms articulated by those with more or less overwhelming power; thus, I am reduced to something less than a fully autonomous, intrinsically valuable agent. Here is one way of thinking about this: I cease being an end unto myself. Importantly, my transformation is facilitated by a particular power relation since my boss controls resources that are needed in common and wields great influence across the scope of the corporation's social landscape. Thus, when my supervisor becomes my superior I then become a subject rather than an employee. A relation of hierarchy has is now marked by dominance. How do hierarchies become systems of domination?

One prominent social theory highlights three steps in the process. First, as noted, "societies tend to be structured as systems of *group-based social hierarchies*."[21] This might typically come about in a number of ways, such as by a Durkheimean division of labor, wherein persons take on roles according to function and over time some functions become more valuable to society than others.[22] However, while the division of labor offers a functional explanation for social differentiation that can ostensibly be justified by exactly that—socially necessary functions—social groups often exhibit what is referred to as an arbitrary-set system wherein they are divided by salient, socially constructed markers such as intelligence, family lineage, or, in the case of American sociology, skin color.[23] And these clearly have no necessary relation to valuable functions and roles.

Subordination begins to set in when one social group, as defined by the relevant salient marker, comes to occupy a position of authority or power. What facilitates group ascendancy? On George Orwell's anthropomorphized farm, one group led by the pigs and ultimately solely by Napoleon, seems able to articulate a justificatory narrative and subsequently institutionalize it as the shared common narrative.[24] Initially the pigs are ascendant because they seem to possess or at least are willing to exercise valuable skills that place them in a position of leadership (they are functionally valuable). However, in time, they leverage their skills and the goods they produce to justify a simple but powerful slogan that seems to normatively justify their ascendancy in a manner that is unrelated to their function and which the rest of the citizens of Animal Farm are in a weak position to resist—all animals are equal but some are more equal than others. An important lesson imparted by Orwell is that groups desiring social and political power understand the efficacy of narratives, even when they do not reflect justifiable social lessons. In *Animal Farm*, the story of the animals' first battle with humans becomes a rallying point for all the animals, and in each telling the pigs are portrayed ever more gloriously in the fight against the animals' former collective enemy, human beings; hence, the idea of legitimizing myths, which "consist of attitudes, values, beliefs, stereotypes, and ideologies that provide moral and intellectual justification for the social practices that distribute social value within the social system."[25] Legitimizing myths are important because they are the means by which ascendant groups assign to themselves positive social value while portraying others (setting the terms of social value) as justifiably possessing lower standing. Without legitimizing myths, hierarchy is merely stratification. With legitimizing myths, hierarchy becomes grounded in superiority and inferiority and formal distinctions become laden with norms.

So we have an understanding of how hierarchy becomes domination and why some groups succeed at dominating. How do they hold on to their position? One persuasive answer is somewhat surprising but provides an effective explanation. Jim Sidanius and Felicia Pratto observe that hunter-gatherer societies, which gather resources and produce mainly for subsistence, are rarely marked by pronounced hierarchy. Rather, societies marked by clear systems of hierarchy generally tend to be those that produce surplus goods, including noneconomic ones (i.e., the arts). Let's consider this a bit more closely. Among the defining characteristics of modern societies that produce surpluses are technological development, education, infrastructure, political stability. Indeed, surpluses are evidence of advancements in social organization that depend on widely agreed upon norms and expectations and ways of institutionalizing them. In brief, such societies are *institution rich*. As in *Animal Farm*, we will usually find the groups that are able to control social narratives are also the ones with outsized access and influence over institutions; it is also because they have influence over institutions that they are dominant. While Orwell is instructive here—consider that the pigs laid down all laws and had exclusive access to the means of trade—America's racial history tells the story just as well. While white males fought for equality, their opportunity to form a new government while being racists allowed them to at once declare a victory for human rights while denying blacks (and women) those rights. And, as is commonly known, those rights were denied for specious reasons founded upon an array of narrative tropes, such as those depicting the African savage. Importantly, and this is our answer to the first question—how do institutions come to be in possession of bad character?—white males designed "democratic" institutions for posterity while themselves occupying a time and place that sanctioned severe forms of racial subordination by, for example, recognizing slavery. This leads to the next important question: What explains institutional recalcitrance, especially where race is concerned?

Identifying and Assessing Institutional Character over Time

Institutions are responsive to significant social, political, and economic developments such as the move from relatively unregulated markets to the welfare state. However, their responses are often constrained by a limited selection of developmental tracks that are in part determined by institutions' own limited range of options for developmental change. In other words, genuine social, economic, or political progress may be hard to come by because institutions tend to be path dependent.[26] On this view, an institution's future is significantly guided by certain developments in its past. (Here it is helpful to keep in view our earlier discussion of the relationship between ascendant groups and opportunity to institutional access.) Moreover, developments are likely "to stick" on account of their providing positive feedback—increased benefits with an inverse correlative relationship to the cost of deviance from a set course. Path dependence is anchored by a number of mechanisms.

First, there is positive feedback. Consider our regime of corporate profiteering. This is a feature of economic life that would be difficult to eliminate. Why? For one, profits beget wealth for stockholders that raise their esteem, as well as their worth, so they are likely to continue to affirm the importance of profit seeking. Less cynically, profits allow corporations to pursue other interests in other markets or in expanding existing markets. Further, and importantly, the idea of profit also tends to serve the social heuristic of determining desert as grounded in free and autonomous action underwritten by effort— norms and values that mark, if not define, contemporary liberal societies. This is a system of positive feedback—the many interests and functions served by profits agitate for profit being the main engine of modern economic life. Thus, profit becomes an end for action, as well as the means.

Second, new social initiatives have a complicated relationship with institutional development for two quite distinct reasons. On the one hand, they can be inordinately difficult to realize, but on the other, suboptimal or simply bad initiatives might be adopted rather than ones that more closely meet the goals in question. Social initiatives entail large setup costs. One must gather influence and backing, convince dissenters, and overcome competing entrenched interests. Once in place, initiatives provide learning effects such that these initiatives become easier to mobilize and utilize thus require more effort to displace, thus the inordinate difficulty in establishing or pursuing new initiatives. Further, what happens "when the benefits an individual receives from a particular activity increase as others adopt the same option"?[27] The concern here is that institutional goods become more valuable as more pursue them, which only serves to set the processes which beget those goods more firmly in place. Last, agents develop adaptive expectations such that initiatives perceived as unpopular will tend to lose out to initiatives that seem to be "winners."[28] Distinct from a concern over material incentives, this aspect of path dependence acknowledges the space that is often occupied by the interaction of rhetoric or informational bias alongside public opinion, a relation that can work to preempt institutional change. New social initiatives are hard to institute, but once in place or favorably positioned, they quickly gain significant advantages and influence institutional processes.

In the introduction, I said that racial inequality is rightly signified by the term "systemic"—this indicates blacks' life chances are diminished across a very wide range of institutional outcomes. Also, we have agreed with Rawls that the nature of the basic structure is in large part determined by how major institutions fit together. This has a direct correlate in path dependency, since "institutional arrangements induce complementary organizational forms, which in turn may generate new complementary institutions"—the third attribute of path dependence.[29] Thus, thinking historically, and keeping in mind the role of dominant groups in setting narratives and gaining early unilateral influence over institutional development, we might suppose that slavery as an economic institution could never have survived merely as that—it required, thus motivated complementary institutional developments in the realm of politics (i.e., passing laws to return runaway slaves). To extend the example, blacks were denied an education because it would empower them to question the status quo, thus resist it or at least lead them to believe that they had the right to do so.

At this point, a skeptic might insist that I have reviewed an outline of an idea that may plausibly explain short-term, maybe even mid-term stability, but this is a feature of any system in which goods are at stake alongside human interests and desires. In response, we should now note the final feature of path dependence: Institutions are designed for stability, thus are intended to resist change. Institutions ultimately play a significant role in granting society its identity and character over time. And, since they are fundamental to social cooperation they must be reliable and more or less predictable. This is a feature that theorists as conceptually distinct as Hobbes and Rawls both seek to model in their theories of the state and justice, respectively. Imagine if the constitution, for example, could be amended by simple majority votes in the Senate. Society would lack precedents for contentious issues cocnerning fundamental principles that tend to become objects of debate time and again. Another way of thinking about this is by acknowledging that our institutions would be at risk of too accurately reflecting the times, subsequently reflecting swift and possibly destabilizing shifts in patterns of political power. A decade of legislative activity led by a left-leaning Congress would be marked by abortion rights and increased welfare benefits, while possibly being followed by a conservative Congress that reverses these developments for no other reason than that those policies fail to represent its values or the values of its constituents who may themselves be ill-informed or easily persuaded by media or elites. It is easy, then, to imagine the great impact such initiatives and their reversals would have on the stability of markets, a coherent framework of rights, and so on. Ironically, resistance to change poses the opposite danger in the face of certain historically inflected moral issues, such as racial subordination—a robust and resilient institutional status quo that embodies certain kinds of unfairness or social or political asymmetries.

Path dependence is key in explaining the recalcitrant nature of institutional change. Importantly, it provides a rather clear way of making sense of a number of otherwise abstract claims such as the following: Institutions can come to possess bad characters that are not easily shed, thus continue to produce outcomes consistent with bad character over long periods of time. When institutions embody certain practices, that embodiment will likely set limits on future developments or set the terms of those developments; this is a central rather than epiphenomenal characteristic of institutions.

With answers to our two questions in hand, we are now positioned to specify historically evolved power, the first component of the full theory of power:

Historically evolved power is the phenomenon of historically patterned group dominance founded upon racism embodied in path-dependent institutions resulting in robust contemporary inequality that no longer depends on explicit racism.

This is how we get institutional racism without the "racism."

Institutions and the Idea of Character Briefly Revisited

I said above that what allows us to apply the idea of character to institutions is that (1) they display dispositions and (2) exhibit agency resulting in (3) behaviors that are susceptible to moral criticism or praise. This specification was worked out in response to reasonable concerns about whether a morally significant term easily and commonly applied to persons is readily and coherently applicable to entities that seem more "corporate" in their composition. I hope to have assuaged those concerns. But there is one more matter to be addressed. In the following chapter I will present two policy case studies to make vivid the more abstract constructions offered by the theory of power. In moving through these case studies we will want a guide to "what we're looking for" as well as to "what we're looking at" when we find it. Thus, before proceeding, I will state two rules of bad institutional character. These specify criteria for when we might say institutions are displaying bad character rather than merely acting wrongly by accident or as a result of error that is a necessary part of the democratic learning process. In view of the basic values of democracy, institutions display bad character when: (1)they distinctly and systematically marginalize some citizens; (2) and do so under the auspices of and sometimes in the name of democratic values.

This brings us full circle conceptually and positions us for our empirical observations and prepares us for our prescriptive maneuvers. How so? The conception of racial inequality as the problem of social value was offered in response to a core puzzle: the persistence of racial inequality in an era of formal equality and in the absence of widespread explicit racism. The conception states that racial inequality persists because of a first-order cause, specifically, that blacks are not considered equally valuable citizens thus do not receive equal amounts of democratic care and concern as their white counterparts. This manifests itself, in our time, as systemic racial inequality—a form of unjust treatment that is reliably predicted by race, thus some citizens indeed are distinctly and systematically marginalized. Precisely because distinct and systematic marginalization on the grounds of race are values antithetical to a democratic ethos that we tend to otherwise affirm, this is a cause for shame as that notion signals that we, as a nation, have fallen away from our ideals—a flaw in character.

Now we bring in another consideration—that institutions are designed and purport to be vehicles for democratic values and ensure democratic stability and accountability. When they achieve these aims in light of their commitment to democracy, they display good character, and bad character when they fail. What puts them at risk of failing? As stipulated by the theory of power: when their actions fit historical patterns of asymmetrical group relations that are resilient to change. In what ways do we know that institutions are failing on their own account? When they distinctly and systematically marginalize certain citizens, for surely a hallmark of democracy is that some lose out in democratic contestation but do so in ways that are justified because the contests are fair, inclusive, open, and so on. Marginalization will be particularly emblematic of bad character when such treatment is justified (explicitly or tacitly) on democratic grounds. Now, it might be hard to immediately grasp how to make sense of that claim, but I can offer a hypothetical that will later be supported by a historical example. Imagine a polity claims that its stability requires suppressing one portion of its population; that population is not in fact a destabilizing element, but rather reflects and responds to a long history of oppressive social, political, and economic treatment. The misattribution hinges on historically determined social markers such as race, itself a heuristic for assessing deviance. Here, democratic values might be invoked in a manner justifying asymmetrical group relations. However, justifications grounded on this kind of misattribution cut at a basic egalitarian core of what democracy means: equal consideration of each citizen's well-being.

Part II. Socially Embedded Power

Social Positioning and Lessons Learned

We learn our moral and civic lessons in part from institutions, and *which* lessons we learn is in large part determined by our place in the social scheme. Middle-class whites with easy access to high-quality educational institutions and a social network comprised of similarly advantaged persons tend to think that Americans can be self-made achievers if they try hard enough. In contrast, many inner-city black youths find school one of the least worthwhile places to be. Real effort pays off in earning street respect rather than getting a good grade on a book report. Thus, it is entirely possible to place two representative persons who are nonetheless American and get starkly different outlooks on what is worth doing and how best to do it. Strikingly, these outlooks clearly map onto one's position in the social scheme. Making sense of this with respect to race helps resolve the second part of the puzzle of racial inequality: How do we explain racial beliefs on both sides of the racial divide in the absence of explicit racism, on the one hand, and rejecting that blacks are somehow damaged, on the other? As with the first component of the conception of power, let's proceed by pursuing answers to two questions. First, how do persons come to possess bad character with respect to race? Second, what kinds of reasons seem to underwrite the possession of that character?

Earlier I noted that race is commonly acknowledged as a social construct. Importantly, "the idea of social construction is that human beings and their world are in no sense given or natural but the product of historical configurations or relationships."[30] The specification of historically evolved power articulates the institutional mechanics that allow those historical configurations to shape society in the image of social power relations and subordination. But social construction can do further work for us as it helps us understand not only what power relations amount to with respect to material outcomes, but what it means for one's character to be shaped by those relations.

If we reflect on the issue of gender for a moment, social construction does more than stipulate that women are better fit to be nurses and men as surgeons. Beyond determining which functions are appropriate for a particular gender identity, social construction leaves identities susceptible to evaluative judgments meant to justify assigning some roles rather than others. Extending the example, commonly held gendered views suggest that surgery requires objectivity and distance from emotions evoked by sudden developments on the operating table, the kind of developments women are seen as less able to stifle an emotional response against. Meanwhile, (women) nurses stay by our side in a supportive fashion, providing basic medical attention while attending to our more personal needs, maybe consoling our significant others as well. Here, women's being put into the roles of nurse is not seen merely as necessary, but, importantly, appropriate for women.

Accordingly, this sets the background circumstances against which women form a self-conception. Now, I want to hold off the more ethical aspects of these considerations for chapter 4, for the manner in which external norms teach us important lessons with

respect to our place in the social scheme have deep implications for our ability to normatively reason about the good of our lives and that of others. Here, I simply want to sketch
the mechanics of how we come under the influence of social norms and what that looks
like in a more general sense—that is, how social value becomes an operative principle for
persons. We can begin by anticipating an objection to social construction. Consider what
we might call the "sour grapes"[31] objection. When women and blacks make decisions that
seem from an outside perspective disadvantageous to them, rather than invoking arguments revolving around notions like "self-conception," we ought to simply attribute such
behaviors to the fact that society favors certain outcomes and persons adjust their deliberations accordingly. Sure, the objection continues, it is unfortunate that society favors
certain social positions and outcomes, but all this means is that justice ought to concern
itself with institutionally provided opportunities—the rest will take care of itself. I think
this objection only has one shot at being persuasive and that is if we deny persons their
affective capacities in addition to ignoring the way those capacities impact and shape
one's perception of prevalent norms. This is to say, we would have to deny, at least in
part, that a significant aspect of what constitutes maximizing one's conception of the
good is feeling accepted and as if one is doing what one ought to be doing. When society so firmly sets the standards of social value that one's personal ethic mostly reflects
society's normative wishes—when our personal character reflects the virtues and vices
of institutional character—we have moved beyond pure rational choice considerations.
Thus, "social construction affects two key aspects of freedom: choice and subjectivity."[32]
As Nancy Hirschmann argues:

> This construction of social behaviors and rules comes to constitute not only what
> women are allowed to do, however, but also what they are allowed to *be*: how
> women are able to think and conceive of themselves, what they can and should
> desire, what their preferences are, their epistemology and language.[33]

Social circumstances, then, threaten our agency by forcefully imposing social values and
expectations born of unjust relations of power.

An important feature of social construction in the hands of scholars like Nancy
Hirschmann is that while the selves we turn out to be are at risk of being shaped by
relations of power, this does not necessarily entail a blame game (i.e., men are at fault
for endangering or burdening women's agency, or, with respect to the racial inequality,
whites are directly responsible for blacks youths' disparaging attitude toward education). She writes, "The idea of social construction is aimed at understanding much less
overt forms of social production; it is something that happens to everyone, men as well
as women, rich as well as poor, at all times and in multiple ways."[34] So, the trouble runs
deeper. Beyond setting the parameters for persons' appropriate roles and self-understanding, social construction motivates normative beliefs about others and ourselves on
account of the lessons we learn with respect to the place we occupy in the social scheme.

Now thinking about race, we have implicit racism when this kind of belief becomes a standard for judgment and action. One may possess racial or racist beliefs that play a non-trivial role in judgment and reasoning but are not necessarily intentional or consciously mobilized forms of reasoning. On this view, whites learn their lessons on account of the way society has come to value, or at least not disvalue, whiteness.[35]

The idea of implicit racism has been well-rehearsed elsewhere, thus I am not so interested in describing whites' views, though I will be concerned to specify the moral disadvantage implicit racism gives rise to. I will trust that those with implicitly racial views suffer from a kind of bad character that justifies their being subject to principles of racial justice. What is less discussed is how blacks come to hold a kind of bad character on account of racial disadvantage. I stated above that we learn a great deal of our normative lessons from institutions, and here Mary Waters's research is particularly helpful.

In *Black Identities*, Waters offers a study of the similarities and contrasts in the life paths, experiences, and beliefs of first- and second-generation West Indian immigrants. Specifically, the study inquires into the identities taken up by each of the two generations.[36] Particularly valuable is her attentiveness to the historical backdrop against which West Indian societies have developed (along with variation within that broad category) and their view of social practices surrounding race and their beliefs about race and skin color. A central point is that West Indian societies engage in racial stereotyping, but the colonial history of West Indian countries provides for a background importantly different from that of the United States. Waters highlights some main features, of which a few especially help ground the importance of studying American racial identity. First, these countries have white minorities, and while these minorities are highly influential in political and economic circles, their numbers do not easily allow them or their skin color to be seen as the most desirable personal feature within those societies. Second, what follows is that power in these societies is represented more evenly across the skin color spectrum; the basic idea of "blackness" holds comparatively less sway.

However, American blackness insinuates itself into and shapes the lives of West Indian immigrants, particularly the second generation. First-generation immigrants tended to hold the view that American blacks allow race to define their life chances, thus preventing them from working harder to improve their lives. When these immigrants arrived in the United States, a high premium was placed on family life, education, and personal effort, all of which they perceived as being undervalued by American blacks.

It is particularly interesting, then, that the second generation, growing up in mostly segregated and poor areas of New York City began to exhibit key differences in their views of race. Waters notes that the children of immigrants were immediately exposed to conditions American blacks have come to know as normal parts of their lives: segregated housing, crime, lower incomes, and poor educational environments. Further, "the dilemma facing the children of the immigrants is that they grow up exposed both to the negative opinions voiced by their parents about American blacks and to the apparently more favorable responses of whites to foreign-born blacks."[37] So they come to quickly experience a "standard" view of blacks—as a group of persons whose identity character traits are fundamentally undesirable, as of lower value.

The dilemma here is important because the children of immigrants ostensibly have options. They can choose to identify with American blacks, or they can choose, to varying degrees, to prioritize their ethnic heritage and keep American "blackness" at a distance. I want to focus on the group that chose to embrace an identity of American blackness to hone in on the startling ease with which this generation seemed to take on exactly those character traits their parents criticized American blacks for possessing and then strengthen the argument by taking up an objection to my strategy.

Mary Waters observes:

> The first generation is likely to believe that while racism exists in the United States, it can be overcome or circumvented through hard work, perseverance, and the right values and attitudes. The second generation experiences racism and discrimination constantly and develops perceptions of the overwhelming influence of race on their lives and life chances that differ from their parents' views. These teens experience hassles by police and store owners, job refusals, and even attacks if they venture into white neighborhoods.[38]

Importantly, "while the American-identified young people come to terms with their parents' images of American blacks, they do not do so in a vacuum. It is not just their parents who criticize black Americans. These youngsters are very aware of the generalized negative view of blacks in the wider culture."[39]

Crucially, and where character enters the picture, "These [teens] adopt some of the 'oppositional' pose that American black teenagers have been observed to show toward academic achievement, the idea of America, the idea of opportunity, and the wider society."[40] Thus, for instance, the American-identified teens, sitting in underperforming, mostly black high-schools, tend to conclude that the Civil Rights Movement resulted in few actual gains for present-day blacks. Maybe more crucial is that they tend to reverse many of the gains or undermine the efforts made by their parents to provide a better life for them in the United States than they might have had in their country of origin. The point here is twofold. First, second-generation immigrants are seemingly exposed to negative views of blacks from multiple angles. Second, they can "choose" their identity, and in choosing to be American black, they adopt dispositions that immediately work against their own betterment; seemingly, these dispositions are significantly motivated by the normative racial dynamic to which they are constantly exposed. Waters concludes, "The result of the these different worldviews is that parents' view of an opportunity structure that is open to hard work is systematically undermined by their children's peer culture *but more important, by the actual experiences of these young people.*"[41]

Now for the objection: By focusing on teens that chose to identify with American blacks I have stacked the argument in my favor. After all, second-generation immigrants who chose to maintain close affiliation with their country of origin, as well as those who embraced American society but prioritized their ethnic heritage over American black heritage often, for instance, tended to perform better in their classes. The argument would conclude that blacks thereby can achieve as they please, so responsibility for their lives lies with them. However, the strength of this objection is only topical. Indeed, once we understand the basis of this argument, we more fully appreciate the problem revolving around how character is formed, how we come to be in possession of the character we have, especially if one is black.

It is true that ethnic-identified teens (those who, like their parents embraced the promises of American society and the value of hard work) tended to do well for themselves. However, notice what this required—almost wholesale distancing from the idea of American blackness. These teens reported taking pains to signal to others, particularly whites, that they were of "a different stock" than American blacks. Strategies included cultivating an accent in preparation for a job interview and carrying a map of one's home country on a key chain in hopes of prompting a conversation that would reveal their ethnic origin. The life of these teens, it turns out, is tinged with oppositional attitudes—they define themselves in opposition to a framework with which, by being socially attentive, they have learned is of lesser value and worth. They then bank on the value of being not American black—on their view it is entirely worth the effort to purposefully deny that identity.

So, with respect to character from the perspective of observing public lessons that attend one's social place, we can appreciate how powerful prevalent social norms and values must be such that the very idea of (American) blackness is nearly repugnant to first-generation and second-generation, ethnic-identified immigrants. While it might be said that this group of teens chose to identify otherwise, the power of race had enough of an impact to signal to those who have a choice that a certain kind of existential danger attends being American black, for the identity of blackness maps on to disadvantage and overall lesser standing. In choosing to embrace this identity, the social baggage with which it necessarily comes must be born by these teens. Finally, it is worth remarking on a fairly obvious point: American-born blacks are just that, so their choice and the distinctness of their options are much less clear-cut. West Indian children can at least make some sense of the options before them, but what exactly would it mean for an American-born black child to choose not to "be" American-born black?

Second, in response to the objection, I think we should be compelled to say that the character of those who chose not to be American black is impacted, regardless of their choice, by virtue of being of color. When we consider the strategies employed by these teens, we ought to appreciate the perpetual internal deliberation to define oneself against "an other." This brings to mind exactly the kind of problem that concerned W. E. B. Du Bois[42]—seeing oneself through multiple lenses in ways that members of the dominant or privileged group do not, or maybe more importantly, is never forced to. So even though these students achieve success where American blacks do not, Waters seems to have highlighted the existential situation for these teens regardless of their success or failures. So, the answer to the first question as to how we come to be in possession of the characters we possess is that our place in the social scheme imparts significant lessons as to what it means to internalize and be the (socially constructed) identities we effect, and these lessons shape our modes of reasoning in response to our place in the social scheme.

Internal Lives and External Reasons

This brings us directly to our second question: What kinds of reasons underwrite the character we possess and employ in our day-to-day lives? I want to begin immediately with a second empirical example, this time from the field of social psychology.

Claude Steele, concerned with the impact of racial identity on academic performance asks the following question:

> From an observer's standpoint, the situations of a boy and a girl in a math classroom or of a Black student and a White student in any classroom are essentially the same. The teacher is the same; the textbooks are the same; and in better classrooms, these students are treated the same. Is it possible, then, that they could still experience the classroom differently, so differently in fact as to significantly affect their performance and achievement there?[43]

Steele's social-psychological research reveals significant differences that map onto race, thus supporting the idea of stereotype threat: "a socio-psychological predicament that can arise from widely-known negative stereotypes about one's group.... the existence of such a stereotype means that anything one does or any of one's features that conform to it make the stereotype more plausible as a self-characterization in the eyes of others, and perhaps even in one's own eyes."[44] Further, "their prevalence in society raises the possibility for potential targets that the stereotype is true of them and, also, that other people will see them that way. When the allegations of the stereotype are importantly negative, this predicament may be self-threatening enough to have disruptive effects of its own."[45] It seems, then, that the kinds of reasons which underwrite the development of a character that reflects the reality of racial inequality are ones grounded in social narratives specifying what marks a person with a particular background as a person of that background. But, this is a bit vague so it is worth exploring the results of Steele and Aronson's studies for they are illuminating.

Steele and Aronson proceed to test the theory by focusing on two groups—women and blacks—in academic test settings. There are a few concepts and mechanics that guide the authors' studies. Stereotype threat is activated when the subject is given a task being performed at the same time that they are given a cue that prompts recognition of the stereotype.[46] Second, the threat is most measurable in a setting in which the subjects are thought to identify with the given task. What does that mean? In this instance, the authors chose Stanford students. Stanford is a selective school, which means that students have very likely already perceived their academic lives in terms of academic achievement. In parallel studies on gender stereotypes, the authors took the extra step of including women who had a strong track record in mathematics. Importantly, the gender and race studies focused on persons already well-positioned to achieve and who we might reasonably think are less predisposed to be burdened by the problem of race or gender. Further, it is less likely that these students, given the kind of preparation a university such as Stanford requires, grew up in particularly adverse circumstances. Thus, their sociological milieu is more likely to have been less obviously disadvantageous than those worse positioned (i.e., the inner-city youth who disparages education). The point I want to draw out is that if the stereotype has observable implications for persons who are less likely to have lived in bad circumstances and who already positively identify with the task, then it seems that racial norms have nevertheless informed the development of a sense of self.

Let's take a look at the studies. The group designed for the purposes of measuring the effects of race were tested given a general diagnostic condition, meaning they were told the test is being administered for the purpose of assessing the student along a particular dimension (though the particular dimension is at this point left intentionally vague). In the first of four studies, a thirty-minute exam was administered, which extracted some of the most challenging verbal examples available from SAT exams. One group was given the exam under the diagnostic condition mentioned above, while the other was told that their efforts would help the researchers solve some other problem; this was the nondiagnostic condition. As it turns out, significant racial differences in performance to the disadvantage of the black students were found when participants were given the test under the diagnostic condition. However, those differences mostly disappeared under the nondiagnostic condition. In brief, this began to suggest that the idea of excellent scholastic performance somehow interacted with race to undermine exactly what the students had exhibited prior to the exam and with which they were likely to identify—excellent scholastic performance.

The authors now wanted to know whether there was a level of anxiety connected to race that mirrored the differences in performance under the diagnostic condition. Another study gave the same exact test (with fewer questions) and imposed a shorter time limit. Here, under the diagnostic condition, blacks answered fewer questions and evidenced less accuracy in their responses, while they performed more or less equal to whites under the nondiagnostic condition.

Next, the researchers began to measure the degree to which race was really doing the work of impairing students' abilities. This was done in two steps across the third and fourth studies. In the third study, the researchers administered a verbal exercise that had two components. One component had words that could be completed in a variety of ways, including racially (for example, _ _ C E [pace, face, lace, *race*]), while the other had words that potentially (but not necessarily) indicated terms of esteem and confidence (for example, L A _ _ [lack, last, land, *lazy*]). Black students tended to provide answers with racial terms, as well as terms indicating lack of confidence or esteem, respectively. I want to pause here to highlight that a major feature of character and virtue is the degree of confidence or esteem we have in our sense of worth and social place. Interestingly, 75 percent of blacks in the diagnostic condition of this study refused to record their race when prompted.

The last study represented the test from the first study but dropped the diagnostic condition. However, one group of students was race primed—given the option of stating their race in a questionnaire—while another was not primed. The results here are telling. Blacks in the race prime condition performed significantly worse compared to whites under the same condition, as well as blacks in the non-race-primed condition. This provided strong evidence that the participants' race destabilized students' sense of self (since they did poorly at a task with which they otherwise identified).

The power of race in these studies can be best appreciated alongside a quick review of the authors' gender study. In that study, participants were told "that the test generally showed gender differences,"[47] while in the race study, participants in the diagnostic condition were told, "various personal factors involved in performance on problems requiring reading and verbal reasoning abilities."[48] Notice that while both blacks and women performed worse under diagnostic conditions in the respective studies, women were the only group to have the variable important for self-evaluation invoked—they were told that the test usually showed gender differences, and as a gender group they did in fact perform worse. But in the race studies, all that was said was that certain personal attributes mattered. Let's consider this a bit more.

What is true for both cases is that neither was specifically prompted to think that their group was the one already suspected of being the worse performer (in terms of prevalent stereotypes, i.e., women are not "naturally" suited for mathematics). In the gender case, the statement that the test tended to show gender differences was sufficiently broad to have been considered by the participants as equally applicable to men as women. However, the theory seems to have force because the stereotype is not random. Recalling examples such as Lawrence Summers's unfortunate remarks in 2005 stating that women were possibly less innately adept at math and science,[49] we appreciate that there is a general perception of women as particularly skilled in humanistic studies relying on verbal skills rather than in the sciences, which typically rely on "logic." Moreover, this perception is public meaning many people know that many others have such a view, and women know that people have this view of them. Last, over the course of their lives, women tend to be treated in ways that reinforce such a divide, whether it be given dolls rather than construction sets as children, or encouraged to be social workers or teachers rather than nuclear physicists.

However, the race study is particularly concerning. How must one experience one's racial identity such that merely being told that the test will assess certain personal attributes causes one's race to be a predictive independent variable of test performance? Why not one's height or eye color? The point I am driving toward is that on the account I have been constructing, the most reasonable way to explain these results is by referring to ones' sense of self. A black student's proven abilities being undermined by simple personal assessment linked to scholastic abilities speaks volumes to the more general phenomenon we saw in Waters's research: Being black in our society shapes blacks' self-conception. For a minimally invoked stereotype to have the observable effect it does, persons must be prepared to be primed—they must already have some view and/or fear of both the way race is viewed in their society; and, it seems they must be vigilant about how they perform as raced agents. Thus, my earlier formulation regarding the kinds of reasons that underwrite the possession of the kind of character we are concerned to investigate was incomplete. It is not merely the case that the kinds of reasons are those grounded in social narratives, such as it is better to be hard-working rather than lazy; rather, they are grounded in social narratives that embody valuational bias against certain identities (i.e., blacks are less intelligent or hard-working).

Jim Sidanius and Felicia Pratto refer to this phenomenon—the way whites and blacks differentially orient themselves toward themselves under circumstances of racial power—as social dominance orientation (SDO): "a very general individual differences orientation expressing the value that people place on nonegalitarian and hierarchically structured relationships among social groups."[50] What SDO predicts, is that persons variously positioned within a society by dint of a given marker have different levels of acceptance of inequality and social asymmetry. Unsurprisingly, the authors are able to produce copious amounts of empirical verification of the hypotheses that flow from SDO: namely that those advantageously positioned score higher on SDO scales.

The implications for character are particularly important. Sidanius and Pratto's analysis confirms that while those better positioned are morally disadvantaged (to be discussed in chapter 4), they are otherwise advantaged in a very particular way—they have higher levels of self-esteem and accept inequality precisely because it enhances their self-esteem. The psychic benefit of self-esteem is a crucial resource for being the author of one's life. In some ways, though not with complete consistency, being on this side of SDO is consistent with having some virtues important for a good character, such as self-esteem. Likewise, it is unsurprising that those subordinately positioned score lower on SDO scales, resulting in what Sidanius and Pratto recognize as in-group bias that ultimately informs practical reasoning—hence, the quintessential example of the inner-city youth who disparages school. However, Steele and Aronson's study indicates that the problem is more complicated, for those students who failed to optimally perform as they otherwise would, did in fact have favorable attitudes toward education. Recall, they identified with their pursuits. I want to conclude by saying that the problem we face, I believe, transcends traditional views akin to self- or in-group loathing. Surely, this is a feature in the lives of some blacks. However, it seems to me the more pressing concern has less to do with what one thinks about one's group under circumstances of disadvantage and more to do with how one develops as a person while in possession of one racial identity marker or another more generally. This is surely an issue of character—if character is the seat of judgment regarding others and ourselves, and that seat is affected by arbitrary social position, then it seems to me that while one is certainly shaped by the position they hold in the social scheme, they also have reason to critically reflect, and when appropriate, resist those affects on their capacity for judgment. In chapter 4, we will come to see the affect one's place in the social scheme has on one's character as symptomatic of normatively significant disadvantages. I will, in light of the previous considerations, specify the second component of power:

> *Socially embedded power is the ability for social asymmetries to affect our sense of self and others such that those better positioned tend to hold beliefs and attitudes that motivate a lack of normative concern for the systemically disadvantaged, while those worse positioned are burdened in developing a full sense of being an equal democratic self.*

Thus, character is at risk of being shaped by the valuational baggage that comes with racial identity.

3

Marshall's Lament

WHAT EVIDENCE SUBSTANTIATES the claim that institutions suffer from bad character in the face of race? In what follows, I lay the groundwork for justifying a series of strident prescriptive maneuvers presented in the final chapter. I take up the problem of justification more fully there—I argue that the appropriate principles of racial justice depend on political justification rather than theoretical justification. The aim of this chapter is to gain insight into patterns of institutional behavior and development. Thus, the shape and content of our claims for institutional reform hinge on understanding basic facts of the problem put in a certain light. The first step in that process was taken by articulating the theory of historically evolved power, which explains the presence of bad institutional character. The theory claims that path-dependent institutions carry forward offensive social practices on account of their historical construction that tends to reflect and embody asymmetrical group relations. Second, we can confirm the presence of bad institutional character when institutions act consistently with the two rules: they distinctly and systematically marginalize some citizens and do so under the auspices and sometimes in the name of democratic values. Thus, we want to operationalize the theory and give an image of the two rules "in action" by revisiting instances in institutional development that exemplify the problem of social value. In doing so, we are better positioned to work effectively at the intersection of the theoretical and the political, a necessary virtue for a theory of racial justice that seeks to address the problem of social value as the racial problem of our time.

Below, I am concerned to delve into the relevant particulars of two major policy areas—crime and welfare—that are representative of the broader phenomenon we typically understand as institutional racism. Each case study focuses on the time period antecedent to the Civil Rights victories in order to assess the problem of social value in the

right way (that is in a more nuanced fashion than allowed by speaking of white dominance). However, the theory of power stipulates that our current practices have deep historical roots. While I remark on some of these roots within each case study, I set a more
general historical scene in the next section by drawing a line from our time to the founding and back by recounting Thurgood Marshall's lamentations regarding our willingness
to unqualifiedly celebrate the success of the American Constitution. In working through
Marshall's laments alongside a series of particular historical observations, the theory of
power displays its explanatory efficacy; additionally, we set out our first insights into how
we ascertain institutional bad character.

MARSHALL'S LAMENT

A brief survey of early colonial history suggests possibilities for America's racial development other than the trajectory it ultimately adopted. Initially, whites and blacks often coex-
isted as subordinated servants. For one observer, "the question with New England slavery is
not why it was weakly rooted, but why it existed at all. No staple crop demanded regiments
of raw labor."[1] Similarly, while staple crops did exist in the South, thus a case could be made
for vast amounts of easily acquired labor, it is not clear that that labor had to be black labor.
And it certainly is not clear that abject black oppression was entailed by that need.

There are no easy explanations for why black identity became the object and embodiment of oppression. However, the convergence of culture and political power offers some
clues. Indeed, as historically evolved power stipulates, the answer lies in whites' socially
and politically dominant positions alongside their monopolistic access to institutions
early in America's development. This is important because slavery in the form that we
have come to know it (as more absolute than indentured servitude) did not begin as a
strictly racial phenomenon. For instance, well-documented but less discussed is England's
trade in Irish slaves.[2] England emerged triumphant from the Hundred Years War, with
its power extending widely around the globe, as well as deeper into the colonies. As
noted by historian Winthrop Jordan, the English at this time also moved away from a
culturally binary to a concentric worldview. Imagine a circle containing tracks marked
off by smaller inner circles, culminating in a final lone circle. The English populated the
center circle and those considered more alien (meaning, non-English) were assigned to
surrounding rings of value.[3] Importantly, this development coincides with the racialization of skin color and identity. Colonists before the end of the seventeenth century
were identified by their religious affiliation (i.e., "Christian"), but by the 1680s the term
"white" took its place. This necessarily broadened who could be considered an insider,
thus whiteness conveyed legitimacy.[4] The concentric circle became reserved for various
white ethnic and national subgroups—now there were different strata of whites, but they
were all accepted as part of the system. Blacks, by virtue of being "black" were relegated to

an entirely different valuational frame resulting in a newly articulated binary valuational scheme: white/black. Thus, while the Irish might not have been considered "as good" as the English, they at least were not black.

Further taking our cues from the theory of power, it is important to note that the emergence of an explicitly racialized worldview was accompanied by a number of institutional arrangements toward the end of the seventeenth century that synthesized norms with practice. For example, a 1661 bill made Virginia the first colony to recognize and institutionalize slavery as lifetime service, inheritable, and based on race.[5] Thirty years later, Virginia abolished Indian slavery, thus *"only for blacks,* then, was slavery considered *the normal condition."*[6] That year, Virginia passed "complementary" legislation requiring freed slaves to leave the state.[7] Meanwhile, in South Carolina, "the planters demanded that their legislative assemblies regulate Negro slavery, but what they wanted and got was unfettering of their personal power over their slaves and the force of the state to back it up."[8]

These kinds of institutional developments were not limited to the southern colonies. In 1671 Massachusetts passed legislation making slavery an inheritable condition. And things were no better in New York: "Under English rule, the slave laws were in many ways as severe as the regulations in the plantation colonies."[9] Moreover, blacks' status certainly cashed out in race-based disadvantage: "The poverty of free blacks is…explained by the fact that New York, like all of the colonies, treated [freed slaves] as outcasts and fenced them in with numerous restrictions."[10] For instance, though agriculture could provide a way to earn a living, blacks could not own property, thus they were effectively denied entry into the economy. Thus, the emergence of race as a normative category of human value converged with the institutional will to reify and sanction racial norms resulting in state-enabled racial subordination. Moreover, whether by making slavery inheritable or by limiting the property rights of free blacks, the end result was the same: Beyond being disadvantaged at a particular moment in time, institutional commitments ensured that black disadvantage would endure thereby hampering future generations' ability to reliably acquire and mobilize resources.

It was apparent that by the end of the seventeenth century, not only were blacks marked for social marginalization, but the machinery of government would willingly mobilize to make that marginalization, a product prevailing social norms, a political and economic reality. This machinery continued to operate on the terms of the newly formulated and adopted racial status quo as the Revolution approached; indeed it became strengthened as our democratic institutions began to take shape for this was the institutional and social inheritance bequeathed to the founders. Rather than the founders working from a tabula rasa, the new national story began in medias res.

So it should not be surprising that two hundred years later, Thurgood Marshall, the first black to serve on the Supreme Court, was skeptical of celebrating the US Constitution bicentennial. In fact, it might be said he lamented its celebration. To engage in celebration would be to affirm a level of social and political achievement above and beyond the shortcomings of early American history. But it seemed to Marshall that American institutions were continuing to fail to live up to the ideals set for them in the face of race, what we have diagnosed as a case of bad character. In a speech before the San Francisco Patent and Trademark Law Association, he stated: "In this bicentennial year, we may not all participate in the festivities with flag-waving fervor. Some may more quietly commemorate the suffering, struggle, and sacrifice that has triumphed over much of what was wrong with the original document, and observe the anniversary with hopes not realized and promises not fulfilled."[11]

Marshall goes on to identify lack of moral vision at a pivotal point in the nation's founding. Failing to "find the wisdom, foresight, and sense of justice exhibited by the framers particularly profound," he indicts the founders for devising an institutional design that "was defective from the start."[12] We can appreciate, then, the analytic usefulness of placing early white dominant culture at the tip of a hierarchical structure during a formative political moment. On this view, formal differential treatment of blacks in the law reflected the reality of black inferiority, the natural order of things—a fundamental hierarchy justifying difference between the races.[13]

United States policy at the time embraced the convergence of racist norms with institutional sanction by legally embodying the principle that blacks were appropriately conceived as property rather than as persons. The United States first expressed its institutional willingness to embrace this idea in the Treaty of Paris, which included a clause stipulating that the British were forbidden from withdrawing from US territory while "carrying away any negroes or other property of the American inhabitants," prompting Don Fehrenbacher to comment, "Thus, almost casually, in the founding document that confirmed American independence, Negro slaves were recognized as property by the United States government."[14]

The acceptance of blacks as property belonging to (overwhelmingly white) slave masters became domestic public policy in the Three-Fifth's Compromise of 1787. The sectional difference resulting in the compromise, which was concerned to settle issues of taxation and representation, seemed to indicate a moral difference over the role and place of slavery in the newly formed republic. However, scholarship has firmly established that the dominant motivation behind challenging slavery was a matter of political expediency rather than egalitarian concern over the status of blacks. Southerners were concerned with losing power on account of the South's numerically smaller free population as compared to the North, so they argued vigorously to have each slave counted as one free person. When the North resisted acknowledging slaves for the purposes of representation, it was motivated by a concern over the political power southern states would acquire through legislative representation—the South's ploy to pad their population numbers was apparent. The North's counter-offer was not a principled denial of black exploitation. They subsequently acquiesced to the South by offering the Three-Fifth's solution, allowing their property claim in blacks to count for some political advantage. On the other hand, the North gained the concession that if the South's property could be acknowledged for purposes of representation it could also be acknowledged for purposes of taxation. So, simultaneously, the property claim in blacks was legitimized by way of providing federal revenue that in no way was intended to undermine the underlying notion of blacks as property.

What is particularly troubling about the continued presence of racial inequality is that at certain points in history American society seemed poised to take on new and progressive directions away from the founding's racial moment. If these new paths had been taken, it is likely that the nation's early bad character would have been redeemed; indeed, it is the effort to overcome moral failures that mark good characters from bad. One such moment was the period following Reconstruction. Yet, Reconstruction, thus black emancipation, never got off to a proper start. At the conclusion of the Civil War, the military was directed to draw up one-year labor contracts that would obligate freed blacks to be employed by members of the planter class. However, it was in practice difficult to differentiate the new arrangement from slavery: Wages were meager, workers labored under an overseer and needed permission to leave the property to which they were contracted to work. This resulted in a set of circumstances startlingly familiar to any former slave.[15] Moreover, among the parameters Lincoln set regarding the formation of new state constitutions was state autonomy to adopt measures dealing with blacks "consistent... *with their present condition* as laboring, landless, and homeless."[16]

And although Lincoln became the architect of the Emancipation Proclamation and Ten Percent Plan, each designed for the ostensible purpose of providing emancipatory opportunities for blacks, racial progress was unable to get a proper foothold. Shortly after taking office following Lincoln's assassination, Andrew Johnson employed four tactics to first stall, and then reverse the possibility of racial progress. Before enumerating these, we should pause to note something important about this moment. Although I have argued that institutions are path dependent, I have also insisted that this does not make their practices determined, thus their nature fixed—at this particular historical moment, we see the interplay between individual agency and the shape of an institution that results in a lost opportunity for history to take a different course. It became clear that Johnson was most interested in reaffirming America's racist character. First, he provided amnesty to former Confederates and restored their property rights so long as an oath of loyalty was taken.[17] Additionally, he chose to recognize Virginia as reconstructed though the state hardly guaranteed blacks' rights. Further, Johnson rescinded the Sherman Act intended to provide blacks with free land, which would in effect "allow them to escape from white domination and achieve economic independency."[18] Last, the Freedmen's Bureau had been created as a temporary measure from the start, but it became apparent to many that the work to be done required more time. Senate Bill 60, proposed by Lyman Trumbull in 1866, was designed to make the Bureau permanent. Johnson vetoed it on the grounds that whites had never received such assistance, the matter should be left to the states, and that such assistance would only encourage irresponsibility on the part of blacks—troubling precursors to twentieth and twenty-first century conservative rhetoric around black poverty, as we shall see below.

So when Marshall, two hundred years later, was troubled that racial disadvantage had endured and resisted formal institutional reform he stated a concern over what seems to be a kind of historical inertia that carried along racial inequality as institutions shaped themselves to the times while easily evoking a sense of historical precedent. Marshall further expands our historical institutional view of racial inequality by indicting the institution of which he was a part—the Supreme Court. He notes, for instance, that Chief Justice Taney reaffirmed America's commitment to the racial caste system in his *Dred Scott* opinion, which denied Scott the right of American citizenship.[19] At issue in the *Slaughter House Cases*, decided in 1873, was whether the federal government could intervene on behalf of New Orleans butchers seeking to restrict that state from creating a corporation that, among other things, would fix prices. Although the complaint was argued on the grounds of equal protection and due process granted by the Fourteenth Amendment, the court decided that police powers were relegated strictly to the states, making the issue a local one. This would impact the lives of blacks most as it left the enforcement of rights up to constituencies that, with respect to race, were hostile to the idea and ideal of black equal rights. More explicitly the decision handed down in the *Civil Rights Cases* of 1883 denied the application of the Fourteenth Amendment to actions of private entities, thus the complainants' claim that the government was committed to acting against unequal treatment in hotels, theaters, and similar accommodations was rejected.

These decisions helped set the stage for decades of Jim Crow and provided grounds for claims to "states' rights" during the Civil Rights Era another half-century later. Marshall observes, though the Civil War eradicated slavery and the Fourteenth Amendment made equal protection national law, "almost another century would pass before any significant recognition was obtained of the rights of black Americans to share equally even in such basic opportunities as education."[20] Thus, Marshall importantly highlights that the moral failures following the reunification of the union remain with us in our time. And they do so not merely as cautionary tales; they actively shape the racial landscape, and these failures arise "from the contradiction between guaranteeing liberty and justice to all, and denying both to Negroes."[21] That basic contradiction succinctly describes the state of America's ill-conceived commitment to truly good principles for nearly two hundred years after the founding. And, racial inequality remains persistent—so it seems Marshall both laments the past on account of the present, and the present on account of the past. This represents the backdrop for the public normative political lessons we learn as democratic citizens under a regime of racial inequality. In turn, it makes the polity and its institutions susceptible to bad national character. Thus, "when contemporary Americans cite 'The Constitution,' they invoke a concept that is vastly different from what the framers barely began to construct two centuries ago."[22] It seems Marshall also means to suggest that Americans invoke an ideal that is incompletely manifest in our society, as well as inconsistently motivational for achieving institutional reform. This is what seems to trouble him. This is his lament.

So far as Marshall's general complaint resonates—a complaint I have identified as remarking on the character of the nation—we might yet desire a view of particular institutional developments that more clearly lead to our current racialized policies. Marshall's lament serves as an insightful pivot from the theory of power to historical observation. Yet, we are aiming to move toward a series of prescriptive maneuvers that appropriately track the nature of racial injustice in our time. So the trick is to make good on that need without relinquishing history's lessons. I propose we do so by focusing on two case studies that represent two contrasting institutional functions—punishment and provision to the needy—whose genesis can be shown to have deeper historical roots but whose practices evolved in the midst of the Civil Rights Era and continue to disadvantage blacks in the twenty-first century, thus operate under a similar logic despite the ostensible functional contrast.[23] I turn now to a study of crime and welfare policy to substantiate the claim of institutional bad character as a significant driver of the problem of social value.

THE POLITICAL DEVELOPMENT OF RACIAL CRIMINAL JUSTICE

The theory of power says that group asymmetries are underwritten by unilaterally articulated social and political norms. These groups have overwhelming access to major institutions that tend to reproduce the substance of those norms. Consider, then, the following offered by Sidanius and Pratto–if outside observers "wanted some quick and easy way to determine which…social groups were dominant and subordinate, they would merely need to determine which groups were over- and underrepresented in societies' jails [and] prison cells."[24] And this is important because "institutional arrangements for dealing with criminal offenders in the United States have evolved to serve *expressive* as well as instrumental ends.… In the process [they] have created facts"—a process emblematic of the legitimizing narratives fundamental to group domination.[25] The reason often articulated with respect to controlling crime is that doing so secures a degree of social order necessary for democracy to function. This in itself is not objectionable. However, if blacks have been victimized rather than merely overrepresented, then the institution of crime control is paradigmatic of two rules of bad character: It distinctly and systematically treats blacks unfairly and does so on what it claims are democratic grounds.

As earlier observed, the backbone of social dominance theory is a fundamental anthropological/sociological axiom: "All human societies tend to be structured as systems of *group-based social hierarchies*."[26] The reproduction of social hierarchy, as well as disproportionate control over and access to institutions, is an indicator of dominance. Sidanius and Pratto locate the critical juncture of race and social dominance in the use of official terror—"the public and legally sanctioned violence and threat of violence perpetrated by organs of the state and disproportionately directed towards members of subordinate groups"[27]—while Vesla Weaver helps us understand the political developments under-girding the most recent major shift in our approach to crime policy; developments that have had serious implications for present racial disparities in incarceration and punitive severity.

With an incarceration rate at roughly 714 per 1000,000, the United States is the most punitive nation in the world; and, with only "five percent of the world's popula-tion, [it] has nearly a quarter of its prisoners."[28] While this suggests a generally overreach-ing approach to crime control, the question of whether crime control has also become a method of social control crystallizes when we realize that although blacks constitute only 13 percent of the population, they make up half of America's prison population. The ques-tion becomes even more urgent when viewed in the context of a historical trend wherein black representation in jails stood at a quarter in the 1930s and at a third in the 1980s.[29] Is there a way to trace a historical line to the present-day fact of racially disproportionate incarceration?

America seemed poised to provide improved conditions for blacks at two important junctures, and at these moments we also notice significant developments and innova-tions within the institution of criminal justice. The first juncture occurred shortly after Reconstruction. During slavery, the idea of repression through the use of penal codes was unnecessary. Slavery was an overwhelming form of domination. Further, as Gottschalk notes: "The institution of slavery made it ideologically difficult to acknowledge the dif-ference of a white criminal class and to legislate for its control. The association in the South of crime with race made it impossible to embrace rehabilitation, the purported *raison d'être* for the penitentiary."[30] However, slaves' freedom after the Civil War posed a challenge to threatened whites. Rather than rehabilitate black criminals, they were dealt with through a private sector partnership resulting in the convict lease system.

Christopher Adamson argues that "convict leasing appealed to governments not sim-ply because of its fiscal utility.... In a real sense [it] was a functional replacement for slav-ery; it provided an economic source of cheap labor and a political means to re-establish white supremacy in the South."[31] On the one hand, the convict leasing system expressed economic functional continuity with slavery in that free or extremely cheap labor was provided to producers of goods. Thus, it was not uncommon for blacks to be arrested without cause or on the basis of false accusations, or for blacks in some instances to receive sentences almost ten times as long as those for whites for the same crime.[32] Indeed, "to supply the demand for convict labor, sheriffs arrested blacks for misdemeanors and vagrancy."[33] Recall here a lesson from chapter 2 regarding path dependence—that certain institutions motivate the development and/or cooperation of unrelated but complemen-tary institutions.

However, convict leasing supplied resources for another historical productive sys-tem: white supremacy. Democrats' "coded attack on crime, corruption, high taxes, and big government were subtle methods of promising whites that something like the sta-tus quo ante could be restored."[34] Moving beyond coded attacks, Mississippi passed the

Pig Law in 1876, which extended the number of crimes that could be classified as grand larceny, thus ensuring excessively harsh penalties for crimes that were likely to be committed by blacks. At the same time, spending programs that would have helped vagrant or destitute blacks were eliminated. Blacks found themselves institutionally hemmed in, increasing the likelihood of directly facing a system intended to maintain control over them.

We should note that convict leasing was not a short-lived reaction to emancipation. Douglas Blackmon tells the story of a young man—Green Cottenham—arrested in 1908 on the charge of vagrancy. An initial sentence of thirty days of hard labor was extended to six months when he proved unable to pay certain prisoners' fees. Cottenham was subsequently sold. U.S. Steel Corporation paid Shelby County (in Alabama) $12 a month to cover his fees. In turn, he was sent to a mine where, due to poor working conditions, six prisoners died within Cottenham's first four weeks and sixty died before the year was out.[35] Not only were state governments engaged in trading blacks' bodies nearly forty years after emancipation, criminal justice served as the center of both supply and demand. Moreover, state officials neglected to enact any oversight—the lives of the prisoners were worth only as much as their monthly fees. In observing the partnership between the private sector (private capital) and government (democratic governance), we should recall the general narrative with which this chapter began alongside the theory of power. While crime policy is a particular institution, the private/public partnership is made possible on account of an overarching logic and an overarching set of institutional commitments entailing the suppression of black liberty to the benefit of white supremacy. At this moment white supremacy remains important because the underlying logic was explicitly in service to white domination and that norm was reflectively affirmed by a great many Americans. The overarching logic was possible because of whites' early access to institutions that proved recalcitrant to change, as well as ready conduits for historically articulated racial norms.

The second significant historical juncture that presented improved prospects for blacks was the Civil Rights Era, and this pivots us toward the nuances of race in our time. The theory of *historically evolved power* says that we can explain contemporary racial inequality by positing path-dependent institutions that carry forward historically explicit racial norms in policy outcomes. As institutions slowly adapt to new historical and social milieus, they also impact society by reintroducing subtle manifestations of historical precedents, such as racism and racial subordination—they continue to teach normative lessons of a certain kind. This period, and the decades leading to our time, are concerning for a particular reason. While convict leasing was certainly abhorrent, it was, in retrospect, an entirely plausible development. Although Emancipation resulted in blacks' freedom from slavery, the Constitutional amendments that followed were not sufficiently supportive of Emancipation's substantive aims. Moreover, those who had been defeated—Southern Democrats—had regained nearly complete political control and would naturally turn a blind eye to the injustice being perpetrated against blacks.

However, while racism was alive and well in the 1960s, its explicit institutional support had eroded significantly. Additionally, when we consider social developments in the late twentieth century, we must admit that the observable racial climate is a vast improvement from Selma, Alabama, and Chicago in the 1950s and 1960s. Yet, as noted above, incarceration continues to exhibit significant racial disproportions, thus suggesting a regime of official terror not altogether unlike that found in the period following Reconstruction. How might we understand, then, the racialization of crime policy for our time, yet also appreciate its historical nature?

Vesla Weaver argues that a significant part of the origin of the modern carceral state can be located during the years that make up the second historical juncture representing hopes for black improvement—the years surrounding the Civil Rights Era. While wide-ranging legislation was established to provide blacks what they had been promised during the first Reconstruction, the United States began its ascent toward building a massive carceral system. As she observes, "the death penalty was reinstated, felon disenfranchisement statutes from the First Reconstruction were revived, and the chain gang returned."[36]

Weaver's theory of *frontlash* formalizes the development of this process as it took shape into the 1960s, and importantly, the implications that development holds for contemporary trends in crime policy and their implication for incarceration rates. *Frontlash* is anchored by the premise that politics can be more than reactionary—politics can be creative—and institutional design may be the canvas upon which pivotal political actors can simultaneously express their adaptation to a changed political and normative landscape while mobilizing that landscape's constitutive parts to their own interests and preferences.[37] The theory hinges on the use of the then newly articulated norms of democratic egalitarianism to justify radically inegalitarian and unfair practices of social control, thereby upholding the two rules of bad institutional character.

The theory has three main components.[38] First, though we often think of politics as unfolding through a negotiated dynamic, there can certainly be clear losers and winners (i.e., the victory of the Civil Rights Movement marked a clear defeat for conservatives). Second, the presence of what Weaver terms a *focusing event* can provide a point of entry for losers to use their politically creative abilities in reestablishing their preferences and agenda. She identifies a statistical rise in crime, in part attributable to a growing youth population and better means of measurement, as such an event. Crucially, another focusing event was the increasing occurrence of race riots. This is, of course, ironic, since riots were largely a response to racial oppression in the first place. Third, the losing contingent develops a monopoly on an issue, which can be mobilized using newly developed normative language and expectations in order to swing the political process back in its favor. Weaver calls this *issue capture*—conservatives mobilized fear around riots and used the recently ascendant and accepted language of equality and citizen's rights—the same language mobilized by the Civil Rights Movement—to argue that riots were not only disruptive, but criminal in nature. The mobilization of the crime issue alongside the success of Civil Rights evokes disturbing comparisons to the efforts after the first Reconstruction to control the newly emancipated black population. Hence, the development supports the main idea of historically evolved power—the evolved continuity of racial norms embodied in institutional practice, in this case, that of criminal justice.

While riots are materially destructive and socially disruptive, race riots were indicative of deep-seated outrage against an unjust system. Rather than seeing riots as a discrete reactive phenomenon, they are better understood at the extreme of a continuum of political and social protest. It is here that maybe one of the most important aspects of Weaver's account plays a significant role—the criminalization of riots entailed the depoliticization of legitimate political grievances against a severely unjust state of affairs. But this depoliticization was itself a political move. For instance, Southern Democrats sought to, and succeeded at, collapsing the distinction between peaceful protests and riots, thus making all forms of (black) resistance a threat to social stability. The institution of law and criminal justice was then mobilized to maintain the same structural status quo that was being challenged for it was also the means by which blacks had been oppressed for over a century.

We have good reason to question whether the concern with riots as criminal was sincere since prior to their occurrence, Southern conservatives in Congress had already been seeking to link crime to race.[39] For example, there is extensive evidence from the Congressional Record illustrating the explicit discussions over the extent to which progress on the Civil Rights issue might be perceived as a reward for blacks' willingness to disrupt the political status quo.[40] Thus, peaceful forms of protests such as the Freedom Rides of the 1950s were portrayed as deviant. Senator Russell Long, for example, argued that Martin Luther King's letter from the Birmingham jail encouraging civil disobedience was the manifesto that led to race riots.[41] Another argument that linked crime to racial equality was that integration would lure "crime prone" blacks to white neighborhoods, thus undermining the rights of whites. At the dawn of significant social and political justice for blacks, conservatives began the process of institutionalizing official terror on the grounds of racial terror. Ironically, while conservatives resisted civil rights on the grounds of states' rights, their actions simultaneously revealed a strategy to federalize crime control.

This is important—if we were to take Lyndon Johnson's engagement with crime during his first two years as a barometer, measured by legislative activity or public rhetoric, it seems the federal government was uninterested in federalizing the crime issue.[42] Prior to the 1960s, it had remained uninvolved in crime-fighting, even though the rate had risen 66 percent in the prior decade.[43] Although Johnson had been initially uninterested in crime, factors such as Goldwater's mobilization of the issue prompted him to pay it political homage, and then, as we shall see below, reverse course and take decisive action. Moreover, riots were a real phenomenon that frightened the average white American, with many looking for a strong stance on it.

Despite Johnson's early commitment to a root causes approach to crime (wherein crime is explained as caused by structural disadvantage, thus is addressed at the socioeconomic level), conservatives had proven too successful at (1) energizing a concern with crime as something to be dealt with through punishment; and (2) binding it to race, both explicitly and implicitly. In capturing the issue by leveraging the language of democratic rightness, they set the tone for America's character with respect to crime policy, for nothing in the logic of democratic rightness entails marginalizing and portraying as deviant blacks' concerns over and responses to injustice. Not coincidently, Johnson's root causes approach was disparagingly leveraged with respect to welfare policy. The main argument brought to bear by conservatives revolved around the notion of a culture of poverty, and "these discussions of the behavioral characteristics of the impoverished were consistent with American officials' long-standing preoccupation with distinguishing the worthy from the unworthy poor and were particularly useful to the conservative effort to emphasize and enlarge the latter category."[44]

By the time the Harlem Riot broke out in 1964, a common rationale for adopting a punitive stance was that granting civil rights to blacks would only reward lawlessness, just as welfare would encourage laziness. Thus, in almost lockstep fashion, the pursuit of civil rights became entwined with lawlessness and crime. However, the Civil Rights Movement had succeeded, and, subsequently, political losers became creative, since direct racial confrontation became foreclosed. The Movement had been too strong, momentous, and overdue to be rolled back. The issue of crime was in turn used to link race to a social malady; and the federal government was mobilized to create the infrastructure, processes, and conduits for the punitive turn in the United States.

In March 1965, in response to growing pressure resulting from successful conservative issue capture, Johnson sent Congress the most expansive federal crime bill in US history. The proposal contained provisions for the Law Enforcement Assistance Administration (LEAA).[45] The LEAA developed into an administration that distributed funds to local agencies and states, so long as certain benchmarks were achieved, in an effort to get crime under control. While such strategies were openly and explicitly linked to racial domination after the first Reconstruction, the new strategies were articulated mobilizing the powerful language of equality and fairness—the language largely responsible for the success of the Civil Rights Movement. This is important and provides a key insight as to why racial inequality has become increasingly complex. Whereas, during the first Reconstruction, it was still acceptable to speak of blacks as members of a distinct subclass, that option was unavailable after the success of the Movement. Thus the use of the language of rightness and goodness mobilized for the purposes of group subordination effectively recast progress as historical retrenchment.

The acceptance of that language eased the public conscience but the choices and actions that followed indicated a terrible character failing. The LEAA took shape under the guise of helping to secure the American polity generally, but it ultimately was instrumental for increasingly casting blacks as social deviants from which society needed to be protected. The stark racial disparities in criminal justice we see today have their roots in a marked and aggressive expansion in the infrastructure for controlling crime. For example, let's consider the above "so long as" qualifier. The structure of LEAA funding provided tangible incentives for state law enforcement apparatus to mobilize. Of the many results, local agencies were motivated to capture and prosecute criminals as proof that the funds were being used properly, and, importantly, as reasons why more funds would be needed. Simultaneously, the LEAA denied funds to agencies tied to anti-poverty programs or initiatives, removed provisions for drug rehabilitation programs, all while mandatory minimums were being introduced into crime policy.[46] These developments are perplexing, for as Michael Tonry observes, "in 1967, the President's Commission on Law Enforcement and Administration of Justice concluded that measures directed expressly at crime and criminals could have little effect without much larger simultaneous efforts being directed at crime's underlying social and economic causes."[47] In other words, institutions were falling away from their ideals.

Nevertheless, the LEAA ultimately and rapidly evolved into a powerful agency, propelling the growth of the carceral state at a breakneck pace. In the years 1969 (two years after the commission's report), 1970, 1973, under Richard Nixon's watch, funding for the LEAA was $59 million, $268 million, and $850 million, respectively.[48] The LEAA provided block grants to states contingent upon fighting crime; increases in policing, arrest, and prosecution rates were taken as indicators that states were earning their money. In effect, the LEAA incentivized and subsequently rewarded investment in the US's carceral apparatus. And, since 1973, imprisonment has increased by a factor of six.[49]

The LEAA should not be taken as solely determinative for the ensuing development in crime policy and racial outcomes. Rather, I pause there as a way of highlighting the introduction of certain political interests and social beliefs that, patterned on prior asymmetries, encouraged the evolution of crime policy and the development of an institution that arguably set us on our current track—this is a rather ideal embodiment of historically evolved power. The institutionalization of the LEAA is a paradigmatic example of how path-dependent institutions continued to set the tone of a national character that embodied the vestiges of our racial history. Here, one might invoke the democracy-at-work thesis and say that the development of crime policy is indicative of a properly functioning democracy. This is based on the presumption that voters respond to rising crime, signal their concern to political elites, who then ramp up the government's response to crime. On this view, then, racially disproportionate outcomes are almost purely epiphenomenal at best, or an unhappy outcome of an otherwise race-neutral endeavor at worst. However, Katherine Beckett provides significant empirical evidence discounting the democracy-at-work thesis. Indeed, by analyzing patterns of public opinion in relation to elite political rhetoric and media coverage, she concludes:

> In sum, from 1964 to 1974, levels of political initiative on media coverage of crime were significantly associated with subsequent levels of public concern, but the reported incidence of crime was not. From 1985 to 1992, political initiative on the drug issue—but not the reported incidence of drug use or abuse—was strongly

associated with subsequent concern about drugs. These results indicate that the extent to which political elites highlight the crime and drug problems is closely linked to the subsequent levels of public concern about them and thus suggest that *political initiative played a crucial role in generating public concern about crime and drugs.*[50]

Tellingly, the second time period mentioned by Beckett, 1985-1992, a decade after the LEAA went into full swing, coincides with the War on Drugs, notable for its stark racially disproportionate outcomes. For example, in the early 1990s, while whites represented roughly 50 percent of crack-cocaine users, they represented only 10 percent of the convictions. Meanwhile, blacks were only 40 percent of the users and represented over 80 percent of the convictions relating to crack-cocaine.[51] The Human Rights Watch reports disturbing continuing trends. In 2003, for thirty-four states reporting, 25.3 per 100,000 whites were admitted to prison for drug offenses[52] compared to 256.2 per blacks; roughly ten blacks were admitted to prison for every white person.[53] Some argue that the War on Drugs was particularly odious because its distinct racial impact was predictable.[54] This is problematic because "In the nation's largest cities, drug arrests for African Americans rose at three times the rate for whites from 1980 to 2003, 225% compared to 70%. This change is *not* explained by corresponding changes in rates of drug use."[55]

Nor, as Beckett concludes, does public opinion explain the severity of sentencing, since it tends to trail elite and media opinion-making practices. (Notice the relevance of this observation for the contention that institutional character plays a role in shaping personal character.) Nevertheless, the racial subtext of these practices remains powerful today. One scholar is perplexed by the fact that white-collar crimes rarely result in significant hard time, though these criminals commit crimes that may affect hundreds if not thousands of people, which "is a far cry from the demand for 'three strikes and you're out' for crimes for which most of those will be black."[56] Whether it is the differential application of the death sentence[57] or the fact that the likelihood of a black person being arrested for a drug offense rose from twice as likely as whites in 1975 to four times as likely in 1989,[58] it is apparent that criminal justice plays a distinct role in black lives. Maybe the most straightforward statistical heuristic is that today, one in three black males between the ages of twenty and twenty-nine are under state supervision.[59]

Crime policy and punishment, as the two arms of the institution of criminal justice, are fundamentally forms of social control. Crime policy fulfills this function by articulating bureaucratically explicit guidelines for the administration of justice. It determines what counts as deviant behavior and the right method of extracting society's due as a crucial component of liberal democracy. Punishment fulfills this function by translating abstract ideals and policy procedures into corporeal reality by either removing deviants (imprisonment) or eliminating them (death penalty). Although Western societies rely and champion criminal justice to secure social stability, we have seen that a status quo of group subordination is served equally well by this institution. On this view, historically informed institutions rearticulate principles of fairness and justice in such a way that what we get is quite the opposite: distinct unfairness underwritten by a stated commitment to principles of democratic rightness. Thus, the substance of the ideals of rightness collapses in the face of race—a cause for shame.

WELFARE AS WE (OUGHT) TO KNOW IT

When Bill Clinton promised to "change welfare as we know it," he was in conversation with history. Less than twenty years earlier, Ronald Reagan tapped into and reinforced the public's racialized view of the undeserving poor by invoking the image of the black welfare queen during his 1976 presidential campaign.[60] Although a Democrat, Clinton's promise resulted in the most restrictive and punitive welfare measures since Aid to Dependent Children was initiated. A brief historical survey shows, however, that welfare reform under Clinton simply came full circle. Although Roosevelt's New Deal initiatives transformed the Democratic Party into a friend to the needy, thereby revolutionizing the American welfare state, the transformation came with historical racial baggage. Social conservatives resisted any possibility of giving blacks the means of reshaping the prevailing social or economic regime. As with crime, welfare readily abided by the two rules of bad character. Blacks became distinctly marginalized, and over time, the processes set in motion by that resistance transformed into a self-sustaining trend of first, opportunity denial, and then, stigma, thus marginalization became systematic. Moreover, while the welfare state grew out of a recognition of a duty to help the needy, that aim was used to shift blacks out of the category of needy and instead challenge their deservingness, a challenge blacks today have not yet been able to overcome.

Below, I trace the arc of welfare's racialization with particular focus on the ways in which the mechanisms guaranteeing racial disadvantage and stigma have been embedded in the institution and have continually remained in conversation with racial history and norms. In the previous section I contrasted the institutions of crime policy and welfare as those that punish and aid, respectively. Although the racialization of crime policy is certainly wrong, it might nevertheless, against the background of slavery, be unsurprising that the arm of government responsible for control has been working against blacks for some time. But what about the arm of government meant to take care of needy citizens? How did welfare become racialized? And, what were the sociopolitical contours of that racialization? As with the crime case study, I will begin with some observations on conditions and events leading up to the Civil Rights victories. These will provide background on the genesis of a decisive racial shift in the 1960s. As per the theory of power, institutional development linked to historical narratives and tropes weighed heavily on the chance for blacks to gain the rightful benefits of welfare free of stigma. And, as noted just above, this difficulty exhibits all the signs of playing by the rules of bad character leading to racial disadvantage.

The Social Security Act of 1935 established precedents for today's major social spending programs. It was conceived in acknowledgment of the fact that free market industrialized societies are susceptible to periods of economic suffering and levels of inequality that threaten the well-being of their own members. These conditions called into question the desirability of laissez-faire economics and provided a clear mandate for government aid. Although the Social Security Act was clearly needed, the shape it ultimately took was far from inevitable. Indeed, its passage was the first sign that America had not quite turned the corner on race.

The Lundeen Bill and the Townsend Bill were live alternatives to the Social Security Act. Each was informed by a slightly populist, egalitarian reaction to the social and economic vulnerability exposed by the Great Depression. The Lundeen Bill explicitly disallowed discrimination based on race while offering unemployment insurance without restriction on any occupational group and was to be funded by taxing the wealthy.[61] Its measures were so popular that thousands of union locals endorsed it while garnering one million signatures in a supporting petition. A New York Post reader survey at the time showed that 83 percent of the readership preferred it to the Social Security Act.[62] The Townsend Bill had similar redistributive potential as it proposed that a 2 percent tax on all financial transactions be placed in a fund providing a $200 monthly stipend to all persons over 65 years of age. The idea was twofold. From a normative point of view, financial institutions had been complicit in the greed fueling the Depression, and, pragmatically, the stipend would compel older workers to retire and make room in the workforce, thus reducing unemployment.

The Townsend Bill would have resulted in a $2,400 a year unconditional grant to recipients and held economic emancipatory potential for blacks. To appreciate that claim, consider a snapshot of black economic dependence at the time. Women in the South earned between $2 and $4 a week for various kinds of menial labor ($8 to $16 a month), the main kind of labor for which blacks were hired. Sharecropping, which not only provided blacks with little income but often saddled them instead with year-end debt, absorbed 44 percent of the black agricultural workforce compared to only 16.4 percent of white agricultural workforce.[63] In the North, which also sought to exclude blacks from obtaining jobs requiring skill, women cooks earned an average of $579 a year with men earning $788 a year; meanwhile, the minimum comfortable wage at the time was $1,500 to $3,000.[64] This means that the blacks doing best were still earning only 32 percent of what the Townsend Bill promised. So, given the deep structural disadvantage for blacks, proposals such as the Lundeen and Townsend Bills were not merely radically redistributive but seemed to express equal social and economic consideration to blacks.

It is then important to note, as one New Deal historian does that "the Social Security Act was not born from a movement of average Americans." Rather, "it was drafted by government experts in the fields of economics and social welfare.... Of the three bills, the Social Security Act was the only one that discriminated against African American workers."[65] The Social Security Act was divided into two categories of programs, one for the industrial labor force comprised of Old-Age Insurance (OAI) and Unemployment Insurance (UI), and the other comprised of means-tested programs, Aid to Dependent Children (ADC) and Old-Age Assistance (OAA).

Considering the labor programs first, OAI was intended to provide retired workers with a means of subsistence after having contributed to a national fund during the course of their employed lifetime. However, the mechanics of the system introduced distinct burdens on blacks. In 1935, the year the Act was passed, more than 75 percent of blacks in the United States lived in the South, with a significant portion of them sharecropping.[66] However, the Senate Finance Committee and House Ways and Means Committee were comprised of thirty-three Democrats, seventeen of whom were southern.[67] Since the South had been a relatively uncontested one-party region, Southern Democrats easily attained seniority on congressional committees placing them in highly influential positions. They were well aware of the potential these programs held for blacks and, thus, the possibility for upsetting the social dynamic institutionalized by Jim Crow. For instance, OAI, paid directly to recipients from the federal government, offered $15 per month, which was more than a sharecropper might see in the course of a year.[68]

So far as benefits go, a program intended to merely stabilize the typical poor American had the potential to immediately and significantly improve blacks' quality of life. The programs offered bargaining power for demanding equitable compensation in agricultural work or opting out of the southern economic system altogether. But a great portion of blacks would not be given that opportunity. The legislation made sure to exclude benefit provisions for laborers in two occupations in which blacks were most overrepresented: farm work and domestic work. Nationally, 65 percent of blacks fell completely out of the program's guidelines.[69] Even when blacks had managed to pay into the system through working in an approved labor sector, their benefits were lower, since they had historically been denied competitive wages.

The Lundeen and Townsend Bills were never brought to a vote. Mary Poole tells us though "supporters of the plan had secured enough votes to substitute the Townsend Bill for the Social Security Act on the House floor; they were only prevented from doing so by the passage of a gag rule that prohibited the addition of amendments to the Social Security Act."[70] House Democrats passed a rule requiring the number of necessary votes for a measure to make it to the floor be raised from 145 to 218. All other contingents, including seventy dissenting Democrats, opposed the measure. The gag rule, which was the fallback option for preventing the bills' consideration on the floor, was then implemented to protect the Social Security Act in its then current form. It was passed in June 1935, with racial disadvantage structurally institutionalized in what was otherwise an egalitarian initiative.

The New Deal extended government's helping hand into many aspects of American life, but not into every American's life. For example, though the Agricultural Adjustment Agency provided subsidies to promote crop yield reductions in order to stabilize and boost the price of cotton, which had declined dramatically, subsidies were provided directly to farmers with no oversight as to how the benefits were shared with sharecroppers. Needless to say, many farmers denied their sharecroppers benefits. The National Recovery Administration (NRA), which allowed employers to pay employees differential wages for the same work, thereby allowed employers to openly practice wage discrimination (which would impact benefits received under other programs). Moreover, the NRA also excluded occupations such as agricultural and domestic labor from its program.

What we know as welfare[71] today, then, has its roots in a regime of racial practices and the racial dimension became more prominent over time, culminating with ADC's (AFDC) transformation into TANF and GA under Clinton. Robert Lieberman's work on the racialization of welfare policy provides clear insight into how welfare was different from other spending programs from its inception, and how its administrative structure provided for its continual racialization. Consistent with the main claims of historically evolved power, he writes, "Attention to the role of institutions in the construction of racial inequality suggests that the status of racial groups in society results not necessarily from the mobilization of racist ideology but from the normal workings of social and political arrangements."[72] This is important because "African-Americans…rarely have been widely included as honorable recipients of broad policies of social provision, and they are disproportionately segregated into the weakest, stingiest, and most politically vulnerable parts of the welfare system."[73] It is worth noting that Lieberman's indictment of social and political arrangements closely mirrors the sentiment that institutions display morally culpable agency, thus are susceptible to character assessment.

Lieberman's main analytic contribution to understanding the degree of racial disadvantage historically built into welfare consists in explaining how the interaction between various levels of institutional structure produces a range of unfavorable outcomes for blacks. The benefit structure can range from egalitarian to discretionary. A policy's financing structure can range from contributory to noncontributory. Finally, the administrative structure may be comprised of many substructures: level of government (national or state); policy permeability (easy access for the purposes of change or closed); policy environment (administratively stable or unstable); and, last, client contact (are taxes withdrawn by the state and automatically distributed at some later time or must clients approach the institution first requesting help). It turns out that of the three institutions Lieberman studies (ADC, UI, and OAI), ADC has all the ingredients for repeating a deep history of racial bias. ADC is noncontributory so it is the most redistributive of the three policies—it takes from the well-off and gives to the less advantaged; it is open so it is easily amended, which leads to it being the least stable of the three; clients must approach the state for assistance, so it is the most evaluative and punitive; last, and on many accounts, most importantly, it is parochial and entirely discretionary—it is managed at the most local level as compared to other programs.

How has this structuring of the most visible need-based program continuously interacted with America's racial dynamic over time? What have been the implications of this interaction? Historically evolved power leads us to expect that the explicit racial motivations that subordinated blacks in earlier policies become embodied in institutional processes that slowly adopt over time, but nevertheless carry history with them.

As America moved past the Great Depression, one trend continued while another began. First, blacks remained systematically disadvantaged with respect to welfare and this disadvantage had precedent. The Federal Emergency Relief Administration (FERA) could be considered an ADC forerunner (as well as earlier programs aimed directly at mothers, as ADC was). It was responsible for coordinating other New Deal programs and providing aid to the needy. As ADC would later be, it was parochial and discretionary. The result, for example, was that average monthly relief in New York was $49.06 per month, compared to Virginia's $17.65 per month, which itself was relatively generous by southern standards.[74] In "Jacksonville, Florida, Negro families on relief outnumbered white families three to one, but the money was divided according to proportions of the total city population. Thus, 15,000 Negro families received 45 per cent of the funds and 5,000 white families got 55 per cent."[75] This trend carried over almost immediately into ADC. Lieberman notes that by the late 1930s "seven Southern states that had an ADC program awarded benefits to black children at a lower rate than their proportion in the population."[76] For example, 37 percent of Louisiana's children were black but only represented 26 percent of its clients; for North Carolina, the proportion was 30 percent vs. 22 percent; in South Carolina 48 percent vs. 29 percent; in Alabama 39 percent vs. 24 percent.[77] In the 1940s the national average benefit was $13.40 per child per month—in Arkansas, the grant averaged $3.52 per black child, while Louisiana offered $4 per black child.[78]

The second, newly developing trend was the growing association of blacks with welfare while blacks were portrayed as undeserving and lacking the American ethos of personal responsibility and hard work. Welfare consequently became the least favored part of the Social Security Act. From a structural point of view, there were features of the institution that contributed to its growing stigmatization. First, while the government picked up one-half of the states' cost for OAA, it only picked up one-third of ADC. This signaled the federal government's comparatively weaker commitment to welfare while simultaneously providing a cause for resentment among local constituents, since their states were picking up a large portion of the bill. At the same time, it was exactly because ADC was premised on giving to the needy in general, and that racially exclusionary provisions such as those in UI and OIA had not been built into ADC, that blacks were equally if not more than likely to be ADC recipients and especially dependent on ADC since these other programs often turned them away.[79] It was not until blacks began to depend on the government for their needs to be met, and that this dynamic became publicly visible, that welfare became the unwanted stepchild of the newly developed welfare state.

One factor that put welfare in the spotlight was the rapid and substantial growth of ADC's rolls in general. By 1957 ADC had more claimants than any other Social Security program.[80] And, particularly, there was a marked increase in black participation. While blacks were only 2 percent of the northern population in 1920, that number swelled to 7 percent by 1960.[81] Specifically, in urban areas—areas associated with ghettos and destitution—blacks were 12 percent of the population. While they made up 13.5 percent of the rolls in 1936, they comprised 45 percent by 1969.[82] In both instances, black representation had ballooned by triple digit percentages. The increase in black ADC representation, however, was not merely a function of black migration. For example, the 1939 Amendments to the Social Security Act added a survivor's benefit to OAI, which relocated many white mothers *away* from ADC, hence black percentages rose, on the one hand, because blacks were significantly underrepresented in OAI, and on the other, whites had a chance to exit from the program reducing demographic diversity.

While we cannot offer a causal story between the two following facts, they do indicate a general racial climate with which welfare became bound up. In 1964, 68 percent of northern whites supported the government's role in pushing integration, but in 1966, the same year in which ADC roles dramatically increased, 52 percent now felt the government was pushing integration too fast.[83] Gilens's research on the media's role in racializing welfare helps fill out the picture of the American perceptual landscape with respect to welfare. He points out that though blacks averaged 29.5 percent of those in poverty from 1950 to 1995, they comprised 53.4 percent of the images in media stories on poverty.[84] Parallel to the remarkable reversal of opinion concerning government's role in pushing racial integration, Gilens finds that "the percentage of blacks among pictures of the poor jumped from 27 percent in 1964 to 49 percent in 1965."[85] In that same two-year time span, media coverage trained a critical eye on antipoverty efforts, quick to focus on mismanagement in the Office of Economic Opportunity and issues in related offices such as the Job Corps program.

American society and its government seemed to be at a crossroads. On the one hand, the welfare state came into being because the Depression made it clear that a democracy without an institutionalized safety net exposes its citizens to an undue degree of risk on account of others' financial dealings. On the other hand, blacks had won their rights but their formal equal entry into the polity was attended by many generation's worth of disadvantage—it would have been unreasonable to think they would not need the country's help getting on their feet. However, welfare proceeded to abide by the two rules of bad character, evidenced by a series of developments taking place between the late 1960s into the early twenty-first century. Indeed, it became increasingly clear that blacks were systematically marginalized and that this treatment was underwritten by invoking certain democratic ideals (i.e., personal responsibility).

The years immediately following the initial moment of welfare racialization produced seemingly conflicting initiatives. This conflict indicated a juncture at which welfare seemed caught between fully endorsing aid to the poor and helping under highly qualified conditions. One initiative, the Work Incentive Program (WIN) was established to promote the idea of responsibility among the needy. In recent years, this idea has been rightly associated with conservative rhetoric masking a deeper desire to remove blacks from government assistance and to dissolve any social contract in this regard between the government and the poor. However, we should not casually dismiss efforts to encourage

ADC recipients to take ownership of their well-being solely on account of the strategy originating in conservative quarters. Part of what it means to respect others is to attribute to them a degree of agency, as well as putting in place a schedule of expectations. WIN instituted the thirty-and-a-third scheme, under which recipients could still claim aid while keeping the first thirty dollars and one-third of earnings. Additionally, it was designed to provide job training and daycare for mothers with children.[86] However, an otherwise reasonable invocation of personal responsibility showed itself to be empty rhetoric—job training never got off the ground and daycare was underfunded. At the same time, caseworkers had discretion to determine when a recipient was refusing to participate in training without good cause, as well as latitude to determine instances of parental absence at home.[87] As Lieberman notes, guidelines were so loose that two case workers could easily reach and justify two conflicting decisions about a recipient's eligibility. The welfare system was increasingly becoming the site of a battle over the right response to poverty, as well as an ideological battle over who constituted the deserving. In some senses, we might think that the problem of race drove a wedge between assessments of need and desert, without which the welfare state might have operated as fairly as a democratic institution ought.

The second initiative, the Family Assistance Plan (FAP), intended to aid the working poor, was formulated by Nixon early in his term. This plan, too, seemed to hold great promise for welfare recipients. It provided $500 for each of the first two members of a family and $300 for each additional member. It was meant to encourage work, since full benefits could be claimed up to an annual salary of $720 and for each dollar past the limit, benefits were reduced by fifty cents until they reached zero.[88] However, Nixon's plan was devised in response to the race riots that had shook America the preceding summers. Thus, Quadagno points out an inconsistency when she asks: If FAP was only meant for families and the majority of persons participating in riots were young, black, single males, in what ways did this constitute a response to the riots? Motivated by the Moynihan report, which located black instability in the single-parent home, the FAP was in fact an attempt to engineer the black family structure by inducing black males to marry.[89] Moreover, it was deigned to provide enough support to allow women to stay home with their children, thereby institutionalizing black patriarchy. The point became moot—southern conservatives would not allow the FAP to pass, for their constituents had been wielding welfare as a tool of coercion by removing from the rolls blacks who participated in voting drives or who registered to vote. Ironically, liberals had been completely sidelined and FAP was a competition between racially biased conservative policy agendas.

The costs of the institution's bad character were significant. By the time Reagan was elected president, it was acceptable to misrepresent the egalitarian intention behind welfare by invoking images of irresponsible, money grubbing, black mothers. In other words, democratic principles of inclusion and reciprocity were invoked to unfairly and distinctly portray a particular identity group as beyond the bounds of democratic care—the two criteria for determining institutional bad character. Moreover, the 1980s saw the re-emergence of culture of poverty arguments fueled by Reagan and the conservatives' own disdain for public assistance. However, while particular individuals certainly influenced the discourse around welfare, it is important to keep in view structural issues as these help us to continue tracing the development of bad institutional character; though people appear on the national stage and even influence policy, institutional practices have staying power beyond public utterances, thus keeping in mind Lieberman's various distinctions in social security policy structure is helpful. For example, the idea of workfare, which at times mandated single mothers to leave the home, hence their children, for training and work, made a reappearance. Less federal support meant states had to carry a larger burden for a program that continuously was seen as helping the undeserving. Workfare programs were pivotal in helping financially struggling states to keep their budgets in line.[90] As one scholar observes: "Despite evidence from previous programs...that workfare neither provided meaningful employment opportunities for any single women nor removed large numbers of them from the welfare roles, it was evolving from a cranky conservative notion to one with increasingly broad support."[91]

However, it turns out that it was not the idea of helping the poor in general that upset Americans. Gilens's media research finds that during the Reagan recession the pendulum swung the other way. The early 1980s "saw the lowest percentage of blacks in magazine portrayals of the poor of any time since the 1960's."[92] Moreover, in 1982 and 1983 the percentage of blacks in pictures of the poor dropped to 33 percent, nearly twenty percentage points below their forty-five-year average. Coincidental with the change in visual representation was a change in the content of the stories. Rather than expressing doubt and popular rage with welfare, the news became concerned with how national economic conditions were contributing to the plight of the poor as more of those in poverty became white.[93] This development is particularly ironic, for as Jonathan Simon notes: "By the 1980's, Reaganism as an ideology had delegitimized the project of helping the poor. Such assistance was perceived as making things worse. The best thing government could do for the poor on this account was impress upon them just how responsible they were for their own problems."[94] Simon here indicts the nation on account of normative hypocrisy—somewhere along the way, responsibility was forgiven and excused when whites were hit by the recession, highlighting the ways blacks were susceptible to distinct and systematically, marginalizing treatment. Importantly, the reader should recognize that this represents a paradigmatic instance of the problem of social value—the core normatively relevant attitudes, dispositions, and actions functioned appropriately in the face of white needs (thus, it cannot be the case that there was a blanket denial of the welfare state) but failed in the face of black needs. This failure was founded on marginalizing blacks on account of legitimizing narratives; and this asymmetrical failure also clearly indicates a cause for shame as it betrayed other principles to which Americans and institutions otherwise took themselves to be committed.

In 1994, Republicans took control of both the House and Senate for the first time in forty years, just as Clinton made his promise to "change welfare as we know it." However, while welfare did change, the most familiar aspect of those changes[95]—the racialized norms which underwrite blacks' lower standing in the social value scheme—were those which would once again call into question the principled integrity of the idea of welfare. Aid to Dependent Children, the embodiment of welfare as an institution, was split into two new separate programs: Temporary Assistance to Needy Families (TANF) and General Assistance (GA) for the needy poor. As indicated by the term "temporary," among the changes wrought upon welfare was the first ever implementation of hard time limits. The idea of training was revived, but recipients were mandated to take a job after one year. The changes also embodied socially conservative clauses. Teen parents were required to live with a parent or guardian, and states could compete for a $20 million bonus if they eliminated "illegitimacy." Entitlement to childcare was eliminated, and states could choose to institute mandatory drug testing. Maybe the most detrimental change was the shift from open funding to block grants as needs arose– fixed sums of money the states could appropriate as they saw fit. Institutional character remained marred. While the parochial nature of welfare had always been problematic, the above clauses alongside the shift to block grants gave states even more incentive to exercise the discretion allowed by welfare's parochial nature. This resulted in shortening the hard time limits on welfare receipt, as well as exercising subjective judgment as to whether a recipient had made good faith efforts to make good on his or her "individual responsibility plans."

Recent studies confirm continuing patterns of explicit racial disadvantage, especially at the level of state policies and outcomes. One study holds constant recipient income, education, the state's percentage of urban development, the poverty rate, and party control (which party runs the state). In five separate models racial independent variables are introduced: percentage of black population, percentage of black and Hispanic population, racial attitudes, and the number of black elected officials. Each time a racial variable is taken into account by the model, there is a correlative reduction in benefits paid by the state.[96] A separate analysis finds a significant relationship between percentage of black AFDC caseloads and the likelihood of a state adopting (what might be considered punitive) restrictive work requirements, time limits, and responsibility waivers.[97] As the percentage of black AFDC caseloads rises, so does the likelihood of a state's adopting a waiver: "In states where the relative number of black AFDC families was largest (70–90 percent), the probability of adopting a waiver was five to six times greater than that of states where the AFDC population was predominantly white."[98] It bears mentioning that the Clinton administration allowed fast-track processing of waiver requests, which encouraged more applications for waivers.

There is also collateral damage to take into account. Not only are blacks left holding the historical baggage and stigma of race but also in those states where blacks are only 50 percent of the AFDC cases there is a tendency to request these waivers, and other groups, including whites themselves, are pulled into the racial framework. Indeed as the American financial crisis became particularly acute at the end of 2008 and beginning of 2009, some became concerned that states were dropping people from the rolls precisely when the poor needed welfare the most. The *New York Times* reported, "Ron Haskins, a former Republican Congressional aide who helped write the 1996 law overhauling the welfare system" was concerned. He said, "The overall structure is not working the way it was designed to work. We would expect, just on the face of it, that when a deep recession happens, people could go back on welfare."[99] It is significant that this concern is expressed by a conservative politician. More significantly, it signals a fascinating feature of the theory of power. An agent who had been a part of writing the policy openly acknowledges that the institution has somehow "gotten away" from the intended design, indeed taking up history's worse lessons quite apart from what it was intended to do. Indeed, Haskins's comment resembles something of a lament—a troubled wondering as to where and how American institutions came to fail in unexpected ways in the face of stated and accepted commitment. How, Haskins seems to ask, does our institutional character allow for this kind of morally significant failure?

CONCLUSION

Historically evolved power is predicated upon the idea that racial norms, institutional design and development, and path dependence converge to produce robust patterns of racial inequality. This part of the theory of power—the institutional component—is intended to direct our attention, moreover, to the temporal dimension of this convergence. Taken together, it explains dynamic and long-standing injustices—it explains how once overt and explicit racism, openly sanctioned by institutions, can become implicit and unintentional in our institutions, yet produce results consistent with historical precedent. The importance of history is immediately apparent—historical precedent is that blacks were not moral equals to their white counterparts. Thus, as the conception of social value stipulates, the mechanisms articulated by historically evolved power allow us to understand the particulars of the above historical case studies as not merely being instances of political mistreatment, on the one hand, nor white supremacy, on the other— rather, we get a clearer, theoretically valuable picture of institutional recalcitrance, as well as a nuanced understanding of how racial norms transmitted over time distinctly serve to mark out social spaces and the normative values accorded those spaces. If we think time, racial norms, and institutional design make bad bedfellows that need to be separated and maybe reconfigured into a more appropriate partnership, then we had better have a grip as to how that relationship began and how its more mundane yet significant practices took shape. I hope to have done that in the above. We have explored criminal justice (or the law) and welfare (understood at the more general level of social provision). It is remarkable to see clear parallels in terms of racial injustice. One institution is intended to control and extract punishment, while the other is intended to provide for those in need at various stages of their lives under various conditions; yet both display symptoms of socially disvaluing black identity in our time. More than remarkable, it is morally problematic that much of what seems to account for development of policy for these two institutions is race.

Thus, we arrive at the issue of bad institutional character. Recalling that its two rules are that citizens must be distinctly and systematically marginalized and that that marginalization typically be justified on democratic grounds, there should by now be little question as to whether institutions have displayed bad character. The theory of power explains *how* institutions are at risk of developing bad character; the two rules provide parameters for confirming its presence. Crime and welfare policy have and continue to treat blacks in a systematically unfair manner and do so by invoking various democratic principles of right and goodness. For example, by focusing on civic cooperation, black responses against oppression are subsequently framed as deviant rather than registering a legitimate complaint legitimately. Similarly, with respect to welfare, by invoking the American ethos of personal responsibility, justifiable black claims on public resources are framed as un-American, since these claims are portrayed as grounded in laziness and other related vices. The value of the two case studies have been that they do more than confirm bad character, but additionally show that institutions have had the opportunity to redeem themselves. Sadly, few such opportunities have been made good, but that such opportunities exist ought to forestall the despairing conclusion that path dependence in the light of historically begotten asymmetrical group relations is equivalent to sociopolitical destiny. This conclusion is important for it will help identify the kinds of policies we ought to pursue, as well as prepare us for coming to terms with the necessary scope of those policies if we want to overcome the problem of race in our time.

Before we can take that final step, we need a final piece of the puzzle to get the complete picture. The second component of the theory of power (socially embedded power) further stipulates that persistent and pervasive racial circumstances contribute to racial inequality in another way—by affecting our character as members of the social scheme structured by racially problematic institutions. We in very large part learn our socio-normative lessons from the institutional regimes within which we find ourselves. Needless to say, they have been unjust toward blacks. What does that mean for the kinds of democratic agents we have become and might yet become? Socially embedded power holds that our normative orientation is shaped by our place in a social scheme marked by domination and subordination. If we are to articulate principles of justice that closely map on to the problem of social value, the theory of power is a good start but we will further need to understand in what ways the social places we occupy affect our capacity for moral and ethical reasoning: our ability to show appropriate normative concern toward others and ourselves. My position is that bad institutional character creates social places that beget moral and ethical disadvantage among whites and blacks, respectively. Overcoming these disadvantages is as important as institutional reformation, for persons populate institutions, and they are also each other's neighbors. If we each remain unaware of the nature of our normative shortcomings, racial justice will face difficulties regardless as to whether institutions adopt rules of fair play.

4

The Souls of American Folk

CRASH, AN AMERICAN TALE

In 2004, *Crash* became one of a number of movies to employ a technique we might call narrative dispersion. (*Crash*. Dir. Paul Haggis. 2004. DVD. Lions Gate. 2005.) Movies using this technique present multiple cross-cutting narratives that intersect, deconstruct, then reconstruct each other in an effort to examine the workings of a meta-narrative on a particular theme. While *Traffic* (Traffic. Dir. Steven Soderbergh. 2000. DVD. Polygram USA Video. 2001.) was interested in the politics and sociology of the drug trade on the American-Mexican border, and *Syriana* (*Syriana*. Dir. Stephen Gaghan. 2005. DVD. Warner Home Video. 2006.) was concerned to explore the vagaries of corporate globalism in the age of the "War on Terror," *Crash*'s distinctive contribution was that it employed a complex narrative structure to explore a similarly complex social phenomenon—American race relations.[1]

The movie centers on a twenty-four-hour period in Los Angeles, one of the US's most diverse and densely populated cities. It is in light of these two features that Don Cheadle's opening line resonates: "It's the sense of touch... [His partner: "What?"] Any real city—you know—you walk, you brush past people, people bump into you....In L.A., nobody touches you. We're always behind this metal and glass. I think we miss that touch so much that we crash into each other just so we can feel something." What *Crash* tries to come to terms with is: Why does it take a crash rather than an extended hand to be in touch with strangers? Important in Cheadle's line is the idea that in some senses we *want* that touch. He invokes the imagery of people behind metal and glass which is consistent with the persistent rigidity of American social relations—we are in some senses bound off from each by the social structure we have each inherited even though, through the glass, we can see beyond those boundaries, thus the potential of social emancipation. Thus, the invocation of glass suggests a transparency that allows us to see beyond our current limits; limits that are marked by real obstacle—transparency is not immateriality; yet, while the obstacle is real, it can be broken or demolished. *Crash*'s secondary aim is to suggest that while crashing often produces bruises of an emotional, maybe even psychological sort, we should prefer to crash lest a plural society be marked by apathy at best, persistent bigotry at worst.

One of the striking features of *Crash*'s characters, and the feature that allows the movie to resonate with viewers, is that each protagonist is capable of appreciating the duties that arise from sympathetic human connection. A daughter preempts her father from doing something for which he may never be able to forgive himself, and a son (Matt Dillon as an explicitly racist cop) agonizes over how to relieve his father's physical misery. The problem, however, is that Matt Dillon's character seems openly resistant to acknowledging the humanity of persons from outside his social sphere and is only driven to talk to a racial stranger in Danielle Allen's[2] sense when a situation of life or death forces him to realize the shortsightedness of his bigotry. But Matt Dillon's on-screen persona is the exception—most of the other characters come close to being attuned in the right way to the idea of owing others respect and normative concern. However, they often seem confused about *why* others are owed this acknowledgment. This basic confusion is a burden at those moments when they ought to acknowledge strangers as deserving of normative care and concern. And, at times, they are also confused about *why* they should or *how* they can acknowledge the fullness of their own humanity. Consider the following three scenes.

Scene 1: After eating dinner in one of Los Angeles's tonier neighborhoods, Anthony (Ludacris) and Peter (Larenz Tate) walk down the street with Anthony complaining that the waitress failed to offer him coffee because she "knows" blacks don't leave big tips. The debate on racial stereotyping is merely a precursor to the next: Why did the white woman walking toward them (Sandra Bullock) suddenly grab her husband's arm? Anthony believes it is because she fears young black men in urban attire. Although Anthony offers a series of reasonable arguments on the irrationality of white fears in the proximity of black urban youths, he and Peter nevertheless fulfill the woman's fears by taking her and her husband's Lincoln Navigator at gunpoint.

The next day, as Peter and Anthony are walking down an alley in their LA neighborhood (decidedly less tony than the previous night's haunt), Peter cordially greets a local thug named Mo-Phat. Anthony is indignant at Peter's behavior: "Man robbin' purses from old ladies, and you all, 'Hey! How's it going, Mo-Phat?' That nigga will steal teeth from a cripple, man." Peter thinks Anthony is being a hypocrite: "You calling *him* a thief? And we do what?..." Anthony has the conviction of his principles: "The man steals from *black* people! The only reason black people steal from they own, is because they terrified of white people."

Scene 2: Police officers Tom Hansen (Phillipe Ryan) and John Ryan (Matt Dillon)— both white—are in their patrol car when a call goes out for a stolen black Lincoln

Navigator (the one stolen by Peter and Anthony). A black Navigator drives across their view and John decides to pursue even as Tom cautions him that it is the wrong car—the plates do not match. Nonetheless, the driver and passenger are black and John is looking for a reason to harass. After inspecting his license and registration John asks Cameron (Terence Howard) to step out of the vehicle. His wife, Christine (Thandie Newton) can't believe the treatment they are receiving. Cameron pays the price for her justifiable outrage. John first roughs him up then, after "subduing" Cameron, subsequently proceeds to indiscreetly fondle Christine in a mock attempt to check her for weapons in all places he thinks she could hide one. John proceeds to exercise his dominance by extorting an apology from Cameron as he watches John violate his wife: "Now you say you're a block from home.... Now we could use our discretion and let you go with a warning, or we can cuff you and put you in the back of the car." Cameron, a television executive, understands that the combination of race and a criminal record nearly amounts to an existential death warrant for a black man, so apologizes. Tom, watching from the sidelines, is sufficiently disgusted that he requests a new partner that same night.

Tom's and Cameron's paths are meant to cross again as Anthony attempts to carjack Cameron the following day once again putting Cameron in the crosshairs of the LAPD. Cameron remains so embarrassed and belittled by his previous experience that he counsels Anthony to remain hidden as he unadvisedly exits his vehicle seeking a dramatic confrontation with the group of officers who have cornered the car (they do not know Anthony is in the vehicle, hiding). Tom, recognizing Cameron and recalling the injustice perpetrated against him by his former partner jumps into the line of fire. It is important for what is to follow that he does this without knowing one way or another whether Cameron has indeed committed a crime—he thinks it is entirely possible that Cameron has again been stopped for no reason other than his skin color. But he does understand Cameron's anger, as well as the danger he is facing by venting his justified anger on a pair of trigger-happy LAPD officers (one of whom is inexplicably armed with a shotgun). Tom diffuses the situation, preventing the increasingly likely possibility of a violent end, allowing Cameron to drive off with Anthony who is still hiding in the passenger seat.

Afterwards, Cameron proceeds to drop Anthony off on the next street corner. Before handing him back the pistol he previously wrestled from him, he observes him with angered pity: "Look at me. You embarrass me. You embarrass yourself." Anthony exits the car wordlessly and it is clear he is in part ashamed for having violated his own principle by attempting to rob another black man. Cameron's quiet admonishment has called Anthony to account to himself for his misdeeds.

Scene 3: The evening of the same day that Tom has saved Cameron from near certain death at the hands of the LAPD, Tom—now off duty—is driving through the valley and notices a lone black youth, who turns out to be Peter trying to hitchhike to the other side of town (and otherwise unrelated story lines cross yet again). Tom stops and offers him a ride—the scene is titled, "Miscommunication."

As they ride along, making small talk about the weather, Peter remarks on the country music playing on Tom's radio: "This is some good music."

"Mmhmm" (Tom seems to think that Peter, as a black man, is being sarcastic if not patronizing)

"No really. I'm starting to understand it. I wrote me a country song myself just yesterday."

"I bet you did…" Tom rebuffs Peter's attempt to form a bond.

Tom then notices a stain on Peter's shoe and a tear in his jacket. This raises his suspicions so he proceeds to interrogate him a bit more closely regarding his presence in the valley. Peter lies, saying he was in town to go ice-skating. He then tells Tom that he always wanted to be a hockey goalie, at which Tom laughs. Peter, hurt, asks: "You think that's funny or something?" The chance to develop genuine rapport quickly begins to evaporate. Tom insists that Peter is having fun at his expense although Peter indeed does like hockey. Tensions escalate as Peter tries to make a last effort to bridge the difference between him and Tom. He notices that Tom has fixed a statuette of St. Christopher—the patron saint of travelers—to his dashboard, a practice in which Peter also engages. He begins to laugh at the coincidence but Tom thinks he is now being openly mocked. Peter reaches into his pocket. Tom draws his gun and shoots Peter dead only to realize that Peter merely wanted to show that he had the same statuette in his own pocket. They did have some things in common after all.

SETTING THE SCENE II

The above scenes provide a strong foundation for making sense of how personal character falls short of racially relevant moral excellence on both sides of the racial divide. Importantly, on the one hand, this coming up short strongly contributes to persistent racial inequality, but on the other, carefully considering how and why it falls short further suggests the possibility of redemption. I think it is best to focus on Tom and Anthony. These characters, on the one hand, seem to comprehend the demands of justice and also seem sensitive to being motivated by the needs of others, as well as attentive to how the injustice they are capable of perpetrating affects others who do not deserve that treatment. On the other, their respective moral characters seem flawed in an important sense.[3] In the next section I will more fully explore the kind of flaws they exhibit and specify those as moral and ethical disadvantage respectively. For now, let us revisit Tom and Anthony's stories as a way to frame the subtle dynamics of what it means for one to have a flawed moral character.

Officer Tom Hansen should be understood as not simply inconvenienced by his partner's racial bigotry but, rather as in disagreement with it. He realizes from the outset that John merely intends to wield his power over Cameron and Christine and he realizes that they are different kinds of people—John seems to enjoy not merely his authority as a police officer but his opportunity to parley that authority into white privilege if not white dominance. Indeed, Tom's determined effort to save Cameron from himself and the LAPD later in the film should be understood not merely as the right course of action when an honest cop witnesses the danger posed by zealous co-officers armed with shotguns. Rather, he is largely motivated out of recognition of having been in some sense complicit in the injustice perpetrated against Cameron during their first encounter. Nonetheless, later that evening, although Tom ventures to offer Peter a ride, it is clear that there is a gulf between the two of them, and the movie's writers and director would have us understand that the gulf is mainly created by Tom's inability to open himself to Peter's own efforts to bridge the gap between them. Tom's reticence results in tragedy. His behavioral affirmation of the gulf between him and Peter functions to make him deeply suspicious of Peter so that an otherwise minor disagreement escalates to the point of Tom, a white officer, needlessly shooting Peter, a young black man—an uncomfortably common occurrence in contemporary American society. It is important for what is to follow to concede that when Tom shoots Peter, he crosses a significant moral threshold that in some sense ought to place him beyond the reach of our own sympathetic concern for his racial shortcomings. His actions may prompt us to respond to him with the same disdain we readily express with respect to John. But there is a point I would like to make in order to hold on to Tom as appropriately emblematic of the kind of morally disadvantaged agent that should nonetheless be looked upon as owed our moral attention as compared to John who places himself on the other side of an important moral divide from the outset (I will explore this distinction below).

We might be able to hold on to the more basic sense that Tom is indeed a burdened potential racial egalitarian by reimagining the scene as one in which Peter is walking down the road, and instead John drives by, and rather than stop, he purposefully ignores Peter's situation, while muttering something to the effect: "I won't help these people if they can't help themselves." Indeed, this kind of action would be entirely consistent with the racist John has shown himself to be. However, Tom *does* stop in the middle of the night to help a black youth, and we are never given a reason to believe he stops other than that he wants to help.[4]

I want to suggest, then, that Tom's difficulties do not arise out of cultivated bigotry. Indeed, his genuine concern to help Cameron holds off attributing to him an explicitly racist stance. However, his later unease in close proximity to a black youth he voluntarily picked up on the road indicates that he is not quite prepared to view black identity through a lens of neutral value. On the one hand, he dismisses the mere possibility that Peter could like hockey, on the other, more problematic hand, Peter is viewed as incapable of genuinely valuing the things Tom does (i.e., country music), thus when he tries to identify he surely must intend to belittle Tom in some way. But for all that, Tom picks Peter up in an area the latter refers to as "not exactly pick-a-brother-up territory." Tom agrees not merely with the empirical description of Peter's observation, but in a manner that can only be captured by observing actors in motion, his expression indicates the unfortunate nature of the truth of Peter's observation. In all, Tom's inability to act consistently from racially egalitarian motivations, even as he realizes the value and content of those motivations, marks him as morally disadvantaged.

What of the black characters in *Crash*? Is there a parallel analysis describing their normatively important characterological shortcomings? In my Scene 1 above and in other scenes in the movie, Anthony seems susceptible to a twenty-first-century case of Du Boisian double consciousness. He expends a fair bit of energy trying to persuade Peter of the deep-seatedness of white privilege and the way it corrupts the culture blacks tend to rely upon as an important social resource. For example, he claims that whites benefit and materially profit from blacks rapping about killing and selling each other drugs. In other words, Anthony is a theorist of false consciousness. Further, Anthony is fully aware that the day he robs members of his own race, he in fact becomes a part of the problem. However, Anthony's disavowal of crime is highly qualified, for he does not disavow it because he thinks it impedes pursuing a good life in general or being virtuous. Rather, he endorses crimes against whites as merely one way to survive in a world he perceives as racially rigged against him. Anthony clearly has a sense of justice, an ethical compass about what it means to act rightly. It is also clear that he is confused about what it means to *consistently* act from that sense of justice in a manner conducive to achieving an ethically good life marked by integrity. On the view I sketch below, he is ethically disadvantaged.

Racial justice importantly depends on the persons inhabiting the social scheme having the right moral and ethical outlook so that they do not merely see the reasonability of principles of justice but can be moved to act from those principles themselves. What is crucial about the cases of Tom and Anthony is that while neither intends to be a part of the reason racial injustice persists in the twenty-first century, it is also the case that neither clearly sees how they already are implicated in perpetuating that system on account of their shortsighted moral and ethical outlook and the practices begotten by that outlook. Importantly, if we were to imagine back stories for each character, we would also realize that they have crucially learned their normative lessons as a result of their place in the social scheme—and since these places are carved out by institutions, the lessons have been purveyed under the aegis of bad institutional character (as explored in the previous chapter). The aim of this chapter is to operationalize this series of observations in a manner conducive to offering a robust philosophical theory of racial justice. In doing so, I will specify the ideas of moral and ethical disadvantage to complete the picture of bad national character I began sketching in the course of the previous chapter's review of institutional marginalization of blacks. To preview, these ideas will be fundamental not merely for assigning responsibility but for appropriately articulating the bounds and practices of the account of perfectionist politics I argue is necessary for neutralizing the problem of social value—an account of politics that seeks to neutralize the kind of character flaws that prevented Tom from granting Peter due respect and concern and the kind of character flaws that prevents Anthony from showing himself that kind of respect and concern.

Tom and Anthony: The American Condition

I have chosen to focus on Tom and Anthony because I think they illustrate and exemplify the core of America's racial problems. Consider, on the one side of Tom and Anthony, genuine racial egalitarians—these are not people who need a theory of justice to direct them to treat others and themselves as they ought to be treated. Their actions are already consistent with deeply held principles and beliefs. On the other side of Tom and Anthony are those like John or worse. The worst of this bunch will never willingly come to the conclusion that blacks are their equals. It is telling that it takes John being faced with the option of saving a black woman or watching her be engulfed by flames—a gruesome death—to express interracial care. But few bigots and racists get such an opportunity to see the error of their ways. It is a fortunate thing, then, that they do not make up the majority of Americans who fall on the wrong side of the racial divide. Rather, people like Tom tend to be the norm, and as we observe Tom, especially in his actions toward Cameron and his initial desire to help Peter, we see that while he certainly is not a racial egalitarian 'all the way down', the potential exists for him to achieve something like racial enlightenment. Similarly, as Shelby argues, many black youths such as Anthony tend to make rational choices given the fact of systemic inequality—these are 'objectively' bad choices that nonetheless express remarkable consistency with tenets of justice, such as reciprocity. While not every black youth is cornered in the ghetto—recall Claude Steele's high-achieving Stanford students—Anthony's way of being is nonetheless categorically familiar as the main issue is the difficulty he has in consistently acting from an ethical consciousness that guides him appropriately inside and outside his immediate sociological circumstances.

What is the most effective and appropriate way of analytically characterizing the above phenomena? This question can be divided into two components. The first is practical: Even if positing the problem of character as central to racial justice is well-grounded, how can we determine and make good on its legitimacy for that purpose? This question is given full consideration in the next chapter. A proper approach to that question, however, depends on an answer to another, with which this chapter concerns itself: What are the proper diagnostic concepts that will allow us to clearly assess how it is that we fail to value blacks or ourselves depending on our place in the social scheme?

Below I specify the concepts of moral disadvantage and ethical disadvantage. They are entailed by the socially embedded component of the complete theory of power offered in chapter 2. There I laid out a conceptual framework that explains the persistence of racial inequality in contemporary times in the absence of explicit racist norms and practices. We will recall that the main claim of socially embedded power is that persons under the influence of institutional practices, and the norms those practices sanction, tend to develop a complementary sense of themselves and others within the social scheme. Specifically, the hypothesis derived from the theory is that whites will tend to view their position, laden with advantage as it is, as the default evaluative position. The implications of this are manifold. First, such a position will impact evaluations of blacks. If from one perspective hard work is all it takes to make it in America while the reality is that race undermines that principle with regard to black efforts and aspirations, then blacks will surely come across as lazy when they receive welfare, for example. Second, such a position, as already noted, has implications for policy preferences—welfare will be seen as the refuge of the undeserving, so support for it is likely to be minimal.

The theory has something to say about this problem on the other side of the racial divide. Blacks do not merely have less access to material resources and life opportunities, but their place in the social scheme presents a skewed social phenomenology which itself shapes beliefs and action. On the view of socially embedded power, the influence of the norms sanctioned by institutional practices, as well as the place given by the social scheme, places obstacles in the way of developing a sense of self on a par with whites. A simple but effective illustration is captured by Claude Steele's work showing that the excellences developed by relatively advantaged blacks at Stanford can still be adversely impacted by race in ways not present for white students. I want to suggest for the purposes of guiding our understanding that here the virtue of knowledge attainment and use is impacted in a manner that has implications for realizing a plan of life.

The importance, then, of introducing the ideas of moral and ethical disadvantage is that they allow us to assess the ways in which whites are burdened in expressing full and equal normative regard for the lives of blacks; similarly, we can assess the ways blacks are burdened in developing a robust ethics which inform character as undergirded by virtues. Taken together, this pairing of character disadvantages is sure to make trouble for our democratic integrity. This distinction between the two types of disadvantage amounts to more than terminological parsing. The key point, with respect to moral disadvantage, concerns the ability of those better positioned in the social scheme to be able to both acknowledge genuine injustice and be able to perceive their duties towards others as members of the social scheme that perpetuates the injustice. With respect to ethical disadvantage, the primary point of concern is not whether blacks are acting badly. Rather, the term is meant to open an inquiry into the quality and kinds of resources they have available to them with respect to being able to conceive and pursue a fully flourishing life within a social scheme that has marked them out as of lesser social value. In both cases, the fact that these are disadvantages is meant to indicate that a successful partnership between institutional and personal reform is fundamentally important and promising for achieving racial justice on the view of social value. Further, the idea of disadvantage preempts concerns about the immutability of determinism or alternate explanations such as psychological damage (with respect to blacks).

MORAL DISADVANTAGE

The idea of implicit racism has been and remains important to contemporary race studies.[5] The idea was developed in response to an interesting and problematic development in studies of American racial attitudes. As the twentieth century gave way to formal racial equality and a more pronounced public intolerance of racist discourse, individual dispositions toward race seemed to change. Gone, for the most part, were the days of calling blacks "coon" and "nigger." Moreover, there seemed to settle into place a public norm that partaking in such behavior was not merely socially ugly but morally wrong. History seemed to buckle under the weight of what Barbara Herman calls, "new moral facts."[6] By this she means, moral precepts having the force of truth that are learned by agents for the first time. Indeed the idea of blacks as equals seemed to be a fact of an entirely new kind. Herman suggests that people tend to act badly in the face of new facts. However, racism seemed to be dying, so if Herman is right, what of that bad behavior?

Enter implicit racism—racial attitudes have ceased to result in fully reflective behavior, but the basic beliefs and stereotypes surrounding race remain a part of the typical person's belief structure. This in turn manifests at times in unreflective behavior that is racial after all, such as when Tom dismisses the possibility that Peter can share his interests just as Peter is trying to form a bond. I am not presently interested in exploring the psychological structure of racial beliefs, important as that knowledge may be. I simply take for granted that implicit racism is a well-enough established phenomenon, the general contours of which are by now commonly understood. Rather, I want to mark out the normative importance of the kind of phenomenon implicit racism is. It seems to me that there are two things to be said about it. The subject of implicit racism—in this case, Tom—would disavow the beliefs that motivated him to flee. That is to say, he finds the undergirding racial beliefs repugnant and would prefer to not have them. Notice that Tom reflectively disavows the overtly racist nature of his partner's actions, yet is unable to overcome his own racial reasoning as he is easily suspicious of Peter's sincerity. Further, implicit racism, as illustrated in this example, motivates dispositions and actions in response to, if not toward, others—the nature of our actions toward others is the heart of moral inquiry. Thus, Tom rebuffs Peter's various overtures.

So what kind of phenomenon is implicit racism? It is a feature of normative deliberation within the agent which bypasses deeply held principles in favor of particular normative heuristics that prompt a disposition, attitude, or action in violation of what it would mean to treat a person of color as a moral equal. This is why it qualifies as a moral disadvantage for it impedes a more desirable goal that is affirmed by the agent that is yet difficult to achieve on account of overriding influences. This characterization recommends two points of inquiry that will help settle the role moral disadvantage plays in a general assessment of, as well as a response to, racial inequality. First, what is unique about moral disadvantage as compared to immorality *simpliciter*? Second, what are the mechanisms by which people come to be disadvantaged in this way?

To first note what is unique about moral disadvantage, let's recall Tom's partner, John, who we witnessed harassing Cameron and Christine and who we imagined as likely to have driven by Peter while uttering a denigrating comment he believes to be true. Why is John an interesting contrast? He is an out and out racist because he is clear on his beliefs. He has cultivated a view of blacks that he reflectively endorses and puts into practice whenever possible. In one scene, John calls his father's health insurance provider as he is suffering without much aid from the medical establishment. The woman—a black woman—is herself at the mercy of institutional bureaucracy and is less helpful than John desires just as he becomes increasingly irate. He asks to speak with her supervisor and she informs him that she is the supervisor.

"What's your name?"

"Shaniqua Johnson."

"It figures." She hangs up on him, knowing that he has racially insulted her—John has taken the chance to remind her that her name is an indication of her race and her race is an indication of a lack of basic competence and worthiness. John is not confused in the least bit about the relationship between his principles, beliefs, and attitude or actions. John is happy to endorse his racial views and act upon them.

The main difference between Tom and John is that one is distinctly immoral while the other is morally problematic. John's morally offensive actions arise from reflective intentionality and are offensive because they offend against precepts of respectful treatment that are settled by a view of persons as having inherent moral worth—worth that it is wrong to deny on the basis of arbitrary facts such as race or gender. Further, and crucially, his actions are consistently affirmed all the way down to the structure of his beliefs.[7] While John's actions are intentional, as well as consistently and explicitly offensive, he poses little concern for us from the point of view of moral evaluation. His views and actions are repugnant and that is all there is to be said. The more serious problem, then, is the rest of society—people like Tom—insofar as there is a disconnect between the principles and beliefs they hold and the dispositions and actions they display. One scholar characterizes this condition as the ordinary vices of domination: "Given the pervasive injustice of oppression and given the high level of participation in maintaining structures of oppression and the difficulty of unlearning traits associated with domination even for those who become critical, I see unjust and other vicious people as fairly ordinary."[8] Why do these vices[9] and people like Tom qualify as ordinary? Recall that I offered in chapter 1 a weak interpretation of Charles Mills's invocation of white dominance—institutional structures informed by our history of race wherein whites are beneficiaries simply by dint of the nature of institutional processes and outcomes; further this position allows whites to view society as it is structured as the default norm, thus underwriting their beliefs that all it takes to make it in America is hard work, thus allowing them to view blacks as unwilling to work hard while simultaneously being able to deny racist intent. The result is persons socialized into systems of advantage that are far from racially neutral, and indeed, propagate offensive moral norms. This is part of the morality of everyday life for the advantaged.[10]

To be subject to the ordinary vices of domination means that the relationship between reflective autonomy and morality is often sullied by the circumstances within which we find ourselves and the practices to which we are a party. The unique moral quality of moral disadvantage consists in a precarious balance between the fact that we are influenced by these factors and tend to live our lives by the lights of that influence, and yet, we are not completely passive because we retain the ability to denounce that influence upon reflection. Moral disadvantage then occupies a problematic space in normative evaluation for it resists being categorized as resulting from reflective intentionality, but, on the other hand, exactly because the results of moral disadvantage are susceptible of being disavowed by its agents, we are not disposed to simply forgive and forget. In fact, we hope for and demand disavowal. Let us now consider the mechanisms by which moral disadvantage settles into our souls.

Barbara Herman remarks, "Our success in becoming autonomous and self-regulating agents will depend, in part, on the moral character of external social structures. One *finds* oneself in institutions with complex histories; one is *partly constituted* by values one absorbs from different parts of the social order."[11] Herman's claim is consistent with the basic proposition set forth by socially embedded power, that institutions, themselves carriers of historical norms, transmit those norms to persons who then go on to carry those with them through the course of their lives, and the presence of those norms have implications for our moral character. Socially embedded power challenges more generally the view that personal and institutional character develop along independent moral tracks. Rather, the theory suggests that a fair degree of interdependence makes moral disadvantage a reality for our social and political lives.

The best way to grasp the mechanics of moral disadvantage is to begin at the end: by considering behavior that displays moral disadvantage and work back toward beliefs. Tom extended a helping hand to Peter but was consistently unable to allow Peter to form a social bond with him. Tom's inability to see Peter as a social peer is not incidental. We first imagine the kinds of images Tom has been exposed to of blacks who only wear urban attire and only listen to "black" music (recall Anthony's complaints that contemporary rap actually benefits from the exploitation of blacks). Second, Tom is doubly positioned in an interesting way. First, professionally, he is bound up in a series of practices and ways of viewing society that are racially inflected. As we think back on the previous chapter, the institution of criminal justice does not merely produce outcomes, but it socializes those who participate in it, cop and criminal alike. But Tom is also a citizen when out of uniform. Even if he resists John's actions, he nonetheless absorbs racial lessons of certain kinds in his everyday life. What if we pressed Tom to tell us a story about the inconsistency between his willingness to help Peter and his inability to connect with him? I doubt he would have one to offer which stood to reason on his own account of what he reflectively believes about blacks. But maybe we can tell one for him. This is how it might go.[12]

As institutional developments have increasingly linked crime to blackness the black body becomes a ready heuristic for social marginalization, if not deviance. Thus, a typically socialized American is likely to have been exposed to public social lessons about which groups of citizens tend to play by the rules thus are worthy of normative concern. Jeremy Kang offers a fascinating metaphor when he refers to one dimension of this process as a Trojan horse.[13] Kang's subject is televised news and he argues that it acts as a Trojan horse because we accept it as a prima facie trustworthy source of good information when we ought not because news coverage of crime is often biased by race. Thus, the Trojan horse news—under the guise of trustworthiness—is actually harmful in being a purveyor of racialized messages. For example, a study of local broadcasts in Los Angeles reveals that crime tends to represent about 25 percent of local news coverage;[14] although violent crimes represent on average 30 percent of typical crimes that result in arrest, they account for nearly three-quarters of crime news; last, blacks tend to be overrepresented in crime news, thus perpetuating the image and idea of "black criminality." If someone like Tom watched the news before becoming a cop, and continues to do so while off duty, this would account for an important portion of the explanation of his inability to accept someone like Peter as a moral equal and instead view him as a possible threat.

Continuing to work backwards, Tom's behavior is based on a belief. But, as socially embedded power insists, and Herman suggests, his behavior is motivated by a kind of belief. What might that be? In brief, Tom believes black men choose to exist on the social margins and are plausibly dangerous; the kind of belief in play is a socially articulated belief marked by relations of asymmetrical power. The philosophical considerations concerning the nature and structure of beliefs are complex. For our purposes, it suffices to characterize a belief as some function of the interaction between what we take to be facts in the world, frames of assessment that we develop over time, and our affective capacities (we often have a hard time believing that which we find distasteful even if it may be true). Kang's characterization of the news as a Trojan horse becomes all the more significant on this view of beliefs, for we can never be entirely sure what is a true fact about many states of affairs—we take it on good faith that some sources can be relied upon. However, this presents a deep problem regarding the relationship between the nature of our epistemic resources and our reflective deliberations. Indeed, it is why some characterize this category of phenomenon as "a sphere of epistemic activity in which relations of identity and power can create a particular kind of epistemic injustice."[15] And this is why Tom is under a moral disadvantage: The beliefs he comes to hold that inform his practical deliberations, which in turn have implications for how he treats others, are out of step with what he would reflectively endorse; but as an agent within a scheme of power—albeit one that works to his benefit—he is poorly positioned to come to fair conclusions about features of his world.

Tom's beliefs, attitudes, and ultimately, actions are informed by social relations of racial subordination. The final scene in which Tom fatally shoots Peter is tragic precisely because it begins by Tom doing something whites might not do ordinarily—extend a helping hand to a black man on a lonely road in the middle of the night. But it ends by Tom doing the worst that whites have historically done and continue to do to blacks: make them strange fruit, for lynching can take many forms. While I have noted above that the violence at the end of this scene should in some senses be taken as imposed by the demands of American movie-making, nonetheless, its structure is deeply instructive for our considerations of character and shame. Tom earlier showed genuine signs of disgust toward John's racism, and he himself on more than one occasion put his own safety on the line to help a black man, but when it mattered most—when Peter was trying to show how similar he and Tom really were—Tom severely fell away from his ideals. To revisit the imagery at the beginning of the chapter, Peter reached out a hand, and Tom found himself unable to touch him; rather though he could see Peter through the glass, he nevertheless, in his heart of hearts, remained behind it. For the purposes of justice it is best characterized as a moral disadvantage. He has no reason to act toward Peter as he does outside of the moral training he has received vis-à-vis his place in the social scheme. And while he clearly has the capacity to understand that better than he does, he can't seem to do better.

ETHICAL DISADVANTAGE

The idea of moral disadvantage has a certain intuitive appeal insofar as its subjects are persons who are often on the wrong side of an important moral question. For many, the question of who is responsible for a just society would end there. After all, blacks, by definition, are the victims of racial inequality—the LA ghetto in which Anthony finds himself is itself a kind of victim of public neglect.[16] However, as the theory of socially embedded power further stipulates, it is not only whites who are affected by the social norms that result in racial inequality. Blacks are also affected in ways that ought to make us attentive to their capacity and readiness to be partners to the theory of justice in the right way. As I have already said, this is neither a claim that we ought to blame the victim or that blacks are damaged—I do not believe our inquiry strictly entails either of these two conclusions. Instead, this is a claim about moral learning—if it is the case that racial norms are widely prevalent and impact whites' beliefs, why should we think blacks are insulated from these effects? Anthony's case is interesting because he has very coherent beliefs about the basics of what Shelby calls civic duties (as he frowns upon robbing blacks), as well as natural duties (he resists listening to rap out of a sense of self-respect). Yet his coherent beliefs do not yield ethical integrity as he readily robs whites; and the fact that he leads a life that could stereotypically land him in jail calls into question the depth of his self-respect.

Character, as we will see shortly, encompasses a range of virtues that all count toward the persons we are in general and indicate our comportment to our own good—character refers to patterns of action and dispositions that have normatively significant implications for self and others. Moreover, many virtues are mutually reinforcing thus forming a web of qualities integral to our being the persons we are. Thus, racial disadvantage likely does more than affect our sense of worth. It is reasonable to suppose that our virtues and their development also face difficulties on account of the moral lessons we learn under conditions of systemic racial injustice.

Tommie Shelby offers one possible view of what these difficulties might be. His argument begins with the idea of ghetto deviance, where deviance straightforwardly refers to behavior deviant from commonly accepted standards (i.e., the pursuit of education and being excellent in that pursuit are both good).[17] Shelby's main concern is to examine how we might assess deviance under circumstances of injustice. For him, there is an important puzzle at the heart of the relationship between deviance, on the one hand, and background injustice, on the other. We, as a society, are in the habit of persecuting deviance, yet, for him, the danger is that deviance might be an entirely reasonable response to the systematically unjust circumstances within which blacks often find themselves. Shelby is concerned, then, to challenge our nonchalance in levying charges of deviance for that nonchalance indicates public ignorance or insensitivity to what it means to exist under conditions of deep injustice.

His first move is to defer to Rawls and note that a main duty entailed by justice is reciprocity; further, reciprocity becomes a duty when the other party also acts according to the rules. Reciprocity, then, is a matter of living up to our civic duties. Shelby concludes that we are half wrong with respect to morally criticizing deviance, for on his view, since the basic structure (major social and political institutions) is unjust with regard to race, blacks are under no obligation to abide by civic duties—if all relevant agents abided by reciprocity, blacks would not be systematically disadvantaged.

However, Shelby does not believe that blacks have no duties to speak of. On his view, although political society owes blacks a just basic structure, blacks owe themselves the chance to be good persons, even under circumstances of injustice. These are natural duties and they are absolute. Shelby, here drawing on the Kantian tradition, settles on the absolute command of natural duties in virtue of the value of human dignity—it is a duty to protect it and cultivate it. Therefore, while a suspension of civic duties may allow for petty theft so that one may feed oneself, it disallows self-disrespect or the cultivation of immoral attitudes that sanction the harm of others. While natural duties are both self- and other-regarding, it is clear that Shelby is concerned with a kind of excellence on the part of persons—on my view of his argument, it is an excellence of character. Shelby frames deviant behavior in terms very close to rational choice—such behaviors are not only justified but make sense within an unjust scheme (i.e., if one's neighborhood unjustly withholds employment opportunities, then it makes sense to simply take from those parties that deny what you need). But it is indeed a virtue—an excellence of character—to curtail actions that serve one's prudentially rational interests in the name of love for others or esteem for oneself.

While Shelby's argument is analytically sound, it does raise an important question: Do the circumstances of injustice permit the development of an excellent character? Do they permit for the kind of human flourishing required by an account of natural duties? Did Anthony have a fair shot of success at developing a different character other than the one he displays given his place in the social scheme? There is a particular way to conceive of the problem, which I will now lay out.

Liberal theories of justice often refer to lives under nonideal conditions as susceptible to the natural lottery. They mean to draw our attention to the fact that we are each born with more or less natural endowments and into better or worse social positions through no choice of our own. If you are born with a high IQ and rich parents, you are fortunate, but not deserving. Likewise, if you are born with a propensity for obesity and poor parents who cannot afford quality health care, you are unfortunate and undeserving of that bad fortune. This is obviously right, but the world we live in is more complex than liberals seem to let on. For example, some would argue that a significant aspect of our life chances are far from natural—they are the product of relations of power across many domains (race, gender, class, sexual orientation). As one scholar puts it, this state of affairs is an *un*natural lottery in that it results in circumstances beyond our control, yet it would be a mistake to say that they are merely happenstance.[18] Indeed, systemic racial inequality has a causal narrative rooted in the purposive development of racial norms and their place in major social and political institutions.

Now, reflections on the unnatural lottery have generally been pursued in order to articulate certain substantive challenges to debates over the nature and implications of moral luck on moral judgment, an area of philosophical concern prominently articulated by Bernard Williams and Thomas Nagel.[19] While the full range of questions is indeed important, there is a particular line of thought that is valuable for us. Natural duties stipulate a mandate to display excellence of character. But the problem of systemic inequality presents a set of particularly oppressive circumstances, leading Tessman to suggest that the integrity of one's ethical compass might be threatened "when there is a certain sort of a self that one ought to be, but the unconducive conditions of oppression bar one from cultivating that self."[20] Anthony is a loser in what is certainly an unnatural lottery, and this seems in part to explain his inconsistent view of civic duties, as well as self-respect.

This is one upshot of epistemic injustice as a mechanism of ethical disadvantage: "Some social groups are unable to dissent from distorted understanding of their social experiences."[21] On this view, blacks who are portrayed as lazy and undeserving are unable to convey to wider society that systematically poor job opportunities and lower wealth in part force their hand in accepting welfare. Public knowledge about the complete features of a set of social circumstances would be able to contribute to a fairer and certainly more complete narrative than the one that is often bandied about. But as Shelby notes, fairness is not exactly a feature of American racial life, especially with respect to institutions. Blacks, then, become an audience to demeaning messages about their own situation and worth. As chapter 2 showed, second generation West Indian immigrants have a choice whether to strongly identify as West Indian or adopt "American blackness" as an identity. As I argued, whichever side the decision ultimately falls on, there is one troubling feature of that decision—it is either in opposition to "American blackness," thus that opposition will structure life choices and identity in ways other identity groups are not forced to do, or it risks adopting aspects of deviance in an effort to sympathize with the plight of American blacks. Further, a call to abide by natural duties runs into the problem of being affected in the first instance by the circumstances that make "blackness" a particular kind of identity in our society—one on the lower end of America's scheme of social value. Now, it might be thought that racial justice calls for intervention into ghettos. After all, that is Shelby's focus and the ghetto is Anthony's home, but we need only to recall Claude Steele's underachieving, yet otherwise high-performing black students whose abilities seem hindered when race becomes an active consideration in their self-conceptualization. This is why it is fundamentally important to conceive of racial justice in light of the problem of social value—the socio-normative position blacks hold in the social scheme rather than their politico-economic position.

I have noted that cultivation of the virtues and good character requires resources and opportunities. In a material sense, and by a metric understanding of systemic racial inequality, these are beyond the reach or in difficult to reach places for blacks. However, there is a more troubling aspect of the problem brought into view by the foregoing reflections: Racial inequality, as the problem of social value, positions black identity as less morally worthy. The fundamental resources and opportunities of concern, then, are those that inform and help cultivate good character on the part of American citizens and institutions with respect to race. The cultivation of the virtues, as Aristotle insisted, is in some sense a matter of fortune, for one must be positioned among peers, family, and citizens in a way conducive to their cultivation. One cannot, in contrast to Kantian moral thought, merely will oneself into goodness without having access to the proper tools and materials required for flourishing. For example, a good character founded on the virtue of being a good friend depends at least in part on cultivating a sense of fairness. It must be a value that we not only affirm in the abstract but that we are able to make sense of in our lived experiences—a crucial resource for learning is not merely being told that fairness is good, but being on the receiving end of it when it counts. Systemic racial inequality puts the ability and opportunity to learn that lesson at risk, since, for example, major social and political institutions are fundamentally unfair with respect to race.

The features of goodness that count in our relations with others count in our relationship with ourselves. This means, one ought not deny oneself a range of identity options simply because one is concerned about social stigma. This means not denying oneself opportunities to achieve academic excellence simply because the powerful ones who oppress you have access to the levers of power. This means that in any instance where being the best persons we can be is a live option from the point of view of what would objectively contribute to flourishing, blacks must be equally able to take stock of their standing as autonomous beings and assess the concept of flourishing in normatively appropriate ways unmarked by racial power—this is the burden posed by ethical disadvantage. For a theory of racial justice to have the relevance we desire from it, it needs to be sensitive—in ways signaled by Tessman and others—to how the circumstances of injustice place obstacles on the path to conceiving of a good life in the right way—that is to say, a way that would be more appealing to the ghetto youth on her own account if circumstances did not influence competing conceptualizations that likely interfere with fulfilling her natural duties.

I want to conclude by remarking on one simple but startling feature of ethical disadvantage. Although ethical disadvantage interferes with the ability to achieve human flourishing, it does not overcome our basic human capacities to achieve something of normative significance that one comes to affirm as one's own accomplishment as informed by one's own sense of the right and the good. Indeed, beyond a desire for acquiring goods or economic gain, gang members, for example, have standing conceptions of fairness, reciprocity, and respect.[22] As does Shelby, we wish for them, however, an outlet for those conceptions to map onto activities and beliefs that in the end do not fundamentally cut against those otherwise acceptable ethical notions. Mothers who decide to make welfare a permanent way of life do so because work requirements imposed by welfare programs often force them to take jobs away from home, thus they are unable to be sufficiently involved in their children's lives. These mothers, whom we would like to encourage to be out in the world learning a wide variety of skills and being exposed to opportunities (if that is what they themselves would otherwise want to do), make the rational choice that welfare allows them to basically subsist while being present for their children. Mothers in these situations are compelled by a basic tenet of justice: treating another as a moral being worthy of a good life. These persons and those in similarly difficult situations make choices that seem at odds with the virtues we typically endorse as good for us. However, in these situations an ethical stance is adopted for the situation that parallels the stance we might expect to be displayed under more favorable conditions. Ethical disadvantage, then, is not blaming the victim, nor does it label blacks as damaged. It is a description that allows us to see that blacks already have the tendency to display ethical virtues consistent with human flourishing but require better circumstances so that proper conceptions of what fairness, love, moral equality, reciprocity, and other constituent properties of justice rightly entail. From this perspective, blacks are already positioned to become partners, alongside whites, to the theory of justice in the way required by the theory.

THE CHARACTER OF CHARACTER IN OUR POLITICAL LIVES

The Idea of Character

We ought to be concerned with the Tom's and Anthony's of our society because the ability to characterize a society as just depends in an important way on it being populated by persons who value the right principles for the right reasons. This requirement entails a particular constellation of considerations—to value any principle for the right reasons in part depends upon moral cognition, as well as various sources of motivation. When we believe what we believe and do the things we do, we are not simply motivated by acknowledgments of duty. Beyond a sense of duty, we endorse and live by a complex array of values that make up our character. The ancient Greeks and moral theorists since recognize these as virtues. While I do not wish to engage in an extended discussion of the virtues per se, the problem we face does require considerations of character—a broader notion often thought to encompass the domain of our virtues alongside the way those inform our moral development, motivations, and actions. We have been discussing the notions of moral and ethical disadvantage as diagnoses for our personal shortcomings in the face of race. We now need to ask: How is personal character important for a theory of racial justice?

As given by moral and ethical disadvantage, the persons we become under our racial social scheme tend to be dissonant with the values of character that we tend to reflectively affirm—expressing respect for persons as moral equals under a democratic regime, for example. We are thus obliged to reflect upon our beliefs and motivations and act in accordingly moral and ethical ways toward others, as well as ourselves. An appropriate theory of racial justice must neutralize the effects of racial power on our moral development.

The notion of character is particularly helpful because it is the idea behind the problem. Let me explain. The ideas of moral and ethical disadvantage are analytic devices that specify the nature of the flaws the typical American needs to overcome on the road to being a racial egalitarian. However, these flaws reside within a more complex framework of individual makeup—our character. A useful way to see the relationship is to imagine a car that handles the road unreliably. It is true that it needs new tires, but it is also true that the drivetrain is badly tuned to such an extent that new tires will likely warp in a shorter period of time than they otherwise would (though the car will handle noticeably better in the short term). Thus, focusing on only the tires will expose one to a recurrent problem of poor handling. Character, as the repository for our virtues and vices, is the regulative mechanism for our ethically inflected practical deliberations. So while moral and ethical disadvantage are important diagnostic tools indicating how the typical American goes wrong in the face of race, our character is where our flaws reside. We always retain the capacity to reflect and choose a different course of action or competing set of beliefs. This is the most fundamental role of character. Additionally, this is the value of conceiving of these disadvantages as burdens rather than as strong/thick determinants of behavior and person formation—we can be better than we are in those moments it counts. But the way must be marked out and we must undergo a degree of moral learning and habituation. Thus, what follows below serves to pivot us toward the call in the final chapter for a perfectionist politics. How might we proceed to conceive of the relationship between character and a theory of racial justice with moral and ethical disadvantage in the background?

Consider that the common guiding question in political thought might be stated as follows: What would make our society a good or just one? Typical answers provided by theorists of justice over the past four decades or so have staunchly approached this answer from the perspective of institutional arrangements.[23] But this will seem odd to the casual yet interested observer. She will ask: What am I to do after a law is passed and my resume fails to generate interest? She will believe that everyday justice depends on the will of local actors to act in accordance with racial justice. Thus, a theory of the good society depends on an account of persons who are good alongside good institutions.

To give content to the relationship between character and justice with respect to race I must first convey the substance of the idea of character. Second, my argument for including the idea of character in the theory of justice—indeed making it pivotal—has not been offered in its fullest light. There may be conceptual reasons as to why character has not played a role in the theory of justice. If so, it might be unavailable with respect to racial justice. I will show that is indeed available with respect to racial justice, but we will have to dip into the tradition of virtue ethics in order to motivate its inclusion in the right way.

I begin with an account of character. Character is appealing because it possesses a certain heuristic property. Imagine for a moment that your partner comes home and seems agitated by the workday. You inquire into the source of the agitation and it is clear that the feeling is cumulative. You are told that there is a supervisor who expects her subordinates to arrive to work on time, but never does so herself. She has chastised co-workers for making inappropriate comments at the office but insists on sharing her weekend's social exploits. She often exclaims, "There is no 'I' in 'team,'" but she displays self-serving behavior when faced with a choice between her own career advancement and supporting subordinates. After hearing this you say: "It sounds like she is a person of bad character." Immediately your utterance captures the cumulative nature of the day's agitation. This result will seem familiar to many readers, but what explains this feature of character? An answer to this question sets the stage for its normative political relevance.

The above example captures three fundamental elements. First, the main agent in it—the boss with bad character—was understood to be acting on her own will. Indeed the agitation resulted from an intuition that the boss acted one way when she could have acted another. Second, the reason why the agitation was cumulative was because the boss's many offenses cohere into a rather complete picture of her as a person. That is to say, it makes sense that she is the same person who does not abide by her own strictures and that she is a person who fails to display loyalty at the appropriate moment. Thereby character depends on the condition of consistency. Last, and importantly, the boss's offenses are not trivial, especially when taken together. Rather, they are offenses precisely because her behavior displays two kinds of normatively important shortcomings. On the one hand, she seems to lack an ethical compass, insofar as her actions are dissonant with respect to her stated and affirmed rules and strictures. On the other, there are moral considerations—her failure to practice what she preaches results in various instances and varying degrees of disrespect and lack of regard for her subordinates. She seems indifferent to the way her behavior may sap workers of morale; and, more seriously, the way her actions may suppress their professional well-being.

The reader is likely to notice familiar themes, for Aristotle associated the virtues, which inform behavior (thus allowing us to assess character), with habits: "The virtues are implanted in us neither by nature nor contrary to nature: we are by nature equipped with the ability to receive them, and habit brings this ability to completion and fulfill-ment."[24] This view is consistent with the first two elements of the case: the propositions that the boss's acts were self-directed and that they displayed evaluative consistency. This does not yet establish that character is normatively significant. However, contemporary theorists have continued to theorize character in just this way. Joel Kupperman, who has worked extensively on the idea, writes, "[character is] a person's normal pattern of thought and action, especially with respect to concerns and commitments in matters affecting the happiness of others or of that person, and most especially in relation to moral choices."[25] Why should we accept character as politically significant? Kupperman goes on to say, "Plainly a good character will include a number of virtues, such as hon-esty, fortitude, considerateness, and willingness to go to some trouble to help those in need."[26] The fit between character and justice with regard to race begins to come into view. If it is true that racial inequality is the problem of social value as denoted by prob-lematic judgments of moral worth of blacks and black lives, then it follows that the idea of (bad) character is in play since racial inequality, in the first instance, seems to funda-mentally revolve around what we are willing to do for, how much we are willing to care about, the extent to which we express acceptance of blacks and these are all judgments about the worth of the persons in front of us—or, as Kupperman says, it denotes our capacity and willingness to go to some trouble for blacks. The political value of character for our purposes, then, is settled by the above morally significant features of character alongside the description of racial inequality as the problem of social value, since the latter idea indicates that despite Americans' capacity to go to some trouble for blacks, concerns arise on account of a marked lack of willingness. And here, we should under-stand the content of 'going to some trouble' to not merely signal material sacrifices or suppression of our own rational self-interest in favor of blacks' interes; it should be clear the problem runs deeper wherein 'going to some trouble' indicates the effort Americans invest in drawing a line of continuity between principles and ideals they already affirm and their modes of comportment that abandon those ideals and principles in the face of race.

Character and Justice

Conceptually, it would be peculiar to exclude considerations of character with respect to the theory of justice for while the idea of rationality seems robust with respect to reason-ing and identifying moral principles—the tact usually relied upon Kantian theories such as Rawls's and his contemporaries'—there is the further question of motivation: Why would I be compelled to do one thing rather than the other? It must be the case that the principles are valid in a way that I can recognize, from my point of view as the person I am. As Herman argues, "moral philosophy depends on an accurate account of what we are like as agents: our range of motivations, the structure of our practical thinking, the different ways we respond to and are affected by circumstances."[27]

Moral philosophy is dependent in this way because so far as morality is fundamental to good human relationships, we require a full understanding of the interaction between our inner normative capacities and external circumstances: "Having a virtuous character, we see different things, or see them in ways that have different practical significance.... And because of the way we come to see what we see, we are moved to act."[28] Thus, even if moral imperatives do in part have independent moral standing, persons do not—we are situated beings who develop habits and learn lessons such that we come to these truths with and through character. And ultimately, our character plays a significant role in the ways we accept, act upon, and fulfill our duties. I want to stress, this is not to say that our ability to recognize duties ought to be determined by a character we already possess, for as Aristotle tells us, the development of character is dynamic and involves a learning process. Rather, this is to say that morality is not unidirectional or unconditional in the way often presumed by Kant (or maybe better put, his more orthodox interpreters). Indeed, the relationship we bear toward it is complex and we are active participants in its practices.

This, then, brings us directly to the need for and compatibility of character in a theory of justice. The substance of any such theory's normative injunctions need to be imagined as necessarily facing the question as to what kind of persons will be party to it, for if we get the answer to this question wrong, the project of justice is jeopardized. The world is not divided between the wicked and the good but is shared, rather, among persons who can genuinely, culpably, but not necessarily wickedly be in moral error— these are the Tom's and Anthony's. As is clear in their narratives, they are in possession of certain basic capacities and beliefs to be appropriate partners to the theory of racial justice—Tom acknowledges his complicity and recognizes institutional wrongness; Anthony understands that robbing similarly disadvantaged persons violates a natural duty. However, it is similarly clear that no amount of merely stressing to Tom or Anthony the rightness of principles of justice will alter the persons they have developed into given their respective places in the social scheme. Rather, beyond their rational reflective capacities, they will have to bring to bear the virtues they already possess, augment them so as to be more consistent agents, and this will depend upon their ability to sympathize, own their shame, and a series of related moral and ethical maneuvers. And it will be the same throughout our polity—persons must be prepared to not merely affirm, but embrace and live by the moral precepts embedded in its principles. If not, the theory is only successful at the level of abstract specification but unsuccessful as an aspirational social and political project, as it seems to me any normative political theory must be.

On the view of social value, discrete measurements of racial inequality—unequal wealth and pay, housing discrimination, political marginalization, and lower quality of education—owe their explanation to black's normative social status. The driving idea is that blacks do not come into view as agents morally worthy of the consideration that would otherwise eliminate discrete instances of racial inequality. Seeing how character is compatible with social justice, I now want to explain why the idea of character is fundamental to understanding and addressing racial inequality.

The theory of power sketched in chapter 2 suggests that the problem of social value works in two ways. First, it removes from society's view blacks as objects of appropriate normative concern. To revisit an example, consider the lower support for various forms of aid and consideration among whites as compared to blacks in response to Katrina. The idea of life-worlds was invoked in this example to illustrate that political life in America is not the same for all its citizens. As evidenced by the empirics, this has practical import for policy preferences if not an understanding of what a policy is actually trying to accomplish. But now there is a further concern. There is a real racial divide that is not merely significant for understanding resource or opportunity inequality. The divide is real for assessing where persons normatively stand in our social scheme. This is the importance of Michael Dawson's invocation of Habermas's idea of life-worlds—it denotes an experiential phenomenon in which persons may inhabit the same political space, but, ultimately, that political space results in such starkly different experiences for the respective parties that they seem phenomenologically distinct.

If the idea of life-worlds is instrumental for theorizing the experience of a racial America, then it will also have something to say about the kinds of persons we are within our social scheme. Recall that the idea of character is tightly bound to habits, as well as moral learning. We have the capacity to develop habits with respect to the virtues and this process is dynamic. While we come to situations with character in hand, we also possess the capacity to walk away from situations with an amended character, a set of improvements that allow us to be more consistent moral agents. However, the racial divide expressed in the proposition that American society is home to distinct life-worlds raises serious concerns about the character of its citizens. Consider just one virtue offered by Kupperman: being willing to come to the aid of those in need. Now consider the difference of 40 percentage points between whites and blacks in supporting government aid to Katrina victims, the majority of whom (as well as the worst hit) were black.[29] Now further consider that this kind of response from whites is unexceptional. Studies illustrating systematic hesitance to interview black candidates or studies illustrating greater support among whites for the death penalty with respect to black offenders provide empirical evidence of a pattern among white racial dispositions that diminish the chance black life interests will be considered equally important or, in fact, equally compelling.[30] This phenomenon is predicted by social dominance orientation as articulated by Sidanius and Pratto and is consistent with Kupperman's claim that character relies upon patterns of dispositions and behaviors. From the point of view of racial justice understood as the problem of social value, it raises serious questions about our social readiness to value black identity as demanded by the strictures of a liberal democracy.

This line of thinking leads to a two-part claim. First, a significant part of the problem with respect to racial inequality is that those positioned advantageously in the racial scheme, as an empirical matter, have likely developed bad moral habits with respect to race. This has important implications for virtues that are necessarily relied upon in a theory of justice. Second, as a conceptual matter, the problem of race is not merely a problem of superficial institutional reform. For example, we might imagine if the sole dimension of racial inequality was income inequality, then legislation mandating income-based affirmative action would be the proper remedy, and, indeed, the only necessary remedy. However, because race is systematic and deeply laden with historically embedded norms, the problem reaches deep down into the structure of our beliefs and attitudes, as evidenced by Katrina respondents. The theory, then, must be prepared to follow the problem into the depths of our souls in the spirit of moral liberation. I shall revisit this point shortly.

Character allows us to speak truth to power in recognizing the undeniable fact that very few of us can stand outside the influence of race's reach. Additionally, precisely because character is not wholly determined by already existing habits, it actually allows us to introduce a liberatory spirit into the theory of racial justice. As I have indicated, the theory of racial justice presented in the final chapter depends upon a brand of democratic perfectionism concerned to shape persons into moral agents capable of embracing racial justice. Chapter 3 indicated that, with respect to institutions, the theory of justice must intervene in path-dependent practices informed by our racial history. With the ideas of moral and ethical disadvantage in hand, the new practices given by the theory of justice must not stop at simply instituting procedural racial fairness. Rather, they must extend beyond institutions to the character of democratic citizens, who like Tom and Anthony, possess a basically functional sense of justice that fails in the face of race. If the Tom's and Anthony's of our society cannot achieve moral excellence on their own, then the possibility of a racially just society seems at risk, thus the need to adopt an approach to shore up our confidence in its success.

CONCLUSION

It seems to me that, as with any disadvantage, persons under the weight of moral or ethical disadvantage need to relieve the burdens on their character. But burdens are difficult to shed without help. More importantly, it is not merely a matter of shedding these burdens but of engaging a path of moral development that does more than simply affirm the right principles with clarity but that also leads us to affirm them in our heart of hearts. It is one thing to acknowledge the duty of reciprocity and another to understand its worth with respect to the life of another who is your moral equal—there is no guarantee that the former entails right action, whether it has the status of a moral imperative or not.

Consider a remarkably poignant passage by Herman:

> A minimal moral capacity functions like many other practical capacities that "license" behavior.... Competence does not make one a good driver, but it puts one on the road responsible for a variety of unexpected outcomes, including some that may be the product of one's own limits or incapacities. We expect that a driver with a blind spot over her right shoulder will, over time, discover the gap in her visual field, appreciate its danger, and compensate for it.... That the blind spot is a fixed feature of her visual field gives her a task, not an excuse.[31]

The task to which Herman is referring is making oneself bring into view the full set of circumstances that might result in the moral equivalent of a car crash. But this is not as easy as it sounds: "The abuser's ability poses special problems: personality deformations, unlike blind spots, can retain essential connections to their history and so to a person's sense of self."

We are not concerned with outright abusers but those who by way of moral and ethical disadvantage have a significant blind spot, and those, who like Tom and Anthony, are not deformed, but are certainly burdened by the way circumstances and the past seem to bear down on their ability to liberate themselves from the social strictures of race—to free themselves from the metal and glass enclosures that are the social positions given by the problem of social value. Herman suggests that if people cannot free themselves, "At some point we revoke a license to drive."[32] This option is not open to us for it only exacerbates the fact that we do not "touch" each other, as Cheadle laments. If democracy relies upon our viewing and accepting each other as co-citizens, we ought to resist promoting apathy and practices of seclusion so far as that is possible. But neither does this mean crashing is the only remaining option on account of our blind spots. What if we imagine, rather, having a morally reliable passenger who can signal when we are in danger of crashing? This would certainly allow us to get to where we want to go while saving ourselves the typically resultant bruises.

This is why the shame alluded to in this book's title and discussed in chapter 1 is an important aspect of our moral lives—it prompts us to acknowledge our moral shortcomings on the view of our own principled commitments. The sense of shame can certainly be generated from within, but if one indeed possesses a blind spot, then it may be left to the passenger to signal those moments when one has driven poorly and invoke shame within the agent. And yet, shame allows one to be a better agent on account of principles to which one already takes oneself to be committed. Perfectionism, as a positive normative framework, is committed to the idea that we can be better persons in a manner consistent with our own vision for what that would look like. And just as it may be necessary for the passenger to provide important cues to the driver in the above example, perfectionism allows others to be an important part of that process, to intervene in our morally relevant erroneous ways. Given the nature of the problem of social value, this seems the right way to go, but is not without its concerns. We need to consider the proper moral grounding of an appropriate perfectionist politics and what its theoretical mechanisms might be. If we can get past that point, the theory of racial justice is then left to imagine its manifestation in policy-making. I now turn to these final tasks.

5

Racial Justice in Our Time

IN 2008, *THE Boondocks*, a newspaper comic strip that had been adapted to an animated televisions series, asked an important question: What would Martin Luther King, Jr. think about twenty-first-century America? *The Boondocks* cut its teeth in print syndication by asking the tough, and because tough, controversial racial questions regarding white privilege so few seem prepared to engage. And, to its credit, though critical of white America, it has had just as much to say to black America about the way it proceeds (or fails to proceed) to deal with racial injustice. The episode in question, "Return of the King"[1] is all the more poignant in light of the series' disposition to questions of race. Instead of trying to assess the Civil Rights Movement from a twenty-first-century perspective, it assesses twenty-first-century America from the perspective of the Civil Rights Movement. The analysis is telling and nicely sets the stage for our last step in formulating a response to racial inequality—articulating the prescriptive recommendations required by a theory of racial justice.

In "Return of the King," the main character, Huey—a black, urban youth who has been sent to live in a dominantly white middle-class suburban enclave—imagines an alternate history wherein King slips into a coma rather than dying as a result of an assassination attempt. King wakes up in 2008 faced with a country that has recently declared war on Iraq. Although he initially regains national renown, he soon becomes a political pariah on account of his questioning the legitimacy of the war. Subsequent book signings are barren events where we find him dozing in his chair. Thus, he encounters a polity somewhat intolerant of reasonable, critical, and penetrating social and political questions. Rather, a kind of materialism has usurped political consciousness. He visits an Apple store and is confused as to whether he needs the 20GB or the 40GB iPod (how small those numbers seem to us today). Thus, it is a country in which maybe we do not ask tough questions because we are easily placated by our material wealth and more concerned with the choice between slight material excess and excessive material excess. Crucially, he also awakens to a country in which blacks seem fixated upon speaking with bad syntax, displaying half-naked women in rap videos, and are more concerned with partying than with protest—all this in the face of continued racial injustice. Thus, it is a country where the oppressed themselves have ceased asking tough questions about a social scheme in which they are systematically disadvantaged. The episode's main argument is that a nation cannot achieve its potential when institutions fail to act with integrity and people do not take seriously the duty of holding institutions to account. What practices would be entailed by taking that claim seriously? This is a question fundamental to theorizing racial justice and my response is a democratic perfectionist project that trades moral mediocrity for racial discomfort as the only way to achieve the appropriate moral excellence made possible by and indeed required for the long-term viability of American democracy.

Huey implores King to tell the people how he sees it—that they have failed miserably as citizens while leaders like King sacrificed themselves in the name of democratic excellence. On his view, King's efforts were expended precisely to imbue democratic self-governance with the integrity demanded by liberal democratic ideals. Forty years after the "success" of the Civil Rights Movement, King observes a persistence in racial shortcomings thus a failure of that integrity, so Huey tells him: "What the people need is the truth. And not the pretty truth—the horrible, terrible, awful truth that hurts people's feelings. The truth that makes people angry and get up and do something." He means to say that the project of realizing a more excellent democracy cannot be achieved cost free—it might be paid at the expense of our civic pride but in the name of an ideal we already otherwise affirm in order to live up to our collective democratic aspirations. I am with Huey on this. So far as I can tell, no society has outgrown a troubled past without experiencing growing pains in order to sustain a better future. Racial injustice replicates a history that continuously makes our nation buckle under the weight of an essentially immoral future; the only way to regain our collective footing is to begin dealing with the truth of the matter. So Huey, a twenty-first-century black youth living in the middle of middle-class white America, demands a vision of a better future. Offering that vision is the least of our concerns. The more pressing demand is an account of the means to achieving that vision, one that I believe depends on democratic perfectionism. Further, on account of the vision being applied to a democratic society, it must also be susceptible to justification—it must be based on the truth of the matter. Huey has provided a helping hand in pressing this claim— the problem of race is the problem of social value and bad national character, and unless we face matters as they are, we risk falling short of our liberal democratic aspirations. The kind of perfectionist project I am interested in articulating heads off the problem of social value by going right to the core of amending our bad character.

Let us begin with a review of the conceptual structure we have built to this point along with some of the main ideas we have deployed to populate that structure. I began by acknowledging but shelving views of racial inequality that take inequality in goods or opportunities as the main concern of a theory of racial justice. My reasoning was that while these maladies are symptoms of a social ill, it is not a diagnosis in the deepest sense. I have argued that to understand where we go wrong with respect to race we have to understand why blacks do not get equal amounts of goods, rather than why blacks do not have equal amounts of goods. My own response, and the main pillar of this book, has been to specify the problem of racial inequality as the problem of social value: blacks do not occupy an equal place in the social normative scheme, thus are not accorded equal moral value. The implication is profound and comprehensive: putting justice into motion for those who need it is inordinately difficult if we do not believe they are morally worthy of our concern and reflective considerations. This largely accounts for the failure of formal equality over the past forty years in bringing blacks up to the status of fully equal citizens in a substantive sense. But precisely because we otherwise affirm the value of substantive equality, our failure in the face of race is a result of a bad national character informed by our history of racial norms that have historically underwritten social, political, and economic subordination.

What does it mean for a society with a history of violently and explicitly subordinating blacks to continue to (mostly nonviolently) subordinate them even when we have generally come to agree that such practices are deeply wrong? The answer I have sought to elucidate is that this is a cause for shame. While we are not morally corrupt, we are in moral error on account of liberal democratic principles we already reflectively endorse. However, because my main aim is to have our society (1) recover and (2) reinstate within persons and institutions the moral principles that already underwrite our otherwise sound democratic practices and values, the theory of racial justice must be committed to a kind of archaeology—an archaeology of our moral spirit such that it leads us to where it rightly intends to go. Revisiting themes in chapter 1, our individual and collective flourishing is enhanced when we confront morally important errors. Hence, the role of shame as a fundamental but background concept for it allows us to reclaim and live by those principles we already affirm. What I intend to do in this chapter, then, is present an account of how a political theory attuned to the problem of racial inequality in just this way would proceed in formulating an effective theory of racial justice.

The above considerations must now be synthesized with some of the observations on power and moral agency to generate that theory. Consider the second major claim of the book, that the problem of social value is operative at two levels. Political history and sociology tell us that our institutions continue to operate under a logic that, while not identical to the explicit racist practices of the past, is continuous with it in morally problematic ways. If we consider our review of crime and welfare policy, we will recall that these major institutions have continuously abided by historically familiar patterns of racial logic. While institutions are not entirely free-standing—after all, they are inhabited by people—they do have a way of developing and operating that is not reducible to the actions and preferences of the persons who populate them. It is on this count that theorists from Sidanius to Rawls can make the claim that institutions have a distinct path of development over time, as well as regiment of practices that are distinctly assignable to entities called "institutions."

This leads to the problem of bad character at two levels. Institutions tend to behave badly in the face of race. The main grounds for imputing bad character to institutions are that although their rules and commitments indicate higher moral ground—the principles that underwrite liberal democracy—their tendencies and public practices do not adequately reflect those commitments. While the idea of applying character to institutions might strike some as novel, it is old hat to apply it at the level of persons—the second level of the problem. By dint of learning bad moral lessons under institutions with bad character, as well as under poor social circumstances combined with lapses in reflective consistency, most persons are in some sense a party to the problem of social value. As argued in chapter 4, whites are not generally racist, but the confluence of an advantageous social position along with easy access to the levers of power render many morally disadvantaged—they are poorly positioned to acknowledge and act upon the moral worth of their black counterparts. Blacks figure into the problem as well, for being the objects of society's moral neglect teaches moral and ethical lessons, and as scholars like Shelby have argued, the circumstances of racial marginalization underwrite attitudes and actions the results of which can run counter to what we typically affirm as ethically sound personal development. Taking the two levels together, then, the character of our society is deeply troubled. But because shame is the appropriate analytic tool to use in motivating the recovery of our moral fiber, we are not beyond redemption. An integral feature of shame is that the resources necessary for such a recovery are within our reach— we basically already affirm the right principles of social morality; they now need to guide us more consistently in the face of race. All this entails that justice talk must shift away from being talk about goods, and instead, about the heart of our national character.

What will it mean for justice talk to shift in this way? This chapter argues that a particular form of democratic perfectionism represents our best chance at realizing racial justice when the constellation of considerations are arranged in the way I have specified. I pause to briefly describe three forms of perfectionism to better situate the concluding positive recommendations.

First, when a person invokes perfectionism, he might be arguing that there are better kinds of goods one should want in life. Such a person thinks that going to a Manet exhibit, for example, represents better artistic consumption than watching *Survivor*. The attendant justice claims are that society ought to encourage the consumption of some goods while disallowing or discouraging the consumption of others. Second, he might invoke perfectionism to make a claim about better and worse life pursuits. This perfectionist might press the claim that surely it is better to be a writer of high-brow literature than an author of romance serials. On this view, doing the latter is tantamount to a waste of one's valuable capabilities, thus is to be objectively diminished. The attendant justice claims here would likely entail a rearrangement of our institutional practices to encourage the pursuit of certain life plans rather than others because some life plans are objectively better in themselves, thus, better for us.

The position I sketch below depends on neither of these—whether cases can be made for the first two strands of perfectionism is a separate question, and worth considering, but one with which I shall not be concerned. Rather, I mean to affirm a third option: this last perfectionist holds that there are better and worse ways to be, better and worse characters to have, and that it is permissible for external agents to enthusiastically nudge us toward these better ways of being.[2] Let us call this *moral-agency perfectionism*. The relevant twist for us is that the values informing what it means to be better moral agents are not given from without—rather, the content of the nudge is currently contained within our national character by way of the moral and political principles that underwrite the liberal democracy we already affirm. The parity between this brand of perfectionism and racial inequality understood as the problem of social value should be immediately apparent for I have been insisting that the problem of social value indicates serious lapses in the national character, thus suggesting that we must be made racially better if our society is to treat blacks as genuine equals in a manner consistent with liberal democratic values.

Below I turn to three tasks. Perfectionism of any sort is bound to be controversial to the contemporary ear, liberal or not, so something must be said about how such an approach might be justified generally. Second, I extend the general justification to inform my more particular program of democratic perfectionism as representing a set of practices that would help achieve the aims of moral-agency perfectionism—a prerequisite for restructuring our racial norms; and finally, I consider what a democratic perfectionist regime would be concerned to accomplish with respect to the problem of social value, and how it might do so, in righting our racial wrongs.

THE NEEDS OF A POLITY

Justification I: Adapting a Perfectionist Stance

Moral-agency perfectionism, as a normative framework meant to ground and affirm certain principles of moral development, which in turn inform actions and attitudes, requires justification as any other framework does. That is to say, if it is to play a role in regulating our lives, and if we are also to affirm certain liberal ideals as fundamental, we ought to be presented with good reasons for affirming moral-agency perfectionism. I think there are two levels at which any normative framework may be justified: *theoretical justification* and *political justification*. The view I will present states that while moral-agency perfectionism might be theoretically justifiable, its normative force is granted by political justification wherein the nature of the problem suggests not only that moral-agency perfectionism is a good fit but that it is the best fit, and that without it, the pursuit of racial justice might well be hindered.

To settle matters, let's begin with *theoretical justification*. At this level, what counts toward justification is whether the framework is internally coherent such that the concepts expressing moral ends are consistent with concepts expressing the moral ideal. For the sake of illustration, let's say we think that human flourishing, mutual respect, and autonomy are three important ideals for morality and we want to argue that hedonism best secures these ideals. What would theoretically justify that position? It would have to be the case that hedonism, which holds that our lives are best when we satisfy our urges and desires as they come to us, is conceptually consonant with the three ideals. That is to say, the content of hedonism defined as the satisfaction of my urges and desires is consistent with the idea of flourishing or showing others due respect. Of course, upon close inspection, hedonism is not so justified, for we often have urges for certain foods, for example, that may be harmful to our bodies. Also, we sometimes have private desires that, if acted upon, could potentially disrespect or cause harm to others. Further, we may think that merely following our urges and desires runs counter to the notion of autonomy as we often fail to have good reasons to indulge in certain behaviors—and this is a bad thing for truly autonomous people ought to be reasons-responsive. Thus, hedonism is theoretically unjustifiable.

The above example is very compressed, but the reader will see my point—the above kind of justification relies on the definition of the terms involved, the content of the ideals in play, and the coherence among them. Above, hedonism fails definitively. However, I have stressed that we must do *political* thought. My insistence that political thought ought to embrace a wider range of considerations (in this instance—considerations beyond definitions, to the way concepts map onto political and social experience) than most thinkers have allowed or been sensitive to stems from the proposition that a significant aspect of (political) morality is informed by lived experience.

Thus, there is a second level of justification to which we must be attentive. What circumstances might justify a particular normative framework? The circumstances we find ourselves in can provide crucial guidance in assessing competing frameworks that all seem to offer something valuable in addressing a particular question. This second level represents *political justification*—the kind of justification that utilizes social and political difficulties as the litmus test for otherwise abstract yet substantive ideas and ideals.[3] I want to focus on why moral-agency perfectionism is politically justifiable. I believe it is so in both a negative and positive sense.

Negatively, we should prefer that moral-agency perfectionism at least not offend against desirable liberal ideals. Following Joseph Raz, a theorist concerned with the relationship between perfectionism and liberalism, let us say that a main liberal ideal is individual autonomy.[4] So, negatively moral-agency perfectionism needs to accommodate our being individually autonomous while being able to press its case for perfecting persons. Can it do this?

Autonomy is essential to liberals because it is the hallmark of individuality and secures political voice, which is fundamentally important for granting the state and its institutions legitimacy. Insofar as liberals prize liberties, property, and the ability to pursue a life of one's own choosing, they necessarily prize autonomy, which is commonly understood as the capacity to build for oneself a scheme of beliefs, preferences, and plans as one gives oneself reasons for preferring one set of those over another set. Therefore, my being autonomous entails that my choice to not believe in God, for example, must recognizably be my own choice for not believing in God—any account I give must be grounded in reasons I affirm by my own lights. What is important about autonomy so understood is that it is possible to say that a person's "own choice" is actually not an autonomous one. That is to say, the fact that one claims ownership of the choice and affirms what seem to be her own reasons is not sufficient to claim autonomy. Imagine I say that I do not believe in God and the reason for not doing so that I affirm by my own lights is that my parents told me not to, and I think they know so much more about the world than I do. In this case I am not acting as an autonomous agent (for the sake of the example, we are assuming that I am of age). Importantly, I could ultimately be right in thinking that refusing to believe in God is good for me. The issue here, however, is that while it is acceptable for me to hold this belief—it may even be good for me to do so—the reasons are poorly grounded as they are derived from the authority of my parents' reasoning based on their experiences. For the choice to be autonomous, their authority on the matter should instead be one data point, so to speak, among many. Thereby, autonomy is consistent with being pressed to revisit my reasons so that they are brought into line with a belief I may affirm nonetheless. It is fundamental to autonomy that there is a direct relationship between my freely affirmed principles and my reasons for acting and believing.

This line of thinking is of a kind Raz employs in overcoming liberal resistance to perfectionism. On his account, the tension between autonomy and coercion is resolved by recasting the conflict as being between freedom and un-freedom. What vexes the typical liberal is that if one chooses to not believe in God and states that that choice is hers, the liberal will fail to perceive a justification for pursuing matters further. But, on Raz's view, this actually results in an abandonment of liberal values, for in the above example, the reasons I claim as my own are not derived from my own reflective capacities, but rather depend on a belief that itself relies on someone else's capacities. On this view, it would be peculiar to say that I am free. Raz writes: "People pursue goals and have desires for reasons. They believe that the objects of their desires or their pursuits are valuable.... This reason-dependent character of goals and desires entails that any person who has a goal or a desire, believes.... that if he came to believe that there were no reasons to pursue the goal, he would no longer have them."[5] He goes on, "A further consequence of the reason-dependent character of desires is that agents do not wish their desires satisfied if their belief in the existence of a reason for their desires is unfounded."[6]

On the above view, perfectionism is thought to be compatible with autonomy because we may be positioned to direct a person toward her own good, not on our account, but on account of that person's own reasons were she to think clearly about the connections between reasons and ends. But Raz has a stronger claim to make that will figure into our concerns over the relationship between character and race: truly autonomous persons are also persons of integrity. That is to say, they do not merely "[drift] along"—they are active participants in tethering their beliefs to their actions and dispositions by way of reasons they independently affirm.[7] This last claim presses us to resist liberalism's preference for a hands-off approach to persons' moral development, as well as the choices that development entails. Our concerns here are limited, though, by a specific case, thus the brand of perfectionism I am endorsing is not concerned with wholesale challenges to persons' belief sets. The relationship between character and the attractiveness of perfectionism is bounded by problems surrounding racial beliefs. Not only are these irrational, but, as suggested in the preceding chapter, they have real world implications for our ability to value black identity as morally equal, thus the ability to overcome the problem of social value. So far, so good. How does moral-agency perfectionism fare with respect to positive justification?

Justification II: Taking a First Perfectionist Step

In *Leviathan*, Hobbes shuffles persons from a nasty, short, brutish life in the state of nature toward a life under absolute rule by the will of the sovereign on account of his view of persons as unable to live peaceably enough among each other.[8] Hobbes's view is founded on a conception of self-interest that runs so deep within persons in the state of nature that cooperation is only or mostly only possible on account of its utility in achieving self-regarding aims. It is a good thing that the social contract tradition generally rejects Hobbes's understanding of human nature, thus allowing democratic theorists to imagine a society made up of a different kind of citizen—one with a view of the social bond as more than a means to get what one wants. Now, surely democratic theorists have disagreed on what democracy amounts to, but otherwise competing views presume the same thing: persons have the kind of character fit for a society that depends on tolerance, communication, and compromise.[9] Otherwise, even the most cynical view of democracy—that positing it as merely a forum for competing interests—would simply devolve into a view of organized conflict that could at any moment dissolve the social bond. Furthermore, historical struggles for self-governance indicate that democracy means something more to us than simply an opportunity to fight, but that is not to say that we are ideal democratic citizens.

For a normative framework to be politically justified in a positive sense, two things must be true. First, it must be able to promote the practice of democracy as a social union among moral equals who, yes, are self-interested, but who also perceive value in living a life in common. Second, and more urgently, it must be able to work from the other side as well—it must illustrate promise with respect to being sufficiently robust in its ability to support such a democratic vision in light of the circumstances in which we find ourselves. The two conditions stipulate, then, that, it must be simultaneously aspirational (future oriented) and realistic (sufficiently aware of the present sociopolitical facts). Thus, it must do more than prove itself democratically acceptable—we must be able to imagine it as capable of challenging our shared dispositions in a manner consistent with more fundamental shared democratic ideals and values in light of the racial circumstances.

Moral-agency perfectionism can fulfill the needs of political justification on the first count. The requirement here is that democracy not be violated in the name of pursuing democracy. On my view, the primary aim of moral-agency perfectionism is to prompt a tighter alignment between our actions and dispositions and our principles. The important move here is that moral-agency perfectionism does not provide its own substantive political principles. Rather, it depends on resources already at hand—as noted above, the fundamental principles of liberal democracy are rarely contested, but it is those principles, when acted on in a consistent manner in the face of race, that can serve a pivotal role in undermining the problem of social value. Thus, on account of the demands of liberal democracy, the moral agency-perfectionist argues that other agents are allowed to push and prompt us to unify our principles with other aspects of our autonomous selves (i.e., practical reasoning and social judgment). This affirms and upholds core democratic tenets, since our aim is to excavate them from the ash of moral error.

Now, the second requirement is both more urgent and more difficult to meet, for it requires a statement of our normatively inflected political needs in light of an interpretation of where our society stands (which in turn threatens to cast the theory as purely consequentialist, which is an undesirable outcome). However, this is less problematic than it seems as we have stated our goal is to politically justify moral-agency perfectionism with respect to racial inequality as (an immoral) feature of our shared democratic lives. That settles the issue of scope, as we are not concerned to comprehensively challenge persons' beliefs and commitments—just those that are relevant to the problem of social value. The concern over interpretation is also less daunting than it might otherwise appear, for we have characterized racial inequality as a particular kind of problem—that of social value: blacks do not hold an equal place in our scheme of normative value as persons holding other identities, namely whites. Hence, the problem of social value defines the relevant circumstances for political justification, namely that the attitudes and beliefs that motivate social, economic, and political practices serve to marginalize black identity and reinforce its marginal moral worth. Further, the arguments running from chapters 2 to 4 indicate that our society at the level of both institutions and persons suffers from bad character, since we fail to uphold the democratic ideals we tend to otherwise affirm— that persons have equal effective rights or that persons are owed equal democratic consideration. On this view, then, political justification is grounded in the validity of our diagnosis of racial inequality as the problem of social value. If that diagnosis is shaky, then so is our justification. However, chapter 2 shows that the diagnosis is not merely reasonable but analytically superior, as well as more politically comprehensive than competing explanations of racial inequality.

The issue of character, then, is signally important for politically justifying moral-agency perfection. Jeffrey Stout writes: "Oppressed peoples have often been in a position to find democratic ideals attractive from a distance, but those ideals are first of all expressions of a democratic culture. They are meaningless when abstracted from the inferential practices and behavioral dispositions of a people in the habit of trusting one another and talking things through in a certain way."[10] Here, Stout is directing our attention to the way attractive normative features of democratic life are emergent properties of democratic practices, and that these practices indicate a kind of character founded on habit—one that allows for trust and open communication. However, there is a warning here as well, and I believe it is embodied in the fact that oppressed peoples find "democratic ideals attractive from a distance." Oppressed persons as much as anyone else, maybe more so, can see the value in democratic ideals, and what poses a problem within a society that harbors oppression is that the subordinated effectively do not have access to the goods those ideals entail. But they are also at the margins of normative concern—there is a failure of character here, for trust and openness become reserved for the dominant and advantaged, a phenomenon marked out by moral disadvantage as elaborated in the previous chapter. But, precisely because these otherwise attractive features of democratic life can be affirmed by both the dominant and the oppressed, we have good reason for wanting to change the character of our society rather than articulate a new set of ideals—thus we seek to eliminate moral and ethical disadvantage.

Danielle Allen shares a related set of concerns. For her, the ethics of shared democratic life require that we be able and willing to "talk to strangers"—"strangers" being persons who stand on opposite sides of the racial experiential divide. Her reflections are motivated by images of citizens struggling to come to grips with the racial upheaval brought about during the middle of the twentieth century, particularly during the integration of public schools across the country. Images of a reporter being kicked by an angry white mob and a lone schoolgirl being ominously surrounded by white students serve as the foundation for Allen to explode old myths about how democracy works and introduce new lessons concerning co-citizenship. One of Allen's crucial realizations[11] is that the mythical notion of democratic "oneness" is wrongheaded. The issue is not whether oneness is a good ideal; rather, the society that we have as a product of our history does not admit of a descriptor or ideal that ignores real divisions between persons and groups. She writes of American political history: "Citizenship taught habits of domination and acquiescence that, in conjunction, produced invisibility and seeming oneness."[12] On her view, oneness under conditions of deep injustice is a rhetorical device that practically masks social injustice and the divisions it begets.

The better way to go, then, is to focus on "wholeness"—a democratic life that accepts differences but in which we identify each other as co-participants in the project of ongoing cooperation for the common purpose of upholding democracy, even as we may disagree about how to best secure that vision. The important move here is that this entails we accept each other as co-participants in a manner recognizably indexed to moral equality. However, because divisions are (here and now) a fact of our social and political existence, we must be willing to talk to strangers—those who are "others" on account of where we stand in the social scheme. Like Stout, Allen believes democratic life depends upon habituation and the possession of certain virtues of citizenship. The issue, of course, is that in a society home to deep injustice, good habits and admirable virtues can come apart from how we actually treat others, thus creating distinct racial life experiences. My argument is that insofar as we are attracted to views like Stout's and Allen's we need to get some preliminaries in place—citizens must be possessed of the right kind of moral agency or character in order to pursue democratic wholeness.

In light of the above, I want to affirm that moral-agency perfectionism is politically justified. For on Stout's and Allen's views, democracy is a tricky business hobbled by extant social relationships of normative racial hierarchy that mark and mar the social character, removing some citizens from moral concern at the same time that marginalized citizens acknowledge the broad value of what the dominant group holds politically dear. No one denies the intrinsic moral appeal of a democratic life of which we see glimmers here and there, sometimes more luminous than others. However, the only way for that life to shine brightest is for its participants and institutions to be ready to take on the habits Stout and Allen recognize as giving rise to democracy's promise. However, habits cut in two directions. Members of the racially advantaged class can at once be habituated to value equality yet be habituated to see blacks as unworthy of realizing that value in their own lives. Habits are born of practices in conjunction with public norms of acceptance and respect that we come to take as settled in the relevant way. If we accept the problem of racial inequality as that of social value, then our ability to treat blacks as moral equality demands depends on the degree to which we are willing to hold persons to the higher standard that already underwrites those attractive democratic ideals. And if we think that that project is hindered in the first instance by a marred national character, we must do more than trade in moral maxims—duty is rarely a sufficient personal reason for doing or believing anything; it is an impersonal command the force of which we may succeed or fail to recognize or acknowledge. We must collectively nudge ourselves to be reasonable—to reliably connect our principles with our actions and dispositions as persons participating in an unjust social scheme. Additionally, insofar as liberals value autonomy, and we accept autonomy as valuable insofar as it is actively engaged in bringing us to be consistent with values we consider to be good, moral-agency perfectionism has a role to play. Envisioning it as part and parcel of democratic practice is the project of democratic perfectionism, a necessary step on the road to racial justice.

THE WAYS OF A POLITY

Lessons Learned from the Past...

What would it mean for a democratic society marked by racial inequality to embrace a perfectionist stance? It is one thing to say that it is politically justified on the grounds that social value represents an important sociopolitical truth. It is another to be clear as to what that justification entails. What are we demanding when we say that our society ought to be organized in a manner that encourages the development of a more excellent moral character with respect to race? Although I have made much about the absence of a theory of racial justice, I am certainly not the first or even an early agitator for a perfectionist inflected argument concerned with race (though I should say this tendency has slipped from view in contemporary work). Frederick Douglass was an early social observer who intimated the political value of democratic perfectionism, and his emblematic statement is to be found in his seminal address, "What, to the Slave is the Fourth of July?" In engaging Douglass I want to bring into more crisp view the demands of a democratic perfectionist stance as motivated by concerns over race. I then want to make a second move—I fast-forward to our contemporary conceptual environment and sketch how Douglass's concerns can be expressed in the language of a democratic theory that promotes the needs of racial justice. In making these two moves I lay the groundwork for a polity to conceive of the project of racial justice as founded on social cooperation. The final section of the chapter thinks about the implications of the first two sections in more concrete terms in elucidating three principles of racial justice as founded on a perfectionist stance.

In 1852 Douglass was called upon by the Rochester Ladies' Anti-Slavery Society to deliver a speech on and about the Fourth of July—Independence Day. Ostensibly, one imagines such an event ought to celebrate the nation's achievements, and in a sense this is exactly Douglass's aim. However, his extolment of America's greatness is qualified by a deep and scathing criticism of what he describes as "these degenerate times."[13] Douglass utilizes the platform given him to make clear that slavery was not only wrong as an offense against humanity but that it signaled a problem of national character, since it existed in a country that at the same time considered itself progressive in light of its fought-for independence from an unjust monarchy. Douglass takes care to pay the American founders tribute. He hones in on the virtues of their resistance to the unjustified oppression perpetrated by the British Crown. He admires the courage and tenacity to fight for the principles of right. And he expresses nothing but the deepest admiration for the founders' identification and statement of truly just principles of political association. He writes: "Feeling themselves harshly and unjustly treated by the home government, your fathers, like men of honesty and men of spirit, earnestly sought redress.... Their conduct was wholly unexceptionable."[14]

Yet, Douglass believed that there remained significant moral lessons for America to learn. It is first important to note that Douglass's address presents a sophisticated analysis of injustice from the point of view of injustice (recalling the engagement with

Rawls in chapter 1, this indicates that it is a genuinely political argument). Jason Frank observes: "For Douglass, race was a consequence of shared experiences of oppression and of shared struggle against oppression.... Douglass claimed to speak from a particular position, or perspective, but the position could only be understood as a relation to the whole that excluded it."[15] Indeed, in his own words, "I shall see this day and its popular characteristics from the slave's point of view."[16] The problem for Douglass, then, is twofold.

The first derives directly from the problem of exclusion, and particularly from the fact that Douglass could still invoke something called "the slave's point of view." Throughout his address Douglass utilizes the possessive adjective "your": "It is the birthday of *your* National Independence, and of *your* political freedom."[17] He asks, "What have I, or those I represent, to do with your national independence?"[18] Although Douglass stands in the same hall with his white audience, in the same country, he is not standing in the same social or political space—there is the slave's perspective and then that of the free citizen in a country in the midst of celebrating the ideal of independence on the grounds of the rights of man. But since Douglass affirms the principles that underwrite American independence, what might we take Douglass to be up to? I want to suggest that, anticipating Allen, he understands that American oneness is a myth—the history of slavery had too deeply marked American society. However, there might be *wholeness*—and for Douglass, the principles that both the free and the slave can cherish alike are the key resource.

But, there is another problem.

> Americans! your republican politics, not less than your republican religion, are flagrantly *inconsistent*. You boast of your love of liberty, your superior civilization and your pure Christianity, while the whole political power of the nation... is solemnly pledged to support and perpetuate the enslavement of three millions of your countrymen.[19]

Here, Douglass explicitly calls our attention to American hypocrisy—our principles fail to inform our practices. We should be clear, though, what Douglass means by accusing the polity of inconsistency. It is not merely a feature of bad bureaucratic administration or even a kind of ignorance. It is a matter of something fundamental to the social fabric.

> You glory in your refinement and your universal education; yet you maintain a system as barbarous and dreadful as ever stained *the character* of a nation—a system begun in avarice, supported in pride, and perpetuated in cruelty.[20]

Notice here the juxtaposition of virtues (refinement, education) against vices (avarice, cruelty)—the result is the problem of national character. So, when Douglass employs the use of "your," he seems to not merely denote who is in possession of the opportunity to appreciate freedom—there is a further critical point, and that is the polity is in possession of bad moral and ethical lessons that perpetuate the inconsistency indicative of bad national character. Americans are guilty of mistaking vices for virtues while claiming to affirm America's basic founding principles of right.

Recalling Rawls, it is also important that Douglass implicates institutions: "The power to hold, hunt and sell men, women and children as slaves remains no longer a mere state institution, but is now an institution of the whole United States."[21] And in a gesture bridging institutional design with culture he adds: "The power is coextensive with the star-spangled banner."[22] Douglass, then, appears to also anticipate the view put forth by the social value thesis—the relations of power to which all in the hall are subject have implications for normative reasoning with respect to racial subordination. In other words, morally problematic racial norms had resulted in systemic moral disadvantage. So Douglass can at once affirm the desirability of the principles offered by the founders although they were complicit in constructing the racial order he was working to undo by suggesting that life as a black man, indeed a former slave, could be a resource to an American dialogue about the moral significance of liberty and the way that significance is at strict odds with racial subordination. This brings to light with particular force a fundamental unreasonableness in America's racial order.

Douglass employs a particular strategy that seems consistent with anticipating both Allen and the problem of social value. During his speech, Douglass imagines being exhorted to spend more time "arguing" and less time "denouncing." Elegantly and precisely, Douglass responds, "But I submit, where all is plain, there is nothing to be argued. What point in the antislavery creed would you have me argue? On what branch of the subject do the people of this country need light?"[23] The answer: on no branch for "all is plain." But we should not take Douglass to be making the point that slavery is wrong *simpliciter*. Throughout his address, he holds in view the promise of America, grounded in universally valid principles of right, alongside its lack of character. What is plain is that one cannot reasonably affirm those principles and simultaneously affirm the rightness of the bad character on display. In making explicit America's falling away from its ideals, Douglass's address is in part predicated on shaming tactics: he seeks to draw out the normative capacities of the audience on account of their own affirmation of principles of right. By at once celebrating the founders and referring to the situation as "these degenerate times," Douglass hopes to shake his audience out of their reverie by reminding them of their reason for convening in the first place. And because his audience requires being reminded of the deeper significance of the event, they should feel shame on account of displaying bad character. Douglass, then, is involved in a perfectionist project similar to the one I am advocating—he seeks to elevate the audience's moral excellence utilizing the resources that already reside in the public fund of norms and in the internal resources of citizens' existing commitments.

If all this is right, Douglass seems to not only anticipate Allen's argument for wholeness or my own idea of social value but also recent work affirming the value of perfectionism for political concerns. For my final move, then, I want to cash out the engagement with Douglass in exploring how modifying the mechanics of recent work in perfectionist democratic theory helps to address racial inequality.

Lessons Learned in the Present…

As I remarked in the introduction to this chapter, liberals tend to be troubled by perfectionist arguments (much less ones that embrace the importance of shame). But, the idea has achieved some traction within liberal theory in recent years. One author defends the practices of some lower level court decisions to stigmatize offenders as punishment for their crimes (i.e., patrons of sex-workers are made to sit on courthouse steps wearing a t-shirt advertising their offense). The view is that sometimes shaming persons is not only more humane (jail can be a very cruel form of punishment), but is a practice to be embraced by a decent society if it strives to call itself just: "A society that strives to be just cannot afford to dispense with powerful tools that can help get the job done."[24] The underlying argument is that certain kinds of private behavior have characterological roots that inform our social behavior. In addition to the comparative humanity of shame tactics, it displays a citizen in front of peers rather than in solitude to emphasize he has offended against the norms we as a society tend to collectively affirm.[25] This seems consistent with my argument for why perfectionism is politically justifiable (though I reject the project of stigmatization in the name of shame). But there are further considerations.

Some recently have argued in response to Rawls's theory of reasonable public discourse[26] that stability demands a perfectionist stance. Rawls notably abandoned key components of a *Theory of Justice* on the grounds that the mechanics securing the conception as one meant to generate its own support over time hence, secure stability, relied on an unrealistic vision of human interests and motivation.[27] Thus, Rawls articulated public reason as a way for persons to bring background motivations (i.e., religious commitments) to the table of democratic discourse and bargaining. However, as David McCabe argues, if we genuinely desire a just and stable society, we will have to come to terms with the realization that not all beliefs and arguments can be welcome comers. If liberalism is to lay claim to being a defender of moral equality and the attendant ability to pursue a good life, and at the same time argue that the state (basic structure) is to be a partner to these principles, then it must take a more committed stand as to what counts as a reasonable conception of the good and what does not.[28] On this view, if a man, on religious grounds, tries to offer a public reason for subordinating the women in his household, that reason should be disqualified without exception—that is what a liberal society requires. However, some believe that the mechanics of a public conception of justice can be turned to resolve the tension between orthodox Rawlsian concerns and instances of value incommensurability.

Corey Brettschneider takes up the challenge by minimizing the distinction between democracy as representing a set of procedures that are meant to be responsive to specified rights, on the one hand, with the articulation and affirmation of substantive rights on the other. On his view, we ought to "recast the idea of substantive rights as an aspect of the democratic ideal."[29] Taking seriously democracy as a robust ideal entails more than conceiving of it as a method for aggregating citizens' preferences. Rather, it acquires the status of a substantive normative theory insofar as it directs our attention to *why* the procedure matters. For example, so long as we think that a virtue of democracy is that it serves as a constraint on state power, the ideal asks, why does that virtue matter for us? The answer for Brettschneider is that it is consonant with rights we take as central for the flourishing of autonomous and free agents.

While Brettschneider offers a compelling argument for favoring this view of democracy, his argument is in service to a second aim. He notes a common criticism leveled against liberalism that is grounded in its tendency to draw a line between the public and the private. This line of criticism originates mainly in feminist theory and the reason feminists press this complaint is that insofar as liberal (democratic) theory claims that personal autonomy to pursue a good life is fundamental to what it means to be a moral equal in a scheme of ongoing cooperation, then it must take seriously the background conditions necessary for that ideal to be realized. Feminists argue that practices of patriarchal power embedded within private practices affect women's ability to achieve the liberal ideal of conceiving and pursuing a good life. Brettschneider thus attempts to develop a liberal approach to the politics of the personal.[30]

The key to understanding the value of Brettschneider's core argument, and the extension of some concerns that I will introduce with respect to race, is to focus on "the personal." For example, we might ask, why not focus on "the private" (i.e., the way fathers raise sons as compared to daughters behind closed doors)? The answer relies on an interesting augmentation of typical liberal concerns. A common source of liberal *esprit de corps* is the value of rights—society must affirm them and persons must respect others'. Brettschneider recognizes, however, that simply relying on rights does not get around feminist concerns about the conditions of home life. To crystallize that view, they want to say something like the following: my husband is not unfair to me or my daughter on account of his prudential interests; rather, his behavior is concerning because he does not morally understand how masculine power dominates and risks distorting the interests and of women and the possibilities for our flourishing. Brettschneider rightly recognizes that a well-ordered democracy relies on more than a person's affirmation of rights. On his view they should also come to endorse reasons for rights. If an errant husband came to see why women are entitled to equal rights and understand the content of those rights, then he would be better positioned to substantively reflect on the effects of patriarchal domination. It follows, he would personally come to affirm those rights, thus be a better man among his wife and daughter on account of that affirmation.

Here, Brettschneider's argument allows us to pivot toward race. Returning to the feminist example, it is entirely possible for a father to state a commitment to rights and and rarely violate his wife's or daughter's rights. For example, he never coerces them to stay home rather than work, nor does he engage in abusive behavior meant to denigrate their moral standing. However, he also never makes dinner and is minimally involved in the raising of the children as he acts by a separate principle that itself affirms a gendered division of labor. It is important that his belief in such a division need not be intended to actively suppress his daughter's and wife's flourishing. But when viewed against the background of other institutional practices that will in fact make that preference manifest in diminished opportunities outside the home for the wife or in the daughter's being socialized into disadvantageous gendered roles the father's preference now reflects a history and pattern of patriarchal domination that raises questions regarding his real moral commitments and the clarity of his moral vision. On this view, the father leads a double-life wherein publicly and overtly he acts and speaks in agreement with rights talk, but his personal beliefs lead to subtle actions that nevertheless are complicit in reproducing gender inequality. This leads Brettschneider to revise the scope of Rawlsian public reason as not merely a means to organize competing reasons in public discourse, but as a means to shape citizens into appropriately disposed democratic participants who better internalize the principles for good public reasons, thus the focus on the personal as compared to the private. He writes: "The double life might allow citizens to retain private *beliefs* at odds with public reason because of political liberalism's commitment to freedom of speech and conscience, however, public reason requires that citizens in the political liberal state be committed to transforming these beliefs to make them consistent with public reason's demand for equality."[31] In other words, public reason, as a democratic political mechanism, must reach down into the self and elevate it to the level of moral excellence demanded by equality.

The relevance of this view for racial inequality understood as the problem of social value that persists on account of bad character for which we should feel shame is readily apparent. Racial devaluation can now in part be described as the result of a kind of democratic double life wherein the polity and its institutions affirm liberal democratic principles but do not act from reasons for affirming those principles. It is important to note that Brettschneider himself does not employ the ideas of character or shame, but it seems to me these are both applicable in very important ways. We may not be justified in describing the father in the above example as "a villain," yet we may also not be justified in clearing him as being a very good person. Why? So far as we take fatherhood to be a role wherein fathers equally help prepare their children for flourishing lives and, so far as we take being a husband a role wherein husbands partner with wives to distribute the burden of raising a family in common, it appears the man in question above leaves something to be desired. Now, because he publicly (and we will assume, wholeheartedly) affirms gender equality, his double life at home represents a falling away from ideals he clearly affirms. Thus, my saying he seems to be not a very good person is a commentary on a feature of his character—a failure to employ practical reasoning, thus action, consistent with his normative commitments. Put differently, a failure to act as one wholeheartedly feels or believes displays a lack of integrity, which we earlier noted is crucial for good character. But notice that precisely because the proper beliefs are in place, shame here is also appropriate—the failure of integrity also represents a falling away from one's own best self, the self that holds the right reasons for gender equality. Again, it is consistent with Brettschneider's argument that so far as it is important to hold and act from the right reasons for rights, equality, and so on, it is appropriate that shame be one mechanism to reclaim one's best or better self.

Lessons Learned for the Future

I clearly am sympathetic to feminist concerns and generally agree with Brettschneider's argument—it seems right that the double life is incommensurable with genuine social justice. But because I am here concerned with genuine social justice with respect to race as predicated on the problem of social value, I think we must embrace a more strident perfectionist stance than Brettschneider seems prepared to embrace. Rights are certainly important, and I agree that coming to terms with reasons for rights is a crucial step in gaining wide support for deep social equality. However, the problem of social value forces our hand in extending Brettschneider's view.

The problem of social value indicates that our social practices, as embedded within a liberal democratic framework, are outwardly regulated by rules and principles meant to preempt categorical inequalities, but fail selectively—that is, in the face of race. Further, given our history of severe racial subordination as founded on denigrating racial beliefs and principles, that selectivity is not merely unfortunate or epiphenomenal—it is reproduced by the very political and social conditions those beliefs and principles generate. It is why West is able to shame us on account of our seeing whites' attempts to meet their basic needs as legitimate while blacks' attempts as deviant and criminal. If we focus only on reasons for rights, we might miss crucial aspects of the problem of social value. We should want to encourage the realization that the reason we think people have a right to adequate nourishment is that it allows them to live a good life in good health. But what happens if some citizens are so far removed from our normative concern that understanding those reasons falls flat for us? Put another way, if society believes black identity is marginally valuable, then the polity might be leading a more sinister double life—and what it needs is not to recognize reasons for rights (or at least not only that), but to understand more precisely the content of their racial beliefs, the sources of that content, the way it insinuates itself into innumerable practices and attitudes, and the implications it has for democratic concern—the ability to talk to strangers. It must come to understand how race prompts us to fall away from our ideals. It seems to me then that it is not sufficient to understand reasons for rights. Rather, we ought to understand *reasons for race*—why does race matter and why does it do the work it does in disrupting our ability to live up to commitments we affirm on our own account? Because it does matter for us—systemic racial inequality in the face of formal equality and contrary public norms—by settling deeply into the belief and motivational structure of the self, a more strident perfectionist stance is required. And because these beliefs are public and undermine the moral ideal of democracy as a political way of life, democratic perfectionism is not merely a good fit for addressing racial inequality as the problem of social value—it is the best fit.[32]

This is why I began with Douglass—though he gave his address over 150 years ago, he would still be justified in describing our time as "degenerate." Were he to deliver his speech today, it is disturbing to think how much of it would remain relevant. Our time may be more degenerate, for what does a society that enacted the Civil Rights Act of 1964 but that is still home to systemic racial inequality have to say for itself? It is a shameful state of affairs. I will argue in the next section for three principles of democratic perfectionism as demanded by racial inequality understood as the problem of social value.

A society committed to eliminating reasons for race must also be committed to arrangements that prompt us to revise the reflective bases of our actions and dispositions, bringing them into line with core liberal ideals we already affirm. We must develop new habits we can imagine helping to facilitate the wholeness Douglass and Allen call for.

THE PRACTICES OF A POLITY

Reimagining the Democratic Project

A particular concern is sure to have settled into the reader's sense of the argument I am offering. Generously articulated, my perfectionist reliance on institutions to lead the way in elevating society's moral excellence is a bit confused—after all, chapter 3 illustrated how two major institutions had engaged in racial subordination, and I depended on that illustration to support the claim that institutions suffer from bad character. Maybe more critically, the reader might think the following: the comprehensiveness of my diagnosis— that society in general suffers from bad character—can lead to the proposition that if we are all in some ways part of the problem, then no one is left positioned to be part of the solution. On this view, it can seem that my prescribed solution is naïve at best, if not disingenuous.

How might we find our way out of a dim room when no one has a light to illuminate a path to the door? This metaphor seems apt as the two above concerns direct our attention to the basic problem of leadership. While I take these concerns seriously and am sensitive (very deeply so, in fact) to the significant challenge our society faces in overcoming racial inequality in light of my analysis of its causes, I believe there is a way out (though I admit, it has the potential to fail as does any human endeavor that relies upon vision, will, and moral courage). To see it, we need to switch metaphors from the dimly lit room in which no one has a light to that of being at sea with a functioning ship that nevertheless needs expansion and redesign as it makes its way to its final destination across an unknown, possibly treacherous expanse.

Otto Neurath was an early twentieth-century linguist who argued that the way we develop language to describe and theorize the world is embedded in our use of it. In other words, it is not a linear process but one where we learn in the midst of being signally ignorant. To shed light on this puzzle, he asked his interlocutors to imagine the following: you are out at sea in a ship that can hazard its environment but nevertheless needs improving and expanding if it is to successfully continue on its voyage. What to do? It is not as if one is going to go back to the point of origin sacrificing how far one has gone already. His solution was that we continue building the ship at sea. This is a remarkably poignant metaphor. Once one has departed from a starting place that cannot meet our needs, on whatever grounds, it is incumbent that we move forward. Moreover, the way to progress often places us in unfamiliar or uncomfortable circumstances—like being out at sea: a great expanse in every direction that requires attention to navigate it properly. This endeavor is attended by perils, as well as promise. As we are at sea, we realize we have further needs. The ship launched successfully but is not adequate. We have some materials on hand and we have learned a few things about how a ship works having been out at sea, so we build and patch mid-voyage. In this way, a ship that was good enough to get us going, but is nevertheless imperfect, can be improved upon without necessarily conceding the progress already made.[33] This is done with lessons learned during the voyage and is done under a particular set of nonideal circumstances—we have a particular ship at hand as a base without the luxury of stopping the process we have begun. We cannot abandon it for we all will drown. We improve it along the way, in fits and starts, with success and sometimes clumsily. I want to say, this is much the way a democracy works.

I think this is a good first step in answering both above complaints, for at their core, they express a very reasonable concern about the possibility of improvement under challenging circumstances that are anything but ideally conducive to the project in question. So far as I can tell, there is no response available from any philosophical tradition that can completely ease this concern. Rather, some traditions, such as the analytic liberal tradition, are in deeper danger of this objection derailing their projects precisely because they do not face the problem of nonideal circumstances. As I pressed in chapter 1, they lose sight of the political. On my account, keeping the political in close view and earnestly acknowledging the problem allows us to take away an important lesson from Neurath's metaphor—democracy has within it the processes and institutions to draw out our best political tendencies, though it sometimes puts into practice our worst as the ship may from time to time be overcome by a hostile environment. But precisely because it is not all bad—in fact, a great deal about our democracy is good—we have materials on hand to refashion and expand a ship that has left port.

This metaphor is important for thinking about race. Douglass got us clear on an important feature of our society that cannot be undone—the ship of American democracy left port as a radically imperfect ship. It was strong enough to bear the weight of a fledgling nation but did so amidst the moral horror of black slavery. As Douglass acknowledges in his praise of the founders, that is no reason to turn the ship around. But that is also not to say we should think the vessel is the best it can be. Indeed, it does not seem fit to get us to our final destination. Race has proven itself a hallmark of American fallibility if not failure, but those on both the side of advantage and disadvantage have good reason to stay the general course of liberal democracy. But we all have duties in making America's democracy a more excellent political vessel.

With these considerations in mind, I believe we have a way of putting to ease the initial complaints. Democracy is stable but dynamic. The trick is to hone its dynamism to bring out the promise of what we want to be stable. We do have a starting place, for what we want to be stable are the morals underlying our founding principles. What must be dynamic, then, are our own attitudes, the lessons we teach and learn, and the will to draw out more fully our capacity for treating blacks as morally valuable co-participants in the scheme of ongoing cooperation. This is nothing new for our democratic experiment, even with respect to race. Although, it has not given blacks what it ostensibly promised, none cannot deny that the Civil Rights Act of 1964 was a crucial victory. The same can be said for other moments in similar movements, such as women's gaining the franchise.[34] Each of these moments highlights our ability to change the course of institutions that in turn teach civic lessons of value and respect. What seems to have gone wrong is that some victories did not alter the course radically enough or did not do so with enough force to prevent old habits from settling back in.

In these final pages I offer three principles of racial justice as grounded in a commitment to democratic perfectionism, but first, a brief word about the place of these principles within a larger framework of social reform. Throughout the book I have strongly signaled a distinction between the project of racial justice as I conceive it (and as I believe we ought) and existing accounts of liberal justice, particularly Rawls's and the tradition he inspired. A first clear difference is that the Rawlsian tradition focuses on distribution, while here I have related social and political justice to claims about character and shame. This might raise the question as to whether I mean for my account below to displace or supplant distributive theories. To be clear, I think that distributive justice is a fine project, and it has its place in any society marked by material inequality. My claim here is not that the project of distributive justice is categorically confused but rather I mean to emphasize its limited ability to account for and respond to social ails outside the bounds of material concerns, and further, to press for the importance of attending to matters of justice outside the realm of distribution. Indeed, the value of specifying race as the problem of social value is that it directs our attention to what are intuitively the prerequisites to achieving distributive justice: inculcating within the polity and its institutions a wide sense of democratic care as part of an aspirational view of achieving the best society we can achieve. Now, there is no promise that my recommendations can do better in the long run, but I offer them keeping in mind that deeper changes in habits and character are required for the needs of race in our time, and these, to my mind, our are best chance.

Finally, the above invites us to revisit a discussion of this book's methodological disposition. I indicated in the introduction that the theory I offer is best identified as a nonideal theory. Whereas theorists working in the Rawlsian tradition typically seek to respond to matters thought to be related to political life without incorporating certain facts or actual experiences of political life, nonideal theory takes some of its most important cues from history, facts of economic distribution, and actual patterns of social marginalization—in other words, my goal has been to present the problem of social value from the perspective of social and political experience rather than as (merely) a conceptual mechanism. This will have some bearing on the prescriptive measures I articulate below. To the point, upon reading them, they might not seem like principles of justice so much as applied maxims, and if they do strike one in this way, then there may be further dissatisfaction, since I do not go on to articulate policy with any specificity. What I offer below I take to be principles of justice; but once one goes in for this language and is also committed to nonideal theory, it also means that the texture and tone of a principle of justice will take on a particular character. Principles of justice within a nonideal framework will have to navigate more explicitly between ideal moral mandates and the social and political obstacles those mandates will necessarily face. Thus, when the principles are articulated, they will anticipate their embodiment in policy by offering suggestions as to how they might be appropriately embodied, but they will tend to favor the moral reasons—as informed by preceding descriptive and explanatory work done in earlier chapters—for their embodiment rather than policy considerations such as legislative feasibility. In any case, the principles of justice below are meant to offer a vision of the kinds of changes needed to achieve racial justice in our time; and, taken together, are imagined as altering the normative fabric of our democracy's shared association such that blacks are appropriately placed in the association's scheme of normative value so that their moral equality with their fellow citizens is readily apparent.

Racial Justice in Motion

The "Real America" Re-Education Act

In 2008, America achieved a milestone that even those of us most skeptical about the notion of racial progress had to admit was significant—we elected our first black president. To boot, his name was exotic—Barack Obama. Subsequently, there was no shortage of pundits who wanted to put race to bed, for we had "obviously" achieved a post-racial America. Those on the Left read a new racial outlook into the actions of the youth vote. Those on the Right convinced themselves that race had mostly been a bogey-man paraded by the Left for the past forty years to extract undeserved goods from the state. But something funny happened along the way to a post-racial America.

John McCain, the Republican candidate, seemed to face a real dilemma. America had just experienced eight years of a deeply troubled Republican presidency, and there seemed to be real power in the youth vote from which he was going to have a hard time benefiting, given both his age and the apparent surge of progressivism in that demographic. There was also the fact that the Democratic Party had presented a black man and a woman as candidates while Republicans seemed fixated on white men. So McCain chose Sarah Palin as his running mate and her most trusted tactic was to rouse middle-America by bashing big city, educated elites (like Obama). Her backlash against what she perceived to be an out of touch establishment was energizing if for no other reason that it seemed to tap into a real anger. What was the nature of this anger?

Palin gave us one phrase, that when put in the context of her audience, tells us an important part of the story of American confusion: "the Real America." For her, and her audience members, this meant, the people who genuinely represent what is good about this country and who hold the right values on everything from abortion to tax policy. The Real America is marked by hard-working folks who do "ordinary" jobs, watch "ordinary" programs, and read "ordinary" things. But a close look at the situation tells us something more about who these folks think the "Real America" is: southern and Midwestern whites who had patiently sat through eight years of failed Republican policies but who had become incensed against the backdrop of the prospect of a black president who at least offered something different than what had been on offer. Further, the rhetoric gave rise to the Tea Party, which did not seem especially shy about employing racial messages in criticizing Obama in twenty-first-century "post-racial" America.[35]

None of this is meant to be a partisan critique—rather, I am making as best I can earnest assessments of a real political situation. We had barely elected a black man when we were insistently reminded that he did not represent the real America—rather it was those that attended Palin's rallies—middle-American whites. One of the important things about these kinds of events is that they are public and seek to teach a particular lesson about what it means to be an American (even what it means to look like an American). Unfortunately, folks who buy this line are simply confused in a manner not so far removed from the Americans resisting school integration that Allen discusses.

I do think that there is an unknown real America, but it is not one Palin would recognize, since she has not been on the other side of the racial divide. Here is one way we would get to know the real America that is consistent with racial experience.

In 2003 Philadelphia made Black History mandatory for all students.[36] The typical American student's exposure to black history typically amounts to a brief study of Martin Luther King, Jr.'s speeches. Martin Luther King, Jr., while obviously a deeply important figure, is also very palatable to contemporary ears for he advocated peaceful demonstration and sought partnerships with whites. Malcolm X, who represented in many senses the apex of black anger at continual abuse, is less often engaged; the Black Power movement is typically reserved for the most enterprising of educators. King is often preceded by a gentle if not tepid engagement with the topic of slavery. After students learn that slavery was (and is) bad, Abraham Lincoln is sent in as the hero who freed the slaves. This lesson is taught with such consistency and earnestness that it was not until quite later in my own life that I came to learn that this view of Lincoln is in need of deep qualification—he was anything but unabashedly racially egalitarian. Indeed, it is not even clear he was genuinely or primarily concerned with black emancipation in a morally appropriate sense.[37]

Schools often do not analyze Jim Crow and how it is that Billie Holiday could sing of "strange fruit" in the twentieth century. Schools certainly do not investigate contemporary racial inequality or use history to shed light on it, as I have tried to do in chapter 3. So, for example, it is the rare instance when a student that comes to learn about the struggle between the "root causes" approach to crime of the 1960s that was ultimately defeated by conservatives, thereby denying American society a chance at deep social change for the betterment of blacks. Courses in the spirit of Philadelphia's fleshed out in the way I am suggesting, adapt a comprehensive view of the black experience can affect the grounds of belief or racial reasoning by discussing a broader scope of change agents (i.e., Malcolm X, thus validating some concerns he expressed that are deemed radical, but were entirely reasonable), as well as explicating inequality more honestly (i.e., the nature of systemic inequality as a function of American historical practices). And, crucially, this is a resource for all children, not just black children. It would be, in other words, an important resource for preempting moral and ethical disadvantage as I outlined those ideas in chapter 4. Policies like this potentially offer the resources, as well as the moment, for students to revise and challenge comfortable if erroneous views of what racial America has and does look like. They would be exposed to the real America. Further, the "Real" America Re-Education Act (RARA) aims to do more than have persons reflect on reasons for rights; along the lines which I challenged Brettschneider's view, it would prompt reflection over reasons for race by having persons revise a more full set of beliefs that order their character in such a way that complexly grounded actions and attitudes regarding race can be challenged. Put differently, the project of democratic perfectionism, while justified by a view of morality we would ultimately come to affirm as our own, is meant to revise the structure of one's moral character. And, this is done in light of what the "real America" amounts to with respect to race—it looks very different than the racially status quo message that is typically bandied about.

The spirit of the policy adopted by Philadelphia schools is to be understood as paradigmatic of the first principle of racial justice (which is to say, I imagine that policy experts could conceivable find other kinds of practices that embody the first principle of racial justice[38]). Its main aim is to shift the grounds of racial understanding. Often, people are in moral or ethical error for the simple reason that they do not have the appropriate amount and kind of knowledge upon which to base their reflections and judgments. If we want to avoid future instances, like the one following Katrina, in which whites disproportionately deny blacks benefits to which they are (morally) entitled, a main resource would be for whites to be able to understand the background against which questions concerning resource redistribution are posed. The RARA also provides goods for blacks. A main ground for aversive attitudes, for example, is the sense that the political system does not work. Maybe more tragically, many youths simply think this is the way it goes for them because "it is what it is." Programs modeled in the spirit of Philadelphia's allow blacks the resources and opportunity to be critical of their political system but to also understand how and why it has done wrong to blacks—that is to say, it presents democracy as a worthy but imperfect project that can serve as an instrument to rectify social ills. Maybe more crucially, young black children could learn that there are a number of legitimate and justifiable ways to challenge the political process from the ground up on account of justice, thus providing a reason to doubt the appropriateness of aversive attitudes or beliefs that effectively suppress a first order desire to achieve academic success.

In brief, then, the RARA and the policies it would give rise to provide a basic good—full public knowledge to aid in the development of being good democratic selves. Persons would be better positioned to be effective partners in sharing a scheme of ongoing cooperation regarding each other as moral equals under circumstances wherein their co-participants were understood to face difficulties and obstacles caused by that scheme in the first instance. The RARA is designed (as would be the relevant policies) to motivate a sense of shared democratic purpose and the duties imposed by both the sense of sharing and the sense of democracy as a moral ideal meant to be fully inclusive on the most morally appropriate terms possible.

The Just Trojan Horse

The epistemic resources given by RARA are fundamental to reordering institutional design, but sometimes we need more pointed messages to counteract bad practices that have long been in play. We need epistemic affirmative action, if you will. To see how this works, we need to revisit the work of Jerry Kang presented in chapter 4.

As we noted, Kang is concerned with the role the news plays in guiding social perceptions of black criminality. He finds that crime is disproportionately covered in local news and that blacks are disproportionately portrayed in crime news. He argues that the news serves as a Trojan Horse because it is a trusted source of public information concealing harmful messages about a certain segment of the polity. While Kang is right to focus on the news with respect to crime, Gilens notes the same trends with respect to coverage of welfare policy. But it also extends beyond the news—television shows and movies are in the bad habit of not merely typecasting actors, but typecasting activities and how they are portrayed. Blacks are commonly portrayed as criminals, and when they are drug dealers, their success is either fetishized or deemed a threat—meanwhile, in the Academy Award winning film *American Beauty*, a local white youth is a major dealer of marijuana but his situation is portrayed sympathetically with drug dealing ultimately providing him a way out of his life (in the suburbs). (*American Beauty*. Dir. Sam Mendes. 1999. Blu-ray. Warner Bros. 2010.) These are subtle messages—black deviance is either glamorous and/ or dangerous; white deviance is necessary and tragic.

The Just Trojan Horse works to actively reshape social perceptions, recasting the relationship between identity and life circumstances. Whereas the RARA is largely educational, the Just Trojan Horse works at two levels: belief reconfiguration and reasonable propaganda.

First, following the concerns set out by Kang, the Just Trojan Horse would sanction monitoring the news and other trusted public media to ensure fair racial portrayal. Here, the idea would not be to prevent factual reporting—if a black man murdered some-one that day, then the fact that the murderer was black would not *in itself* be grounds for rejecting the news story. Rather, if other crimes took place that day by nonblacks, focusing on the story of the black murderer would violate the principle thus grounds for reprimand. Further, news programming is exactly that: programming. Choices are made about what is worth knowing, thus what is worth showing, and because the news is largely a for-profit enterprise, programming is susceptible to market considerations (think about the old newspaper adage: "if it bleeds, it leads").[39] On this view, any outlet's programming department would have to stipulate guidelines of fairness by preemptively committing itself to covering news in the widest possible sense—this is largely motivated by the overrepresentation of crime in the first place, which in turn opens the door to racial and racist messages regarding black deviance.

However, the news is not the only form of public media that distorts. The principle would suppress artistic license to the extent that blacks would otherwise continuously be disproportionately portrayed in problematic ways. Currently prime time shows, for example, police and legal procedurals, and major motion pictures often mirror the news' distorted presentation of crime. On the one hand, while mafia movies such as *Goodfellas* indeed represent whites as violent, there is nonetheless a romanticism and respectability accorded the thugs in these movies. (*Goodfellas*. Dir. Martin Scorsese. 1990. DVD. Warner Home Video. 2007.) When Paulie and his crew finally land in jail, they are shown having a private room to themselves where fresh lobster is delivered and Paulie gets to cook his own homemade pasta sauce with the best of ingredients. By contrast, *Training Day* takes up the issue of severe police corruption. (*Training Day*. Dir. Antione Fuqua. 2001. DVD. Warner Home Video 2004.) Yet, Detective Alonzo is a black officer played by Denzel Washington, while Jack Hoyt—white—played by Ethan Hawke turns out to be innocent, virtuous, and incorruptible. The movie presents an incredible irony: historically the police have been par-ticularly unfair, if not corrupt, with respect to abuse of black suspects, yet here a black man is represented in the force displaying a street thug mentality, while his white counterpart is presented as the beacon of goodness. (It bears mentioning that most of Detective Alonzo's crew is brown, not white—and all of them are crooked.) One surely cannot take a critical look at police corruption and racial abuse and come to the conclusion that the scenario presented by *Training Day* is historically typical. The same applies to police and legal pro-cedurals. When whites are criminals, they often perpetrate "victimless" white-collar crimes while the roles of violent criminals and drug dealers—thereby, the most viscerally danger-ous and threatening—are filled by brown and black actors and actresses.

At the second level, the Just Trojan Horse principle also calls for other kinds of positive measures, namely reasonable propaganda. One such measure would be to actively reach out to persons in an effort to alter social cognition. The typical American would be sitting down for their evening show or sports event, and at some point, rather than seeing a com-mercial, he or she would be exposed to a public service announcement featuring a black per-son making a basic statement, such as: "Be Fair" or "Equality Means All Our Needs Matter."

While brief and simple, such measures would be powerful and radical but not unreasonable. A public medium would be put to use in which moral messages justified by the conditions of racial marginalization would be visually matched to darker citizens. Such measures literally seek to reshape the grounds of social cognition and the way those grounds intersect with normative reasoning. Public Service Announcements could be complemented by other measures more subtle yet focusing on similar aims. For example, as we have seen, crime has increasingly become a racialized sphere of public concern; moreover, almost no political candidate can be elected without being tough on crime. The Just Trojan Horse would demand that every mention of crime would have to be accompanied by statistics outlining employment and housing opportunities in high-crime areas, as well as past policies of public spending. The idea here is to suppress the ease with which Americans commonly divorce "deviant" behavior from circumstance and disadvantage. The goal would not be to justify any instance of black crime but to offer a fuller account of the backdrop against which crimes are committed. Importantly, this is not new to American thinking on deviant behavior, since a typical consideration in legal proceedings involves ascertaining whether the accused might have been under psychological or emotional duress or in his/her right state of mind at the time the crime was committed. And one reason we want to know about matters of duress and states of mind is because we widely subscribe to the idea that agency can always be contextualized within circumstances, and that there are instances where it is imperative that we do so. With respect to the above example of the contextualized information politicians would be required to publicly provide, a main aim would be to get the typical American to not only think about how we should respond to individual deviant behavior but also to consider instances of institutional neglect and public marginalization, as well as civic complicity. The idea is that such measures could serve to trigger appropriate democratic concern by broadening the grounds for judgment. The reason this level of the proposal is pitched as reasonable propaganda is because it would largely justify, when necessary, telling biased stories and promoting targeted messages in favor of blacks, but, on account of our problem of social value, a benefit it seems blacks are clearly owed.

Boondocks Institutions

I began this chapter discussing a particular episode of *The Boondocks*, wherein Martin Luther King, Jr. is dismayed by an America he perceives as having gone off the rails of social and racial progress laid down by activists like himself during the Civil Rights Movement. The key aspect of King's dismay, grounded in a view from 1964, as it were, is that we seem to be enamored with false progress. Our national character is predicated upon an illusory comfort provided by the fact that blacks are not overtly beaten or excluded from practices of citizenship by law. We walk around with amazing gadgets that provide portable music to citizens in moral and political error; citizens who are politically comfortable on account of social status and willing to make a virtue out of practices of subordination. And our major institutions have bad character for that kind of social good is more prominent than one possessing deep moral value—racial justice. King seems to think that we have a thorny problem on our hands that is peculiarly foreign from his perspective. But it seems to me that his dismay and the nature of the analysis on offer provide a final way to instill a more excellent national character.

The Boondocks Institutions principle demands that we go back to holding institutions accountable, that institutions open themselves to such action, and that persons accept the responsibility that comes with being the victims of injustice—what Shelby identifies as a natural duty of the ghetto poor, for example. What might this look like?

Let us begin with a real racial issue that is national in scope but which can be acted upon locally: law enforcement.[40] A major problem with law enforcement revolves around bias, unfairness, and limited access to resources. Unfortunately, because our culture prima facie frames crime as a very straightforward problem—there are things called "crimes"; most people do not commit them, but some do; those who do commit them are bad and deserve punishment—we fail to adequately critically engage the practices we use to fight it and the assumptions that inform those practices. As I reviewed in chapter 3, it is clear that a great deal of bias and unfairness inheres in these practices. So, it is time to mind the store. One way to do this would be to sanction local community action groups, composed predominantly of members of the disadvantaged who tend to be the victims of abusive law enforcement officials and procedures.

It is important to highlight two features of this principle. The first refers to the fact that councils of this nature currently are in existence in various cities and towns in each of the fifty states. Thus, though the principle is aspirational, there is a sense in which it is already in play. My call here, then, for maintaining aspirational aims is to mandate that it be in play nationally in a *uniform manner*—wherever there is a police precinct (particularly one where blacks are a significant portion of the policed population), there must be a council. Further, there is also the issue that this should apply to more than just police matters, but also to local development, so the principle calls for the civic reconstitution of neighborhoods in a fairly comprehensive manner. Second, there are many ways such councils may be structured. As Reenah Kim notes, councils may fall into a number of kinds of structures, and not all of these adequately reflect the principle justifying citizen oversight. Thus, in one model, for example, police officers investigate complaints, which are reviewed by internal affairs and referred to a chief executive who then may turn to a board comprised of some citizens for further review or action.[41] Of course, by the time such a report gets to the few citizens on the board, it is entirely possible that many of the vagaries currently inherent in police practices find their way into the process along the way, thus undermining the substantive point of civic oversight.

One way to get around these concerns would be to imagine restructuring the flow of information in local precincts as modeled on that of publicly held corporations—their records, just as a corporation's financial reports, must be made public to the board on a regular basis (i.e., monthly). Current police practice is that incidents reported to the police generate a "paper trail" that is meant to chronicle the relevant details of the incident and the process used to address it. It is not unreasonable to imagine that, through use of modern technology, all reports can, when appropriate, anonymously refer to the accused, perpetrators, and officers as they are passed on to a local oversight board. In this way, the board can monitor concerning trends in profiling, for example. This is helpful because local residents often witness deviant behavior by folks who are typically *not* targeted by the police, so they can ask, for example, why local university fraternity members are allowed to be drunk in public but a local black man is charged with a misdemeanor for cursing in public. Surely, if the law wants to make something of such behavior, both parties ought to be susceptible to it. (Of course, there is an important question as to whether we tend to overcriminalize, wherein some behaviors are constructed over time as criminal when they in fact pose little public threat.) In addition to concerns about the flow of information, there are questions about who assesses it. Currently, in some instances, council members are appointed rather than elected. But councils are otherwise often less than ideally democratic, with board members coming from a fairly small slice of the local community thus raising questions of representation.[42] While this is a matter for policy makers and policy analysts to take up, the aim as per racial justice would be to design councils to avoid issues of representation raised by practices of appointment or issues that revolve around possibly low incentives for participation for potential participants. If only those persons who are already particularly active and/or are so because they have the resources to do so participate, then the aim of democratizing oversight is put in jeopardy. As with RARA, the main thing here is that such a practice be governmentally sanctioned and supported. Thus, if representation is an issue because some lack resources to participate, then the government is to step in and subsidize participation by compensating wages and punishing companies and organizations if they penalize persons for attending to their civic duty when called upon.

While such boards clearly mandate oversight over a local instance of a national institutional practice, thus keeping it honest (thus helping it achieve good character), it also provides perfectionist benefits to local residents. Members of disadvantaged groups often adopt the ways of being they do out of a sense of alienation. As I noted in the previous chapter, gang members employ principles of justice, such as reciprocity, but they do so in ways that result in morally and ethically objectionable outcomes. Here, good character comes apart from the resources such persons actually possess, namely, a sense of reciprocity that is fundamental to justice. In our example, the Boondocks Institutions principle provides an opportunity to empower the historically marginalized beyond the franchise—if we are honest, voting has very little impact on everyday political affairs. Local involvement in law enforcement practices fosters a sense of control over historically oppressive circumstances and by being entrusted with such responsibility, we easily imagine the typical person attempting to rise to the occasion, thus helping to foster within him or her a greater sense of social responsibility and worth within the social scheme. (It is also important to keep in mind that such practices are meant to work in tandem with those prescribed by the first two principles of racial justice).

This process can be repeated with respect to other concerns, such as local economic development (and, indeed, the principle is imagined as requiring relevant initiatives to be undertaken both systematically and nationally across all social, political, and economic practices that are an appropriate practical and moral fit with the concerns of the principle). It seems to me that in predominantly black neighborhoods, one of two scenarios tends to obtain. Either the local economy is in shambles with little prospect of stabilizing, or, it is on the path to recovery on the back of gentrification, the effect of which tends to be that local black residents are pushed out of their neighborhoods due to rising living costs and into nearby 'bad' neighborhoods in which they can afford to live. This usually correlates with racial segregation, although segregation may not be the intended by-product. By instituting oversight councils, a desired vendor like Whole Foods, for example, can be allowed to set up shop in an up-and-coming neighborhood by agreeing to certain conditions such as employing a certain (high) percentage of local residents. And if those applicants lack certain skills, Whole Foods is obligated to provide sufficient education and training rather than exercise the option to disqualify those persons.

In these and related cases, the main goal is to make the improvement of national character a process of mutually assured success, but to do so, we must be willing to adopt radical views of what it means for democratic citizens to have a say in the way their institutions behave toward them. In doing so, institutions are taught new lessons that improve their character, and in the process of holding institutions accountable, citizens themselves learn new lessons on the value of civic engagement on their own terms. By representing their own real interests, as well as by taking civic action that makes them accountable to the polity, we have a potentially potent formula for ensuring the circumstances of racial justice.

CONCLUSION

Our society is predicated on important democratic values, such as equality and freedom, and the events that made our country possible held the promise of those values being made applicable to all citizens on account of their status as human beings with intrinsic moral worth. That is not how it happened, and it took outspoken critics like Douglass to remind Americans that their character had gone astray, thus that they should feel shame for their role in the presence and persistence of racial inequality. That message is no less potent in our time—over forty years after the passage of the Civil Rights Act, Kanye West makes the serious charge that the president seems to not care about black people and that charge is worth examining closely. Maybe precisely because it happens in our time, the message is that much more urgent.

From the perspective of political thought—an endeavor in the division of social labor meant to do its part in imagining and articulating paths to a better world—there is a good deal about which to be concerned. Our engagement with Rawls and Mills, as representatives of their respective fields of inquiry, illustrates that normative thinkers remain confused as to what justice and race amount to, much less to what they amount to when they are substantively linked to each other. Thus, as I have argued, those of us who are active participants in this slice of the division need to revisit ways of understanding racial inequality—my own suggestion has been to view it as the problem of social value, for that idea indicates the most fundamental factor in how we can explain contemporary racial inequality.

What social value tells us is that history has bequeathed to our institutions and citizens bad moral and ethical lessons as to where blacks stand in the social scheme of moral value. But this realization requires careful consideration, for we must acknowledge that while race remains a serious problem for our society, it is not a problem that exhibits the same characteristics it once did: blacks are not forced to the back of the bus, and it is illegal to discriminate on the basis of race, for example. Nonetheless, blacks remain poorer, in worse health, with fewer or lesser job and educational prospects, and on and on. This all means racial inequality remains an injustice, certainly with a historical record, but it is an injustice for our time. When I say it is an injustice for our time, I mean to invoke main points raised against Rawls and Mills: it is a real political problem, here and now, and it is one wherein invoking historically accurate terms that are nevertheless overly blunt for analyzing the nuanced texture of twenty-first-century racial inequality are less helpful to the project of theorizing racial justice. Thus, in one sense, our time refers to a temporal moment in conjunction with how that moment is appropriately character-ized. But our time also denotes not merely a temporal moment we all incidentally share but, as democratic citizens, it represents a political moment for which we all have some responsibility in making better than previous moments. The time is ours such that we must respect the journey democracy has thus far taken us on, and it is ours such that we improve the democratic vessel for ourselves and for future generations such that when they claim and describe their time they can do so without rehearsing and responding to these same issues. So we must be more analytically rigorous, but we must also be open to concepts and ideas that have real meaning for our moral make-up, thus allowing us to gain prescriptively effective traction on the problem.

Hence, we are back to shame. We know better but we often fail to do better. As we fall away from our ideals, we (may) come to realize that we fail ourselves and our moral commitments. And in doing so, we jeopardize the moral promise of our democracy, for good institutions and good persons must stand side by side, free of the moral and ethi-cal burdens bequeathed by our racial history as grounded in racial power. Shame can certainly lead to uncomfortable feelings. Recall that Huey relies upon the very notion that to make people do the right thing, they first have to hear the terrible truth. On his view, it is the only way to make good on the sacrifices of reform-minded leaders like King. Indeed, leaders like King paid the price of safety and comfort to help set us on the path that we have only partially walked. Can we afford to not achieve the greatness within reach—the singular promise not only acknowledged by Thomas Jefferson, a slaveholder, but also by Frederick Douglass, a former slave? If justice means anything to us, we cannot afford to act as we have been acting, believe as we have become accustomed to believing, or theorize as we have been trained to theorize—race must be made central on account of the shame it should cause us.

Above, I mentioned two lessons West's critical comments teach us—that our character fails us institutionally and personally. These comments are directed toward us, away from West in a manner reflecting Huey's urging of King to take the American people to task, so we may be wary of the possibility that my perfectionist account simply amounts to some of us criticizing and blaming others. After all, West is a member of the polity he takes to task. Isn't he in some way complicit? In these closing comments, let me note one final remark made by him regarding his own reaction to Katrina: "Even me, I would be a hypocrite because I've tried to turn away from the TV because it's too hard to watch. I've even been shopping before even giving a donation." Here West owns his shame indicating his hypocrisy, his awareness of it, and he goes on to outline steps he has taken to rectify falling away from his ideals—and he does this in front of more than eight million people. Racial justice does not require that kind of public confessional—we can make significant gains were we each to follow West's example in the quiet of the night, alone with our reflections. It may make us uncomfortable, maybe even angry to think that race indicates the color of our shame, but that is what it will take to achieve racial justice in our time.

Epilogue

THE AGONY OF A RACIAL DEMOCRACY

MANY WORKS IN moral theory and normative political thought are content to offer socio- or politico-moral diagnoses of issues that are thought to offend against justice. These works tend to present themselves as best efforts to say something meaningful about a problem, and the division of social labor means that someone else develops public policy. That is a fair enough position—I have taken a very similar approach in this book. But there is another kind of afterword the reader might desire, maybe even ought to desire. Namely, what might be left to say about the identified problem in a possible world where the author's prescriptive program has been taken up but has not achieved the goals under the best of all conditions? Put another way: What if the author might be right that the prescribed way forward is the best available but ultimately is not sufficient? Put yet another way: What if the theory fails not because the theory is bad but because the problem is firmly moored in the soul of the nation?

In these final pages, I want to take the time to seriously consider this class of questioning. Being frank (philosophy is not needed for that), American society has a serious problem on its hands: for more than two centuries it has been in the habit of treating blacks as sub-citizens in the best of times, and as sub-persons in the worst. I have argued throughout that for our time, racial inequality is marked by the problem of social value: blacks do not hold an equal place as whites in America's scheme of normative valuation, and this scheme in the first instance motivates and justifies the distribution of goods, opportunities, and respect. In turn, this indicates bad national character. In recent years, it has become apparent that treating blacks as sub-persons, though not the everyday practice it once was, is not relegated to a past time from which we have sufficiently learned our moral lessons. Indeed, institutional practices such as racially unfair implementation of the death penalty too closely mirror the days of Klan lynching. In these final pages I focus on corporeal violations because I think these are the kinds of violations that become most vivid in blacks' minds when reflecting on the nature of American society. Moreover, corporeal violations make most vivid the notions of insecurity, death, and vulnerability. And it is both morally and politically significant that they become vivid under a mode of governance where shared responsibility for stability, the common good, and equal rights and protection are said to be the guiding lights of our shared association.

Theories of justice, even if motivated by a modicum of cynicism, ultimately express some hope about the ability for persons to better themselves and the society they inhabit, and the one offered in the preceding chapters is no different. Yet, hope can be proven unfounded, misplaced, or simply naïve. I think it is philosophically easy to work out the mechanics of a theory conceived as bearing out one's hope (as compared to making it happen on the ground), but it is reasonable to wonder about cases where that hope might be unfounded. I want to ponder something grim, but I think very much worth thinking about because it could be dangerous to ignore. What if America's race problems are so deeply embedded in our society such that no theory of justice could root them out? Rather, what if a wave of black resentment and anger were settled upon as the only reasonable responses to a society that seems unable to get past its sordid racial history? Below, I want to suggest that America's perpetual state of racial suffering denotes in fact our shared democratic agony. And we need to take seriously two senses of agony. The first is prolonged suffering and pain, a state I think we have been in for a long time on account of racial injustice under democratic norms and institutions. There is redemption for this agony and the possibility for it has been marked out by the path set in chapter 5, though I have to admit that positing something like the idea of democratic agony likely presents significant challenges to successfully taking that path. The second sense, and one for which I think the theory I have articulated—no theory of justice, for that matter—could not possibly effectively address, ought to give us collective pause: the moment of pain and suffering before death. What I take up below, hesitantly but I think necessarily, is the following question: Can our democracy die, and what could bring about its demise? Using the recent killing of Trayvon Martin as the cornerstone, I consider how the persistent framing of blacks as dangerous has engendered sanctioned or accepted abuse of blacks. This has initially resulted in continuous distrust among black citizens but we should consider the possibility of distrust becoming resentment, and the possibility for resentment to become action, perhaps violent.

On February 26, 2012, Trayvon Martin, an unarmed black youth, was shot by a gated community resident in Sanford, Florida. The shooter, George Zimmerman, deemed Martin's presence in the community suspicious and having full confidence in Florida's Stand Your Ground Laws, found himself in a confrontation that ended in Martin's death.

The full details of the night remain murky. On Zimmerman's account, Martin disappeared into the shadows only to pounce on him from behind, beating him, thus forcing Zimmerman to defend himself. The narrative that quickly dominated black sentiment, however, was that Zimmerman tragically shot Martin for being black in the wrong place at the wrong time. While many believe there is reason to doubt Zimmerman's story, the deepest shame of the situation is that in one important respect it really does not matter what happened that night. The Sanford Police Department's initial decision not to arrest Zimmerman and blacks' collective outrage are a narrative point in an American story that can teach important lessons about the democratic moment we occupy as a function of past racial practices. Above, I introduced the idea of democratic agony with one sense of agony referring strictly to enduring pain and suffering while the second sense refers to the pain and suffering before death. To see the lessons of this and similar moments, we must ourselves employ a bit of imagination to see the connection between the existential atmosphere begotten by racism and the impact that has on black trust, real social policies, and what sometimes seems increasingly limited avenues for blacks to agitate for full inclusion as moral equals in the polity. To begin, consider with me two "images," two critical reflections on the status and conception of blacks in a fundamentally racially unjust society.

BELIEVING IS SEEING

Image 1: James Baldwin's Debate with William Buckley at Cambridge, 1965

On July 2, 1964, the Civil Rights Act was enacted ending more than two centuries of govern-ment-sanctioned oppression of blacks. On October 26, 1965, standing amidst a dominantly white audience at Cambridge University, James Baldwin traded arguments with social conservative, William Buckley. The question on the floor addressed the relationship between the idea of the American dream and the racial reality blacks faced in America. Baldwin's approach was to synthe-size the facts of American racist history and practices with thoughts on the effects of that history and those practices for whites and blacks, respectively. "It seems to me that the proposition before the house—whether the American dream is at the expense of the American negro…—is a ques-tion hideously loaded, and that one's response to that question…has to depend on where you find yourself in the world, what your sense of reality is—what your system of reality is. That is, it depends on assumptions which we hold so deeply, that we are scarcely aware of them."[1] Above Baldwin frames a question that urgently required an answer in 1965—a question concerning an ideal vision of America where freedom and liberty are assumed to be effective means to one's abil-ity to pursue and live a good life. Unsurprisingly, Baldwin argues that this ideal is made possible for white Americans on account of blacks' sacrifices such as the free labor provided by slavery that allowed America to maintain economic prosperity and the ensuing social systems that marginal-ized blacks' chances of benefitting from that prosperity.

Baldwin's path to offering that conclusion, however, is predicated on reframing the question in a way that preempts the assumption that one can reflect on race and the American dream without first acknowledging that race relations up until Baldwin's time had produced two sets of distinct democratic realities and experiences for whites and blacks. "The Mississippi or Alabama sheriff, who really does believe when he is facing a negro boy or girl, that this woman, this man, this child must be insane to attack the system to which he owes his entire identity. Of course, for such a person the proposition which we are trying to discuss here tonight does not exist." Baldwin's link between normative propositions—whether or not something is just or fair—and one's place in the social scheme becomes particularly forceful. The experiential and cognitive dissonance dis-played by the opposed responses of terror and puzzlement is not a matter of mere disagreement. A shared understanding of the situation each of the participants faces is made nearly impossible by the very conditions that permit the sheriff to consider the black person before him both a viable object for his power, as well as perversely ungrateful for his or her place in a society that systematically abuses and disrespects blacks. For the black boy or girl or man or woman, there is the real threat if not instance of racial abuse. For the sheriff, there is a lack of gratitude and appre-ciation for what he is doing for them, which further depends on his assumption that his place in the social scheme and the actions they justify are not merely allowed but justified—thereby, the sheriff cannot imagine things any other way. His experiential frame of reference coupled with his place in the racial scheme is an impediment to his ability to see the situation any other way apart from his beliefs about the rightness of the system and blacks' lesser moral status. Importantly, this occurs under the auspices of shared democratic life and is indeed made possible by the social structure of that democratic life.

Crucial to Baldwin's argument is the basic proposition that the disparity in perception is grounded in a history and system of power wherein whites have been able to use and dispose of blacks as they see fit. Baldwin's reliance upon the notion of "systems of reality" means to convey that the political structure and processes whites have available to them vis-à-vis blacks produces not merely favorable electoral outcomes, but, a basic structure that affirms whites' higher moral standing, from the cradle to the grave. Blacks, meanwhile, are undeserving and lack positive moral standing, thus available for white judgment. And this complex of systems of reality is underwritten in the first instance by the problem of social value.

The line of reasoning I want to emphasize here is that Baldwin understands that there is a significant relationship between perception, valuing, politics, and practical judgment: what whites believe and feel about blacks has had a great deal to do with what whites have done to blacks.[2] But, as blacks secured the Civil Rights victories at the time of Baldwin's performance, there were sure to be implications for democracy generally that have surfaced in the aftermath of Martin's death. "It comes as a great shock to discover that the country which is your birthplace and to which you owe your life and your identity, had not in its whole system of reality evolved any place for you. The disaffection, the demoralization and the gap between one person and another only on the basis of the color of their skin, begins there—and accelerates throughout a whole life time, until you are thirty and realize you are having a terrible time managing to trust your countrymen." We will see below how important the idea of trust is for blacks' ability to effectively and productively engage American democracy.

Image 2: Saigon— "The Invitation," 3rd verse

The party is in the pen' and the government is promotin' it,
That's the reason I don't be believin' in all this votin' shit.
They bring the coke in this bitch—Ain't no poppy seeds in the in the P's; please!
—It's nothin' but a whole lot of hopelessness.
That's where all the focus is;
Makin' sure the blacks stay in the back—the same place that uhh...scoliosis is.
How could they lie with such compulsiveness?
We just sit around, actin' like as if this is how we supposed to live?
[get the] fuck outta here!—I could swear in 'bout a year
I'll have these suckas explainin' why the hell they still got us here!
Still bein' treated like shit.
Still gettin' beat with nightsticks.—Still attract the heat in my 6!
That's pro'bly why I still drink Bacardi and the gin,
Cause whitey tryna invite me to the party in the pen.
A body'll get yo' ass up in V.I.P.;
And a burner'll get you in without showin' your ID.
The coke,—that'll get you in especially if you cook it up;
You RSVP—to the party in the P-...
...[...] I am the truth!
I ain't one of these kids that lie to the youth—I'm livin' proof![3]

Released in 2011, more than forty years after Baldwin's reflections, Saigon's track shared a historical moment with a number of public offenses against blacks. On New Year's Day, 2009,

Oakland police fatally shot 23-year-old Oscar Grant as he lay face down on the ground while handcuffed in police custody. Although the officer involved claimed Grant was resisting arrest, it was a claim cast into serious doubt by many eyewitness accounts including the account of another young man who was handcuffed on the ground next to Grant. In 2011, Troy Davis, a black defendant on death row was denied a stay of execution despite his defense attorney claiming, with arguably a significant degree of credibility, that more time to mount a case for retrial would exonerate Davis, thereby affirming the integrity of the ideals of our justice system. The claim failed to compel the Georgia Supreme Court despite widespread support—here and abroad—in favor of a stay. Yet, not two weeks later, white defendant Marcus Ray Johnson, also scheduled for execution, was able to secure a stay, hence secure his life. The differential outcomes could do little but cast a shadow over the system's integrity, especially for blacks. One wonders how such a difference could engender trust. In Saigon's estimation, that trust has long been forfeit even in the face of equal formal equality in the twenty-first century.

Accordingly, Saigon's most pressing complaint appears in the middle of the verse. When Saigon asks, "How could they lie with such compulsiveness?" it is a question that calls attention to a source of distrust that feeds into his analysis of the ways blacks "qualify" for discipline and punishment in the final third of the verse. And here, we should take the idea of a lie to work on a number of levels, two of which are most central: first, claims that the justice system is fair; and second, claims that blacks are somehow particularly deviant.

The first two lines underscore how blacks' democratic perceptions can be derailed. Blacks are imprisoned at rates disproportionate to both their percentage of the population, as well as the rate of offenses, so, on this view, government creates a special place for blacks—jail [the pen]. If democracy is importantly about being free and making use of one's liberties, then why would blacks in good faith take part in the American democratic project if they have already been made to believe that that project does not act in good faith vis-à-vis the good of their lives? Putting a finer point on the matter: What could democracy possibly mean to blacks when they are being systematically targeted for coercive removal from the democratic system? (Here, one should keep in mind the fact that most states disenfranchise felons even after they have served their time, debunking the very idea of serving time as "paying one's debt." Permanent exclusion from the electoral process suggests that blacks are constantly in arrears.) On Saigon's view, democracy is used precisely to withhold democratic benefits from, and suppress the development of a proper democratic ethos among, blacks.

Lines three and four call into question the lazy, but popular view that arrests and incarceration merely mirror people's free, if poor, choices. However, Saigon's point is worth taking up. Voices in urban culture have long remarked that while drugs are a blight on blacks, particularly in the ghetto, a striking feature is that none of the base narcotic materials needed for most drugs can be grown or manufactured in the ghetto—much less America. This raises the question: How does cocaine make it all the way from South America, for example, to predominantly black neighborhoods? Moreover, a somewhat lucrative product that is easy to distribute is readily obtainable in precisely those areas where a legitimate small business loan, living wage-paying jobs, and decent, affordable housing are nearly impossible to secure. Importantly, Saigon calls attention to the stricter penalties for crack cocaine—the variant of cocaine that is relatively easy to manufacture in the ghetto. The result in lines five and six: the effective oppression of blacks as if they are a social disease which qualifies them for a schedule of repressions in the final six lines. What is stunning about Saigon's insights is that the problems to which he draws our attention are not confined to ghetto life. After all, Martin was shot in a suburban gated community.

Importantly, the ensuing lack of black trust is fostered by an unholy trinity. First, there is the question of the inherently unfair social circumstances that structure the range of "free" choices available to blacks. Second, once those choices have been unjustly structured, blacks are easily framed and portrayed as a kind of pariah. But third, though the background structure is unjust, blacks can get caught up in racial power simply by getting in their cars and driving around, subjecting themselves, as did Oscar Grant, to the ill will of police officers, who, at the end of the day, act on behalf of a larger democratic society—a larger society marked by systemic racial inequality and a history of black abuse. And, blacks get caught up in just this way on account of the image that has persisted of them as legitimate if not necessary candidates for that repression.

Taken together, Baldwin and Saigon offer a series of claims that cohere into two main points exemplified in the Trayvon Martin shooting and the ensuing reactions. On the one hand is the experiential fracturing of the "America" implied in the American dream. On Baldwin's telling, the America we know is largely a function of an imposition of the reality begotten by a long history of white supremacy. This reality does more than affect real outcomes; it also structures beliefs about value and the standing of blacks in the polity—what I specified in earlier chapters as the problem of social value. Although Baldwin states his case in 1965—one year after the passage of the Civil Rights Act—the crucial part of his argument consists in the genuine confusion whites may feel at black resentment due to mistreatment, though what Baldwin refers to as "the bloody catalog of oppression" is a matter of public record. In 2011, forty-seven years after the passage of the Civil Rights Act, Saigon's claim is that the black body has become easier to target and more frequently targeted, as evidenced by the surrounding cases of Oscar Grant and Troy Davis. And if ever there was a time to distrust—which Baldwin says is a necessary outcome of portraying and treating blacks this way—Saigon's argument suggests: now is that time.

We now have a frame in which to place, on the one hand, the ease with which blacks are depicted as threatening, thus appropriate targets for various uses of force, and, on the other, an increasing deficit of black trust in a system that serves one of democracy's most important functions—keeping the peace. If it is the case that blacks are disciplined and punished—thus portrayed as a danger or threat to citizens—on unjust or deeply questionable democratic grounds, we not only have reason to regard black anger and distrust as reasonable democratic responses but are further positioned to appreciate that the agony caused by Trayvon Martin's shooting and similar instances could represent a turning point in the stability of our democracy—a project that many have reason to believe is not a shared project. But blacks have a reason to be distrustful beyond the too easy proposition that America currently represents a system of white supremacy. It turns out that the real threat to black trust in democracy is that the notion of black dangerousness is underwritten by real policy choices that speak truth to the lie that the American justice system is fair.

SYSTEM SHOCK

On July 2, 1964, the Civil Rights Act was enacted ending more than two centuries of government-sanctioned oppression of blacks. In 1965 the federal Law Enforcement Assistance Administration (LEAA) was created. Revisiting key points presented in chapter 3, its signal purpose was to distribute funds to regional law enforcement agencies in order to better fight and control crime. By

1969 the LEAA had an operating budget of $59 million. By 1975, it was supported by a budget much closer to $1 billion ($850 million). In other words, at the second dawn of black freedom, the federal government institutionalized a set of policies and mandates that today is responsible for controlling and suppressing one in three blacks between the ages of 18 and 29.

The years separating Saigon from Baldwin are marked by public policy changes that give weight to both the analysis of, and the resulting emotional responses to, the shape, scope, and severity of American racial discipline and punishment. In fact, the element of time plays a crucial role, for not only have policies been institutionalized in some distinct sequence, but there are good reasons to believe that an initial moment of racial resentment in response to blacks' victories in 1964 and 1965 has been projected over time. The most recent surge of racial discipline and punishment, thus the continuous and continuously articulated narrative of blacks as public threat, can be traced as a noncoincidental response to the fact that blacks had freed themselves from Jim Crow. Indeed, the irony is that blacks' victory on one front inspired a set of policy developments that have worked to threaten their freedom and safety since those victories.

This is what I am suggesting: the line of argument running from Baldwin to Saigon regarding the relationship between the emergent phenomenologies of a racialized democracy and black distrust of that democracy's institutions—particularly the criminal justice system—are powerful ways to make sense of the moment given by the Martin shooting.

The average American has a view of our carceral state that looks something like the following: police arrest those that commit crimes; if incarceration is high, then it is a direct reflection of crimes being committed; and if blacks are overrepresented in those numbers, it just reflects that they commit more crimes. This reasoning depends upon a number of fairly large, problematic assumptions. The first is that the criminal justice system is inherently racially fair. That assumption has long proven to be false.[4] The second is that blacks in fact commit more crimes, an assumption we noted earlier as requiring significant qualification. But there is a final assumption that only recently has been challenged: that the carceral system has merely responded to the polity's needs. However, there is good reason to believe that rather than being reactive, the development of the carceral system represented a kind of racial victory that created the conditions for its own presence and aggressive expansion as illustrated by the LEAA's astounding growth in the wake of the Civil Rights Act.

On Vesla Weaver's account, blacks' victories in the early to mid-1960s motivated a set of policy reforms that have shaped a large swatch of the fabric of America's penal practices. However, rather than motivating a backlash in response to the Civil Rights Act of 1964, conservatives mobilized racial fear and bias to produce policies that could maintain the pre-1964 racial status quo. The main vehicle of choice for that maintenance?—a reconfigured carceral apparatus that would have a central role in both defining deviant behavior and deviants, and given full support in suppressing both.

Recall the central concept in Weaver's argument is *frontlash*: "the process by which losers in a conflict become the architects of a new program, manipulating the issue space and altering the dimension of the conflict in an effort to regain their command of the agenda."[5] Frontlash has dual importance for our reflections. First, frontlash is not merely an expression of anger, resentment, or ill will. Instead, the 1960s' frontlash was proactive and creative. So the first important feature of frontlash is that a history of racial marginalization found a new way to express an idea of blacks as dangerous, hence targetable. Thus, a certain vision of blacks became institutionally authored at exactly the moment the state was supposed to have made amends for historically sanctioning black oppression. Maybe more ironically, the state now gained the power to punish those who violated blacks' civil rights, but the cost for blacks seems to have been becoming increasingly more subject to punishment themselves.

The second important feature of frontlash is indicated in the very term itself: *front*. On Weaver's specification of the term we ought to take "front" to denote the ways we typically use it when we say something such as: we need to get out in front of the problem. This usage of 'front' expresses the importance of not being left to simply respond but to create the image or scenario we want others to consume or reference. But for that to be successful there must be another mechanic in play: projection over time. As Weaver acknowledges, a backlash is responsive to something that has already occurred. But a frontlash opens future possibilities in accord with the moment that generates the creative impulse. In her words: "We can think of frontlash as water moving swiftly through a path that eventually comes to an end, forcing the water to seek alternative routes or as a weed that after being killed by weed killer mutates into a new variety, becoming resistant."[6]

An important part of the frontlash story consistent with the desire that the old racial narrative have new staying power is that racial conservatives had to couch their arguments in the post-Civil Rights language of equality and liberty. Weaver writes on the concept of frontlash: "Elites aim to control the agenda and resist changes through the development of a new issue and appropriation and redeployment of an accepted language of norms."[7] How so? The Civil Rights Movement put the language of rights front and center in American discourse, and conservatives latched onto that language to argue that the language of rights also meant protecting Americans from social instability begotten by civil discord. Politicians thereby secured one possible future consistent with the past by reaffirming the idea of blacks as threatening.

We ended the section "Believing Is Seeing" by observing the link between the wrongful content given to the idea of black dangerousness, on the one hand, and black distrust of American society, on the other. There is another main reason, tragically ironic, that we should be concerned about the link between public racial beliefs and distrust. While Weaver's account is fundamentally important for grounding contemporary claims about the racial nature of the carceral state's activities and priorities, there is a further interpretive move that brings the problem full circle, and it consists in Michelle Alexander's argument that the current state of the carceral system represents a *new Jim Crow*.

Jim Crow represented an era, as well as a system of oppression, that took the reins of black marginalization from slavery and gave it new life in the wake of the first Reconstruction. It was comprised of a constellation of sanctioned practices founded on the basic principle of social and physical segregation justified by racial designation. Blacks were prevented from mixing with general society lest they should contribute to its degradation. We should particularly take this description of Jim Crow alongside Alexander's reconfigured deployment of it to heart given the feature of separation in the name of prevention and maintenance—what else is the carceral system meant to achieve if not these aims? As Alexander notes, "The United States imprisons a larger percentage of its black population than South Africa did during the height of apartheid."[8]

That the present carceral state represents a new Jim Crow should be alarming. Following the work of Reva Siegel, Alexander notes that American society has consistently responded to moments of racial progress by battening the hatches on white privilege. Moments of racial change engender new rules of conduct and appropriateness, and indeed, these changes are trumpeted by conservatives as proof of America's fundamental fairness, but though "these new rules have been justified by new rhetoric…and a new social consensus…[they] produce many of the same results."⁹ If the purpose of Jim Crow was to control by means of segregation, then one of Alexander's more poignant examples of Jim Crow's most recent revival centers on the War on Drugs. Initiated by Ronald Reagan's administration in the early 1980s, the "war" has been one of the most powerful forces sweeping through the black community. However, recalling the Sentencing Project Report, the "war" is certainly unjust as it has focused on a product predominantly found in black communities though drugs in general can be found just as easily in white suburbs.

Consider this counter-image presented by Alexander:

> From the outset, the drug war could have been waged primarily in overwhelming white suburbs or on college campuses. SWAT teams could have rappelled from helicopters in gated suburban communities and raided the homes of high school lacrosse players known for hosting coke and ecstasy parties after their games.…Suburban homemakers could have been placed under surveillance and subjected to undercover operations designed to catch them violating laws regulating the use and sale of prescription "uppers."¹⁰

But that is not how the War on Drug has been conducted. Instead, the quite literal weapons of the state are more consistently trained on blacks, thus make manifest the story of blacks as dangerous and deviant. One wonders whether one day a sitting president will triumphantly emerge from a helicopter gloriously claiming an end to combat operations centered on the black body. The combined ideas—that the success of the Civil Rights Movement motivated a racially inflected response in the form of the growth of the carceral state that replicates Jim Crow practices—suggest that America's institutions have not kept pace with the moral mandates they set out for themselves and the polity in the form of law and formal rights following the Civil Rights and Voting Rights Acts. To the extent that the preceding is accurate, it represents a fundamental failure of democracy to look after its own citizens equally thus engendering an ethos of equal respect and care. Rather, the past forty years have been marked and marred by a renewed interest in defining black value. This in turn has laid contemporary groundwork legitimizing institutional suppression of blacks, as well as ethically empowering whites, as in Zimmerman's case, to take matters into their own hands. Why should blacks readily trust a society that has quite literally waged asymmetrical warfare against them consistent with historical patterns of social repression in response to the promise of social progress?

AGONY

Agony: (1) Extreme Physical or Mental Suffering

Here is an excerpt from the Sanford Police Report after Officer Ayala identified George Zimmerman: "I then noticed there was what appeared to be a black male wearing a grey sweater…lying face down on the ground. The black male had his hands underneath his body. I attempted to get a response from the black male but was met with negative results.…Sanford Fire Rescue arrived on the scene and attempted to revive the subject but could not. Paramedic Brady pronounced the subject deceased at 1930 hours."¹¹

"It's just very difficult to live with, day in and day out. I'm sure [Zimmerman's] parents can pick up the phone and call him. But we can't pick up the phone and call Trayvon anymore." So said Sybrina Fulton with great emotion in an NBC interview on April 12, 2012.

I began this essay by suggesting that though the events of the night of Trayvon Martin's shooting seem to be inconclusive as of this writing, in the end, it may not matter whether Zimmerman genuinely acted in self-defense. Martin was unarmed, significantly younger, and physically smaller than Zimmerman, who found cause to fatally shoot him. It took American news outlets close to a month to pick up on the story. However, as Martin's story attracted attention, it became apparent that his death was not an exceptional case of an unarmed black youth gunned down. Weeks later, on March 24, Kendrec McDade, 19, was shot by police who justified their actions by indicating that a caller lied about Kendrec being armed. A debate can be had about how police should be prepared to respond to 911 calls generally, but it is notable that both Zimmerman and the caller in Kendrec's case simply presumed the respective black youths to be armed and dangerous and that this presumption in both cases turned out to be fatal.

Public outrage followed the news of Martin's death once the story became widespread, yet two points of racial disparity indicate the source of our democratic agony. White defenders of Zimmerman are quick to indicate that while Martin's death was unfortunate, Zimmerman was within his rights on account of Florida's Stand Your Ground Laws—a set of laws that allow persons to aggressively and forcefully respond to those they perceive as threats to their well-being. But many blacks ask why Marissa Alexander, a black woman who felt threatened by her aggressive husband, was sentenced to twenty years in prison for discharging her gun in her own home. Blacks have been further indignant that she faces severe time, although she fired her gun in the air thus her husband was unharmed. Zimmerman, meanwhile, walked a free man for nearly two months after actually slaying Martin.

Then there is a second racial disparity, and it maps onto displays of democratic care and concern. While Martin's shooting motivated strong outcries and series of marches across the nation, it is estimated that 90 percent of those marching were black, although blacks comprise roughly 13 percent of the population.[12] In other words, Martin's shooting was cause for suspicion of gross injustice perpetrated by one citizen against another, but only a portion of the nation perceived it as such or at least with a reaction strong enough to motivate participating in public protest. With respect to the first definition of agony, how could anyone not diagnose our democracy, its history, and this moment, as anything but a system engendering and experiencing deep suffering, mentally and physically, metaphorically and real as individuals experience pain and confusion, and in the case of the polity as a whole, apathy that is inconsistent with the idea of democracy as a shared project?

Agony: (2) The Final Stages of a Difficult and Painful Death

America, as a political entity and shared society, was born on the back of black suffering; it was underwritten by, as Baldwin says, "a bloody catalog of oppression." The main strand of argument running throughout this essay has been that black treatment persists on account of the story/image/perception of blacks Americans hold in common. The black person as less worthy, likely troublesome, possibly dangerous has continuously motivated and justified aggressive and even fatal actions against him or her. This set of beliefs and perceptions is an essentially American feature rooted in slavery, which received a refreshed telling with the birth of Jim Crow; and, in the aftermath of the Civil Rights victories, the phenomenon of frontlash secured blacks' status as suppressible resulting in a new Jim Crow.

I have also suggested that this long series of offenses and violations, both conceptual and corporeal, prompts us to ask alongside Baldwin and Saigon: How can blacks be expected to trust their fellow countrymen? If the answer is they either cannot or maybe ought not, then there are clear implications for American democracy. Baldwin's concerns resonate today, when in the wake of America's 1960s frontlash, blacks have become a main target of the carceral state, prompting Saigon to deny the value of voting—the very thing almost every democratic theorist can agree is fundamental to defining democratic life. Thus, we would do well to ask a basic yet politically terrifying question: Can our democracy die and can instances like Martin's shooting initiate the final, most painful days? We should hope not, but we should take this question seriously. Indeed, David Banner provides some initial insight as to what might bring on, if not constitute the final, most painful days:

> **David Banner:** Listen to even the things that people are saying about this Trayvon Martin situation, some of the things that the people on the other side are saying. Could you have imagined ten years ago them saying that about a Black child? You're talking about a child. You're not talking about a grown Black man, you're talking about a Black child. That means they don't have any respect! That means that they don't have any fear! Because they believe that either we're not going to do anything or that we can't do anything.
>
> **DX:** So how do you change that? If David Banner could wave a magic wand, how do you change that?
>
> **David Banner:** You can only make America respect you through fear or finance. Those are the only two things that America respects. You either gotta hurt 'em physically or hurt 'em financially. Either way, you make the choice.[13]

Blacks may or may not articulate their views as Banner does. Many might express some variant, in touch with their rage unalloyed by concerns of political appropriateness imposed by a system that may not fully value black rage, legitimate as it might ultimately be. Nevertheless, we should take note of the choices Banner thinks blacks have for responding to institutional racism and realize a serious problem. For blacks to effectively fight back financially—and here I think Banner means "hurt 'em" in terms of, getting goods out of a system that benefits others and to do so at their justified cost—it must be the case that blacks can access and leverage the institutional levers of influence and prosperity just as whites can; it must be the case that America's institutions are fundamentally fair. But there is no good reason to believe this is imminently possible because there is no evidence to suggest that our institutions are in fact basically fair. In a nation where blacks hold $.10 of wealth for every $1 of white wealth, where would that capital come from?[14] In a society where blacks with names sounding remotely "black" are denied jobs in favor of whites, how would blacks access the levers of power?[15]

Tommie Shelby rightly notes that what John Rawls calls the basic structure of America is not merely somewhat unjust but fundamentally racially unjust.[16] Shelby contends that on account of the principle of reciprocity in light of this fundamental categorical injustice, one could reasonably argue that blacks' civic duties are suspended—"The existence of the dark ghetto—with its combination of social stigma, extreme poverty, racial segregation...and shocking incarceration rates—is simply incompatible with any meaningful form of reciprocity among free and equal citizens."[17] Shelby does argue that they have natural duties, primary among them: to seek justice. But if we take seriously David Banner's suggestion that blacks have two options open to them, and we concede that one of those options—the financial option—is not likely to yield significant results, then what is left for blacks to do as America's institutions and citizens continue to perpetrate corporeal violations against them? One should not read this in the first instance as a justification for Banner's other option—a physical response. Yet, if as Saigon suggests, a major question for blacks is: "How could they lie with such compulsiveness?" then continued mistreatment on the order of Martin's death is not helpful in preempting the resentment that could make Banner's propositions a live option. At the very least, Banner's reflections ought to be taken as a stark warning that such a response is not what lies at the heart of a well-ordered and stable democracy, yet it is an option that now, and at all times in political society, we may be forcing on ourselves unless we can learn to begin to exercise genuine democratic care and concern. It is the only way to alleviate the agony of a racial democracy.

NOTES

cℓ ——

INTRODUCTION

1. Throughout the manuscript, I will refer to blacks as the persons owed racial justice, but I want to make clear that I mean "black," as an identity category, to be a bit broader than what is typically meant (i.e., with reference to African Americans). Rather, for our time, I mean the category to be flexible enough to include, for example, dark-skinned persons of Caribbean or South American descent. Why? America has inherited a tradition of social categorization that also affects our social cognition. As a Puerto Rican man who is often mistaken for being African American, I have experienced the kinds of social maladies that someone "properly" defined as "black" experiences. However, I want to emphasize that our current racial issues do stem from a more distinct set of historically articulated identities where "black" and African American (persons of dark skin directly descended from African slaves) were more closely equivalent. I want to say then that our current climate owes its contours to that history, thus I broaden the notion of black in just that way. I recognize that there are difficulties. Let's say we included "black" Dominicans, Puerto Ricans, and so on, how "not-black" does someone in either of these categories have to be to fall outside the reach of the theory, and more crucially, what will the metric be? My response is sure to be unsatisfying: I can't say. What I rely upon is the fact that there is a significant population whose life experiences tend to be closely modeled on the historical black experience on account of their features and/or heritage. And my claim is that those people ought not be left out; I remain silent on the claim as to how many others' experiences are close enough to qualify. For the historical importance of delineating "blacks" as such, see Omo and Howard Winant, *Racial Formation in the United States: From the 1960s to the 1990s* (New York: Routledge, 1994). For a more recent analysis on the present and possible future relationship between skin color and race in America, see forthcoming, Jennifer Hochschild, Vesla Weaver, and Traci Burch, *Creating A New Racial Order: How Immigration, Genomics, Multiculturalism, and the Young Can Remake Race in America* (Chicago: University of Chicago).

2. Here I follow Joel Kupperman's specification of character in *"Virtues, Character, and Moral Dispositions,"* in *Virtue Ethics and Moral Education*, ed. David Carr and Jan Steutel (New York: Routledge, 1999), 199–209. I revisit his work in chapter 4.

3. Glover might be forgiven his oversight given his location in the United Kingdom and my concern about *American* attentiveness to racial injustice. However, I would like to hear explanations from the many reviewers who also failed to catch the absence of race. Thus, I use Glover as a convenient stand-in for the larger issue in America regarding failure to adequately acknowledge racial inequality as a persistent and deep moral problem.

4. See respectively: Ronald Dworkin, *Sovereign Virtue* (Cambridge, MA: Harvard University Press, 2000); Richard J. Arneson, *"Equality and Equal Opportunity for Welfare,"* *Philosophical Studies* 56, no. 1 (1989): 77–93; G. A. Cohen, *"On the Currency of Egalitarian Justice,"* *Ethics* 99, no. 4 (1989): 906–944; Amartya Sen, "Equality of What?" *The Tanner Lectures on Human Value*, May 22, 1979: http://www.tannerlectures.utah.edu/lectures/documents/sen80.pdf.

5. See respectively: David Carroll Cochran, *The Color of Freedom: Race and Contemporary American Liberalism* (Albany: State University of New York Press, 1999); Bernard Boxill, *Blacks and Social Justice*, Revised Edition (Boston: Rowman and Littlefield Publishers, 1992); Howard McGary, *Race and Social Justice* (Malden, MA: Blackwell Publishers, 1999).

6. Glenn Loury, *The Anatomy of Racial Inequality* (Cambridge, MA: Harvard University Press, 2002).

7. John Rawls, *A Theory of Justice* (Cambridge, MA: Belknap Press, 1999), 216.

8. The following view is found in V. O. Quine and is explicitly stated as inspired by Neurath: "In particular we shall find, as we get on with organizing and adjusting various of the turns of phrase that participate in what pass for affirmations of existence, that certain of these take on key significance in the increasingly systematic structure....Our boat stays afloat because at each alteration we keep the bulk of it intact as a going concern. Our words continue to make passable sense because of continuity of change of theory: we warp usage gradually to avoid rupture" (*Word and Object* [Cambridge, MA: MIT Press, 1960], 4).

9. For recent work on this idea, see Philip Abita Goff, Jennifer L. Eberhardt, et al., "Not Yet Human: Implicit Knowledge, Historical Dehumanization, and Contemporary Consequences," *Journal of Personality and Social Psychology* 94, no. 2 (2008): 292–306. See also Lawrence Bobo and Ryan Smith, *"From Jim Crow Racism to Laissez-Faire Racism: The Transformation of Racial Attitudes,"* in *Beyond Pluralism*, ed. Wendy F. Katkin, Ned Landsman, and Andrea Tyree (Urbana: University of Illinois Press. 1998).

10. Martin Luther King, Jr., *"Our Struggle,"* in *A Testament of Hope: The Essential Writings and Speeches of Martin Luther King, Jr.*, ed. James M. Washington (New York: Harper Collins, 1986), 75.

11. Ibid.

12. Up to this point, it may seem that I am relying upon the fact or possibility of a distinct and distinctly unitary "American" philosophy, one that is accepted by all, whose arguments and propositions are common and uncontroversial. Indeed, the notion of shame has been in part justified by the slogan, we know better but fail to do better. It bears mentioning, then, that I do not suggest that there is a distinct comprehensive American philosophy about which we argue over its interpretation at the margins. Rather, I rely on a particular core that none can deny is fundamental to the American political tradition, and that revolves around the ideas that undergird the founding charter: equality, liberty, and freedom. While members of the polity, liberals and libertarians, for

example, may argue whether federal taxes suppress or promote the pursuit of liberty, neither side could make a reasonable case that the pursuit of liberty ought to be modified by dubious social categories such as race. It is this distinction and core tradition that I rely upon. Accordingly, this view informs my use of "we." It might similarly seem contestable that there is an American "we." My claim here runs parallel to the above argument. The project of racial justice and analysis does not depend on Americans uniformly sharing a very similar American identity that would tend to justify the use of "we." Rather, whether or not every American strongly identifies with every other one, the "we" I refer to indicates that persons share basic commitments to the idea of American democracy, and indeed the commitment to that idea is what generates contestation over its interpretation, rather than over the rightness of equal rights, and so on.

13. Some readers familiar with the respective literatures in justice and race may think my choice to focus on Rawls and Mills as the exemplars of the two traditions a bit cavalier. There is work by other theorists that could be considered important, including work cited in earlier footnotes. To be clear, my claim is not that the work of these two theorists is exhaustively representative. Rather, my choice is motivated by the claim that the two philosophers' works are most significantly relevant for our needs. With respect to Rawls, it is well known that his work was largely responsible for reviving liberal theory in the 1960s and 1970s. Further, while liberal theory since Rawls has offered some innovations, it is also undoubtedly true that the field of analytic liberal theory has largely carried on a tradition begun by him. So in this case, my aim is to go back to "the source" rather than to traipse across a landscape covered with a variety of arguments nonetheless sympathetic to Rawls. On the other hand, it is less clear that Mills is representative of the field of race theory in the way Rawls might be accepted as a major representative of liberal thought. My reason for focusing on Mills is a bit different. First, of the theorists working at the intersection of power, normative thought, and race, Mills has most consistently and most extendedly engaged and criticized Rawlsian liberalism, thus it allows us to juxtapose the two theorists as contestants of sorts. Further, within political philosophy proper, Mills has also been maybe the strongest and consistent voice for making race a more central concern to normative theory while remaining sympathetic to the fundamental concerns of the critical race theory literature centering on the relationship between identity, power, reproduction of disadvantage, epistemology, and history. Readers looking to inquire into those works can begin (but not end) with: David Theo Goldberg, *The Racial State* (New York: Blackwell, 2001); Richard Delgado, *The Rodrigo Chronicles: Conversations about Race and America* (New York: New York University Press, 1996); Joe R. Feagin, *The White Racial Frame: Centuries of Racial Framing and Counter-Framing* (New York: Routledge, 2010). A parallel body of work has been done in the field of whiteness studies. Works worth looking into here are: David R. Roediger, *The Wages of Whiteness: Race and the Making of the American Working Class*, New Edition (New York: Verso, 2007); Ruth Frankenberg, *White Women, Race Matters: The Social Construction of Whiteness* (Minneapolis: University of Minnesota Press, 1993); Joel Olson, *The Abolition of White Democracy* (Minneapolis: University of Minnesota Press, 2004).

14. 'Damage imagery' refers to the idea that blacks develop a distorted or damaged sense of themselves and/or blackness in general on account of being black in a society dominated by whites. The idea has its most prominent roots in Kenneth and Mamie Clark's doll tests wherein their study showed that young black girls rejected black dolls and found white dolls more attractive. The implication was that due to racism, black girls rejected the possibility of black beauty, and by extension, the possibility of their own beauty. Kenneth Clark followed this line of thinking in his

Dark Ghetto: Dilemmas of Social Power, 2d ed. (Hanover, CT: Wesleyan University Press, 1965). Clark's view is one that has come under scrutiny in some contemporary work on race and self-esteem. See Daryl Michael Scott, *Contempt and Pity: Social Policy and the Image of the Damaged Black Psyche, 1880–1996* (Chapel Hill: University of North Carolina Press, 1997).

15. See Claudia Card, *The Unnatural Lottery: Character and Moral Luck* (Philadelphia: Temple University Press, 1996).

CHAPTER 1

1. http://www.youtube.com/watch?v=zIUzLpO1kxI&feature=player_embedded.

2. See, for example, Leo King, "Deepwater Horizon Modelling Software Showed BP Cement Conditions Unstable." http://www.computerworlduk.com/news/it-business/3248321/deepwater-horizon-modelling-software-showed-bp-cement-conditions-unstable/.

3. A point of clarification: we might distinguish between moral outrage as a final expression of moral judgment, on the one hand, and outrage as a sometimes appropriate motivational device for further reflecting on a moral wrong. On this view, while it might sometimes be appropriate to be morally outraged at particular racial offenses, it will be mostly inappropriate as a response to racial inequality as a category of offense for reasons I have indicated and which will become clear in the ensuing pages. However, it seems to me that upon realizing and acknowledging the deep substance of racial inequality rage can become one possible trigger for further reflecting on racial inequality to come to some other judgments about the unjust nature of racial inequality.

4. Gabriele Taylor, *Pride, Shame, and Guilt: Emotions of Self-Assessment* (New York: Oxford University Press, 1985), 66.

5. This is a gloss on Taylor's formulation: "She therefore sees herself in a fall from a higher to a lower position" (ibid., 67).

6. Anthony O'Hear, "*Guilt and Shame as Moral Concepts,*" *Proceedings of the Aristotelian Society* 77 (1976–77): 73–86, 77.

7. O'Hear, "Guilt and Shame as Moral Concepts."

8. See, for example, Nancy Sherman, *The Fabric of Character: Aristotle's Theory of Virtue* (New York: Oxford University Press, 1989); Julia Annas, *The Morality of Happiness* (New York: Oxford University Press, 1993), Kindle edition; Rosalind Hursthouse, *On Virtue Ethics* (New York: Oxford University Press, 2001).

9. Sherman, *Fabric of Character*, 6.

10. Christina Tarnapolsky, "*Prudes, Perverts, and Tyrants: Plato and the Contemporary Politics of Shame,*" *Political Theory* 32, no. 4 (2004): 468–494, 476.

11. Ibid., 477.

12. Ibid., 478.

13. See Nicole D. Porter and Valerie Wright, "Cracked Justice," *The Sentencing Project*, March 2011. http://sentencingproject.org/doc/publications/dp_CrackedJusticeMar2011.pdf. Also Michael Tonry, *Punishing Race: A Continuing American Dilemma* (New York: Oxford University Press, 2011).

14. As a procedural note: I will below revert to speaking of shame as a property of persons' moral makeup for the sake of presentational simplicity, but I do not mean to commit myself to designating shame as a property especially unique to persons. I think it is important that we

reserve the possibility to speak about shame on a larger social scale because both persons and institutions bear responsibility for failing to uphold the ideal of basic moral equality.

15. John Rawls, *A Theory of Justice* (Cambridge, MA: Harvard University Press, 1999), 3.

16. Ibid., 6–7.

17. Ibid., 11.

18. Ibid., 216.

19. Susan Okin offers a related complaint when she notes that Rawls fails to treat the family and its practices as sufficiently political in denying that the principles of justice do not need to apply to them as familial relations are founded on affection. See Susan Moller Okin, "Political Liberalism, Justice, and Gender," *Ethics* 105, no. 1 (1994): 23–43, 26.

20. John Rawls, *Political Liberalism* (New York: Columbia University Press, 1993).

21. John Rawls, "Justice as Fairness: Political Not Metaphysical," *Philosophy & Public Affairs* 14, no. 3 (1985): 223–251, 225.

22. Rawls, *Political Liberalism*, 266.

23. Ibid., 269.

24. Ibid.

25. Rawls, "Justice as Fairness," 238 (emphasis added).

26. Ibid., 229.

27. One might here hold the position that justice does not necessarily have to be a response to transgressions. One can work out a conception of persons and argue that justice demands that people are owed some good in light of that conception and justice demands it be provided going forward. I have no serious quarrel with such a view. Rather, I resist that it should have pride of place in our considerations of justice given how persons here and now actually can and do make distinct claims grounded not only in some conception of the intrinsic moral value of personhood but also because of some particular act or event that violates what follows from that conception.

28. Rawls, "Justice as Fairness," 228. [Emphasis added.]

29. Ruth Frankenberg, *White Women, Race Matters: The Social Construction of Whiteness (Gender, Racism, Ethnicity)* (New York: Routledge, 1994), 8. The passage from Frankenberg does double work. It not only poignantly elucidates a critical point but it also performs an attendant point, for one may ask whether I mean to say that only blacks can say something useful about justice. It is worth noting that Frankenberg writes insightfully on race as a white woman, not a black woman. Our intuition here should be that this is on account of her genuine sympathy with the cause of racial justice due to her openness to internalizing its difficulties, thus allowing her to adopt the viewpoint of racial disadvantage. She writes of being involved in second wave feminism: "Because we were basically well-meaning, the idea of being part of the problem of racism…was genuinely shocking to us." And she goes on, "Meanwhile, I was also spending a great deal of time with a friendship/support network of working-class women of color and white women….As I sat with them and traveled their daily pathways—thanks to an unexpectedly profound connection to one woman in particular—an inventory of meanings of racism, of racist behaviors began, de facto, to accumulate in my consciousness" (pp. 3–4).

30. See Rawls, *Theory*, ch. 4, §31.

31. For a historical view, see Mary Poole, *The Segregated Origins of Social Security: African Americans and the Welfare State* (Chapel Hill: University of North Carolina Press, 2006). For a more contemporary focus, see Jill Quadagno, *The Color of Welfare: How Racism Undermined the War on Poverty* (New York: Oxford University Press, 1994).

32. Rawls, *Theory*, 215–216. It is worth noting that Rawls highlights two cases where he thinks nonideal concerns depend upon ideal theory in ways that do not quite map on to the problem of race. The first case has to do with how extensive liberty ought to be—here he is thinking of what it might mean to limit the free speech of hate groups. Second, he is concerned with unequal liberty—paradigmatically, he refers to voters excluded from the franchise or whose votes are given lesser weight. I find it interesting that while it is true both of these depend on a statement of what it means for basic liberties to be lexically prior, thus easily find a home in Rawls's framework, these are nonetheless rather explicit violations of justice. As I will argue, the fundamental problem of racial inequality as that of social value does not conform to these interpretations of what it means for a state of affairs to be unjust.

33. This passage indicates a response to a second possible Rawlsian objection, though I find it to be weaker than that from the four-stage sequence. This second objection says that the problem of social value seems an appropriate target for the social bases of self-respect, and it would further be emphasized that Rawls considers the social bases the most important primary good in the theory. This objection is frequently offered because the term 'social bases of self-respect' seems intuitively promising for it seems to suggest a rather robust restructuring of society such that people are substantively valued in the right way. But the objection fails because Rawls does not conceive of the social bases in this thick sense. He stipulates that the social bases have an objective character, and he further stipulates: "These social bases are things like the institutional fact that citizens have equal basic rights, and the public recognition of that fact and that everyone endorses the difference principle, itself a form of reciprocity" (John Rawls, *Justice as Fairness: A Restatement*, ed. Erin Kelly [Cambridge, MA: Harvard University Press, 2001], 60). There seems to me to be a number of issues with this formulation, one of which hinges on the difference principle being strongly indexed to class—and, as we shall continuously see, racial inequality is not a matter of black poverty. The second issue with a turn to the social bases is that, as Rawls articulates the idea, the social bases presume a just society. Put another way, it is defined in terms of exactly the kind of goals a theory of justice must strive to achieve. Third, the social bases in part call for the "institutional fact" of equal basic rights, but it seems to me that one of the most troubling aspects of racial inequality is that equal basic rights are an institutional fact. Finally, as I shall go on to explain, racial inequality is not merely about what blacks are owed, but about the way the nation must be reshaped on account of the various social places marked out by racial injustice. This means that a theory of racial justice must attend to whites' sense of black value, but I find it difficult to grasp how the development of that sense depends on self-respect in the way Rawls stipulates that idea. In fact, the common complaint from critical race theorists is that whites already have a disproportionately high sense of self-worth and attendant self-referential attitudes. What, then, would the social bases do for them with respect to their ability to deeply understand the dynamics of America's racial scheme? For these reasons, we should reject the objection as troublesome for the proceeding arguments.

34. For an interesting empirical account of the role of white supremacy in guiding American policy making, see Desmond S. King and Rogers Smith, "Racial Orders in American Political Development," *American Political Science Review* 99, no. 1 (2005): 75–92. A notable feature of King and Smith's article is that the notion of white supremacy as a clearly identifiable racial order becomes much more difficult to parse out once we historically move past the general time frame of the Civil Rights Act in 1964.

35. See Charles W. Mills. *The Racial Contract* (Ithaca, NY: Cornell University, 1997), as well as *Blackness Visible: Essays on Philosophy and Race* (Ithaca, NY: Cornell University Press, 1998), esp. ch. 7.

36. Charles W. Mills, *From Class to Race: Essays in White Marxism and Black Radicalism* (Lanham, MD: Rowman and Littlefield, 2003), 179 (emphasis in original).

37. Quoted in Mills, *From Class to Race.*

38. John Gaventa, *Power and Powerlessness: Quiescence and Rebellion in an Appalachian Valley* (Urbana: University of Illinois Press, 1982).

39. Michel Foucault, *Discipline and Punish: The Birth of the Prison,* trans. Alan Sheridan (New York: Vintage Books, 1977).

40. Mills, *From Class to Race,* 217.

41. "Contract of Breach: Repairing the Racial Contract," in Carole Pateman and Charles W. Mills, *Contract and Domination* (Malden, MA: Polity, 2007), 106–133, 113.

42. Mills, *Blackness Visible,* 22.

43. I highlight that Mills conceives of it as a distributive solution because other scholars have attempted to think about reparations beyond distinct material goods distribution. Glenn Loury makes a distinction between reparations in 'compensatory' terms as compared to 'interpretive' terms, wherein recognition for suffering is the aim rather than payment (see *Anatomy of Racial Inequality* (Cambridge, MA: Harvard University Press, 2003), 126). Lawrie Balfour seems to pick up on this angle when she calls for reparations to subsidize a program of national historical acknowledgments of racism and racial injustice in "Reparations after Identity Politics," *Political Theory* 33, no. 6 (2005): 786–811.

CHAPTER 2

1. Amaad Rivera et al., *Foreclosed: State of the Dream 2008* (United for a Fair Economy, 2008). http://www.faireconomy.org/files/StateOfDream_01_16_08_Web.pdf.

2. As indicated at the end of this book's introduction, I here use the predicate 'democratic' to indicate a kind of agent we should be concerned with. Namely, one who has the confidence of being an equal citizen among others such that the ability to share in a morally important form of political life that provides space for autonomous action in pursuing the good of one's life and free participation in the political process is grounded in reasons for believing one's place in that life holds appropriate value.

3. See Melvin L. Oliver and Thomas M. Shapiro, *Black Wealth/White Wealth: A New Perspective on Racial Inequality,* 10th Anniversary Edition (New York: Routledge, 2006).

4. See Marie Gottschalk, *The Prison and the Gallows: The Politics of Mass Incarceration in America* (New York: Cambridge University Press, 2006). For an account of the origins of this development, see Vesla M. Weaver, "Frontlash: Race and the Development of Punitive Crime Policy," *Studies in American Political Development* 21 (2007): 230–265.

5. See Marianne Bertrand and Sendhil Mullainathan, "Are Emily and Brendan More Employable than Lakisha and Jamal? A Field Experiment on Labor Market Discrimination," *American Economic Review* 94, no. 4 (2004): 991–1013. Also see Devah Pager, *Marked: Race, Crime, and Finding Work in an Era of Mass Incarceration* (Chicago: University of Chicago Press, 2007). Although Pager's title topically deals with the ability of blacks with a criminal record to

find work, a significant finding is that in many cases black males with no record still did worse in securing job prospects than whites with a criminal record.

6. See Douglas S. Massey, "Segregation and Stratification: A Biosocial Perspective," *Du Bois Review* 1, no. 1 (2004): 7–25.

7. The reader may be unconvinced by my distinction, responding that an explanation for a real-world problem that affects actual people is certainly one that just is generating an empirical hypothesis. Surely this is right. My distinction, however, is meant to draw a particular kind of line. Justice talk in the hands of policy experts often works backward from material, resource, or opportunity inequality. Policy makers then tend to stop at whether a particular institutional procedure is conducive to adjusting the inequality, so, for example, if urban schools are dilapidated, then maybe the municipal budget needs to be recalibrated. But there are questions as to (1) why urban, black schools are in such a state, and (2) why local municipalities are often unresponsive to clearly bad circumstances? In this sense, so I press, we take a few more steps back to the domain of reasons and values that produce observable outcomes. Thus, the distinction helps us not only reflect on first-order causes—reasons and values—but directs our attention away from distributive measures in the first place, since they are likely to fail if the relevant agents do not perceive or affirm the appropriate reasons or values necessary to treat blacks as equals as per any principles of distributive or allocative justice.

8. Michael Dawson, "After the Deluge: Publics and Policy in Katrina's Wake," *Du Bois Review* 3, no. 1 (2006): 239–249.

9. See "The Negro Family: The Case for National Action." http://www.dol.gov/oasam/programs/history/webid-meynihan.htm.

10. For a representative version of the thesis as it circulated in the past forty years, see Edward Banfield, *The Unheavenly City: The Nature and Future of our Urban Crisis* (Boston: Little Brown and Co., 1970).

11. Tommie Shelby, "Justice, Deviance, and the Dark Ghetto," *Philosophy and Public Affairs* 35, no. 2 (2007): 126–160.

12. This is a line of thinking that informs Lisa Tessman, *Burdened Virtues: Virtue Ethics for Liberatory Struggles* (New York: Oxford University Press, 2005).

13. It is of some note that this view received its strongest statement shortly after Banfield published his book. See William Julius Wilson, *The Declining Significance of Race: Blacks and Changing American Institutions* (Chicago: University of Chicago Press, 1978). For a more contemporary view, see Oliver and Shapiro, *Black Wealth/White Wealth*. While Oliver and Shapiro are not strictly arguing that racial inequality is reducible to wealth inequality, they do take it as central and tend to treat it as a discrete phenomenon.

14. See Devah Pager, *Marked*.

15. Dawson, "After the Deluge," 240.

16. Ibid., 241.

17. John Rawls, *Justice as Fairness: A Restatement*, ed. Erin Kelly (Cambridge, MA: Belknap Press), 10.

18. John Rawls, *Political Liberalism* (New York: Columbia University Press, 1993), 271.

19. John Rawls, *A Theory of Justice* (Cambridge, MA: Belknap Press, 1999), 6.

20. Douglas North. *Institutions, Institutional Change, and Economic Performance* (New York: Cambridge University Press, 1990), 3.

21. Jim Sidanius and Felicia Pratto, *Social Dominance: An Intergroup of Social Hierarchy and Oppression* (New York: Cambridge University Press, 1999), 31.

22. Emile Durkheim, *The Division of Labor in Society,* trans. W. D. Halls (New York: Free Press, 1997).

23. Ibid., 33.

24. George Orwell, *Animal Farm* (New York: Harcourt Brace, 2003).

25. Ibid., 45.

26. Paul Pierson, "Not Just What, but When: Timing and Sequence in Political Processes," *Studies in American Political Development* 14 (2000): 76–77.

27. Ibid.

28. Paul Pierson, "Increasing Returns, Path Dependence, and the Study of Politics," *American Political Science Review* 94, no. 2 (2000): 254.

29. Ibid., 255.

30. Nancy Hirschmann, *The Subject of Liberty: Toward a Feminist of Freedom* (Princeton, NJ: Princeton University Press, 2002), 10.

31. See Jon Elster, *Sour Grapes: Studies in the Subversion of Rationality* (New York: Cambridge University Press, 1983).

32. Hirschmann, *Subject of Liberty*, 93.

33. Ibid., 11.

34. Ibid., 12.

35. See Eduardo Bonilla Silva, "Rethinking Racism: Towards A Structural Interpretation," *American Sociological Review* 62, no. 3 (1997): 465–480.

36. Mary Waters, *Black Identities: West Indian Immigrant Dreams and American Realities* (New York: Russell Sage, 1999).

37. Ibid., 285.

38. Ibid., 309.

39. Ibid., 301.

40. Ibid., 307.

41. Ibid. 310 (emphasis added).

42. W. E. B. Du Bois, *The Souls of Black Folks*, ed. Henry Louis Gates, Jr. and Terry Hume Oliver (New York: W. W. Norton & Company, 1999).

43. Claude M. Steele, "A Threat in the Air: How Stereotypes Shape Intellectual Identity and Performance," in *Confronting Racism: The Problem and the Response,* ed. Jennifer L. Eberhardt and Susan T. Fiske (Thousand Oaks, CA: Sage Publication, 1998), 202.

44. Claude M. Steele and Joshua Aronson, "Stereotype Threat and the Intellectual Test Performance of African Americans," *Journal of Personality and Social Psychology* 69, no. 5 (1995): 797.

45. Ibid.

46. It is important to note that when I say the subjects recognize the stereotype, I do not mean to invoke a conscious activity. Rather, as is the point of the study, certain cues, on some psychological level, bring to the fore the stereotype in question.

47. Steele, "A Threat In The Air." 215.

48. Steel and Aronson, "Stereotype Threat," 799.

49. Marcella Bombardieri, "Summers' Remarks on Women Draw Fire," *Boston Globe*, January 17, 2005. http://www.boston.com/news/local/articles/2005/01/17/summers_remarks_on_women_draw_fire.

50. Sidanius and Pratto, *Social Dominance*, 64.

CHAPTER 3

1. Winthrop Jordan, *White over Black: American Attitudes towards the Negro, 1550–1812* (Baltimore: Penguin Books, 1969), 66.

2. See Audrey Smedley, *Race in North America: Origin and Evolution of a Worldview*, 3d ed. (Boulder, CO: Westview Press, 2007).

3. Jordan, *White over Black*, 86.

4. Ibid., 95.

5. Michael L. Levine, *African Americans and Civil Rights: From 1619 to Present* (Phoenix: Oryx Press, 1996), 17.

6. Ibid., 18 (emphasis added).

7. Ibid., 20.

8. Jordan, *White over Black*, 85.

9. Levine, *African Americans and Civil Rights*, 26.

10. Ibid., 29.

11. Thurgood Marshall, "Reflections on the Bicentennial of the United States Constitution," *Harvard Law Review* 101, no. 1 (1987): 5.

12. Ibid., 2.

13. Philip A. Klinkner with Rogers Smith, *The Unsteady March: The Rise and Decline of Racial Inequality in America* (Chicago: University of Chicago Press, 1999), 24.

14. Don E. Fehrenbacher, *The Slaveholding Republic: An Account of the United States Government's Relation to Slavery* (New York: Oxford University Press, 2001), 25.

15. Levine, *African Americans and Civil Rights*, 91.

16. Quoted in Eric Foner, *Reconstruction: America's Unfinished Revolution* (New York: Harper & Row, 1988), 35–36 (emphasis added).

17. Ibid., 183; Klinkner, *The Unsteady March*, 77.

18. Richard Wormser, *The Rise and Fall of Jim Crow* (New York: St. Martin's Press, 2003), 13.

19. Dred Scott sued his initial slave master, John Emerson, for his freedom on account of his having been left to live in a free state. His first suit occurred in 1852 and focused on a new defendant, John Sandford, the executor of Emerson's estate. Scott lost the federal trial and appealed to the Supreme Court. In 1857 Taney upheld Scott's slave status.

20. Marshall, "Reflections on the Bicentennial," 4.

21. Ibid., 4.

22. Ibid.

23. It is worth pointing out what might be perceived as an imbalance between the presentation of the two cases, namely that the study of crime policy is accompanied by a rather robust explanatory framework while the investigation into welfare seems mostly descriptive. A main reason for this has to do with the nature of the two issue areas. Criminal justice is fundamentally a coercive institution, thus most scholars seeking to explain it, whether intentionally or not, have an operating view of power. Although, as will be seen, welfare has often been wielded as a tool of coercion, few

scholars have theorized it in terms of power. My mobilization of Lieberman's framework of institutional levels in welfare policy is meant to alleviate this to the extent that he offers a schematic of how welfare came to differ from other New Deal policies. The task of theorizing a deeper explanatory framework for welfare, while worthwhile, is too complex to attempt in this space. I rely instead on the reader's acceptance that an analytic description has embedded within it an explanation of the development of welfare policy though I will not always be able to stop and make it explicit.

24. Jim Sidanius and Felicia Pratto, *Social Dominance: An Intergroup of Social Hierarchy and Oppression* (New York: Cambridge University Press, 1999), 202.

25. Glenn Loury, *"Ghettos, Prisons and Racial Stigma," The Tanner Lectures on Human Values*, delivered April 4, 2007, 2 (emphasis added).

26. Sidanius and Pratto, *Social Dominance*, 31.

27. Ibid., 41.

28. Marie Gottschalk, *The Prison and the Gallows: The Politics of Mass Incarceration in America* (New York: Cambridge University Press, 2006), 1.

29. Ibid., 2.

30. Gottschalk, *The Prison and the Gallows*, 48.

31. Christopher Adamson, "Punishment after Slavery: Southern State Penal Systems, 1865–1890," *Social Problems* 30, no. 5 (1983): 556. See also J. Thorstein Sellin, *Slavery and the Penal System* (New York: Elsevier, 1976); Milfred C. Fierce, *Slavery Revisited: Blacks and the Southern Convict Lease System, 1865–1933* (New York: African Studies Research Center, 1994). For a comparative view of the development of criminal justice in the North and South, see Michael Stephen Hindus, *Prison and Plantation: Crime, Justice, and Authority in Massachusetts and South Carolina, 1767–1878* (Chapel Hill: University of North Carolina Press, 1980).

32. Ibid., 54.

33. Wormser, *The Rise and Fall of Jim Crow*, 57.

34. Klinkner, *The Unsteady March*, 91.

35. Douglas A. Blackmon, *Slavery by Another Name: The Re-enslavement of Black People in America from the Civil War to World War II* (New York: Doubleday, 2008), 1–2.

36. Vesla M. Weaver, "Frontlash: Race and the Development of Punitive Crime Policy," *Studies in American Political Development* 21 (2007): 230.

37. Ibid., 238.

38. Ibid., 236.

39. Ibid., 240–241.

40. Naomi Murakawa, "The Origins of the Carceral Crisis: Racial Order as 'Law and Order' in Postwar American Politics," in *Race and American Political Development*, ed. Joseph Lowndes, Julie Novkov, and Dorian T. Warren (New York: Routledge, 2008), 234–255.

41. Weaver, "Frontlash," 248.

42. Ibid., 240.

43. Ibid., 239.

44. Katherine Beckett, *Making Crime Pay: Law and Order in Contemporary American Politics* (New York: Oxford University Press, 1997), 33–34.

45. Weaver, "Frontlash."

46. Ibid., 254–256.

47. Michael Tonry, *Malign Neglect: Race, Crime, and Punishment in America* (New York: Oxford University Press, 1995), 19.

48. Weaver, "Frontlash," 260.

49. Ibid., 230.

50. Beckett, *Making Crime Pay*, 23 (emphasis added).

51. Sidanius et al., "Hierarchical Group Relations: Institutional Terror and the Dynamics of the Criminal Justice System" in *Confronting Racism: The Problem and the Response*. Eds. Jennifer L. Eberhard and Susan T. Fiske (New York: Sage Publications, 1998), pp. 136–168; p. 143.

52. The intersection of crime policy and drug offense is certainly not the only point of concern—it is offered here as one example of concerning trends. However, the drug trade is an interesting case in itself, for, as many have argued, the rise of drugs as a serious problem in America coincides, historically, with the steep rise in urban population. Moreover, the federal government became deeply involved with it just as the Civil Rights Movement came to a close.

53. The Human Rights Watch, *Targeting Blacks: Drug Law Enforcement and Race in the United States*, May 2008, 19.

54. Tonry, *Malign Neglect*, especially ch. 3. See also Marc Mauer, "Race, Class, and the Development of Criminal Justice Policy," *Review of Policy Research* 21, no. 1 (2004): 79–92.

55. The Sentencing Project, *Disparity by Geography: The War on Drugs in America's Cities*, May 2008, 2.

56. Andrew Hacker, *Two Nations: Black and White, Separate, Hostile, Unequal* (New York: Ballantine Books, 1995), 186.

57. Benjamin Fleury-Steiner, *Jurors' Studies of Death* (Ann Arbor: University of Michigan Press, 2004).

58. Loury, "Ghettos, Prisons, Racial Stigma," 21.

59. Weaver, "Frontlash," 230. For a useful analysis of racial disparities in criminal justice effects, see Becky Pettit and Bruce Western, "Mass Imprisonment and the Life Course: Race and Class Inequality in U.S. Incarceration," *American Sociology Review* 69 (2004): 151–169.

60. See "'Welfare Queen' Becomes Issue for Reagan Campaign," February 15, 1976. http://query.nytimes.com/mem/archive/pdf?res=FA0614FB395910728DDDAC0994DA405B868B F1D3.

61. Mary Poole, *The Segregated Origins of Social Security: African Americans and the Welfare State* (Chapel Hill: University of North Carolina Press, 2006), 22.

62. Ibid., 22.

63. Ibid., 18.

64. Ibid., 15.

65. Ibid., 25.

66. Jill Quadagno, *The Color of Welfare: How Racism Undermined the War on Poverty* (New York: Oxford University Press, 1994), 21.

67. Ira Katznelson, *When Affirmative Action Was White: An Untold Story of Racial Inequality in the Twentieth-Century America* (New York: W. W. Norton, 2005), 43.

68. Quadagno, *The Color of Welfare*, 21.

69. Katznelson, *When Affirmative Action Was White*, 43.

70. Poole, *The Segregated Origins of Social Security*, 23.

71. Martin Gilens, *Why Americans Hate Welfare: Race, Media, and the Politics of Antipoverty Policy* (Chicago: University of Chicago Press), 12.

72. Robert C. Lieberman, *Shifting the Color Line: Race and the American Welfare State* (Cambridge, MA: Harvard University Press, 1998), 11.

73. Ibid., 3.

74. Katznelson, *When Affirmative Action Was White*, 38.

75. Leslie H. Fishel, Jr. and Benjamin Quarles, "In the New Deal's Wake," in *The Segregation Era: A Modern Reader*, ed. Allen Weinstein and Frank Otto Gatell (New York: Oxford University Press, 1970), 221.

76. Lieberman, *Shifting the Color Line*, 127.

77. Katznelson, *When Affirmative Action Was White*, 46.

78. Gilens, *Why Americans Hate Welfare*, 105.

79. Lieberman, *Shifting the Color Line*, 48.

80. Ibid., 155.

81. Gilens, *Why Americans Hate Welfare*, 104–105.

82. Ibid., 105.

83. Ibid., 30.

84. Ibid., 113.

85. Ibid., 117.

86. Quadagno, *The Color of Welfare*, 120.

87. Lieberman, *Shifting the Color Line*, 169.

88. Quadagno, *The Color of Welfare*, 118.

89. Ibid., 124.

90. Walter I. Trattner, *From Poor Law to Welfare State: A History of Social Welfare in America*, 6th ed. (New York: Free Press, 1999), 375.

91. Ibid., 375.

92. Gilens, *Why Americans Hate Welfare*, 125.

93. Ibid., 126.

94. Jonathan Simon, "Sanctioning Government: Explaining America's Severity Revolution," *University of Miami Law Review* 56 (2001–2002): 227.

95. Linda Williams, *The Constraint of Race: The Legacy of White Skin Privilege in America* (University Park: Pennsylvania State University Press, 2003), 258–260.

96. Christopher Howard, *The Welfare State Nobody Knows: Debunking Myths about U.S. Social Policy* (Princeton, NJ: Princeton University Press, 2007), 187, table 9.1.

97. Waivers allow states to adopt their own policies for which the waiver is applicable.

98. Richard C. Fording, "'Laboratories of Democracy' of Symbolic Politics?" in *Race and the Politics of Welfare Reform*. Eds. Sanford F. Schram, Joe Soss, and Richard C. Fording (Ann Arbor: University of Michigan Press, 2003), 88, 89, figure 3.1. In same volume, see also Joe Soss et al., "The Hard Line and the Color Line: Race, Welfare, and the Roots of Get-Tough Welfare Reform," 225–253. For a historical account of the impact of fiscal federalism on this policy trend, see in the same volume Michael K. Brown, "Ghettos, Fiscal Federalism, and Welfare Reform," 47–71.

99. Jason DaPerle, "Welfare Aid Isn't Growing as Economy Drops Off," *New York Times*, February 1, 2009. http://www.nytimes.com/2009/02/02/us/02welfare.html.

CHAPTER 4

1. The reader may wonder about using a movie on the heels of engaging empirical facts of history, especially in light of my own concerns for attending to the reality of race. *Crash* is used here for a few very specific reasons. First, though inviting a longer conversation than one that can be

entertained here, we might begin by asking why it is that the typical African-American Studies department devotes a great of its resources for understanding race to the study of literature and cinema. A main reason is that historically, the arts have been one of the few places blacks have been able to convey the experience of race having historically been blocked from becoming faculty, for example. This has, in my view, bequeathed to the arts the status as being a place for the analysis and elucidation of the complexities of black life. Thus, there is way to understand the possibility of cinema and literature serving as a kind of empirical resource. Second, the issue of character, virtues, and so on is what social scientists might call "squishy." In other words, quantifying who has better and worse character on some scale, let's say, is next to impossible, thus turning to strictly social scientific work only introduces another layer of complexity. I turn, then, to a movie that is fairly well-known and that engages in reasonable and imaginative interpretation of a problem that requires more than a little bit of imagination to clearly grasp. Third, it turns out that there is a fair bit of sympathy between my view of how we might get the typical American to face race and that of the movie's writer and director. In his own words: "With Crash, I just wanted to fuck viewers up. I want to sit you down in your seat and make you feel really, really comfortable with everything you believe. All those secret little thoughts you have, I wanted to say, 'Shh, shh, it's fine. We all think that way.' And as soon as you get comfortable, I wanted to start twisting you around in your seat, until when you walk out, you didn't know what the hell to think" http://www.progressive.org/mag_haggis0108. And, extending this sentiment in a manner consistent with this book's concern to activate people's own reflective capacities on their own account: "I don't think it's the job of filmmakers to give anybody answers. I do think, though, that a good film makes you ask questions of yourself as you leave the theatre. The ones that are a total experience in themselves, where you leave the theatre going, 'Yeah, nice film,' I think are failures" http://www.bbc.co.uk/films/2005/07/29/paul_haggis_crash_interview.shtml. In this sense, a good film is an ideal partner to ethical inquiry.

2. Danielle S. Allen, *Talking to Strangers: Anxieties of Citizenship since Brown v. Board of Education* (Chicago: University of Chicago Press, 2004). I engage Allen more directly in the final chapter.

3. I mean to make a very purposeful distinction between "flawed" and "damaged"—the terms are not equivalent. Persons who are damaged are understood as once being capable of functioning along some (psychologically or emotionally) relevant dimension but have been so thoroughly affected by exposure to dire, extreme, or abusive circumstances that there is little chance of regaining the kind of functioning in question. Here, think of a child who watched his father beat his mother so ruthlessly and consistently that he is incapable of giving or receiving physical affection. However, the notion of flawed occupies a less determinative ground. To be flawed retains the idea of having the capacity but failing to fully and/or consistently act from that capacity in the appropriate manner. The distinction is important: flawed individuals, when prompted and upon acknowledging the prompt, can reconfigure their way of being and living in order to correct for that flaw thus bringing them into right relationship with the capacity in question.

4. A second, more cynical point is that violence makes for great commercial movie watching, so we might imagine *Crash*, as novel, wherein Tom rescinds his initial invitation to Peter by expelling him from his car in the middle of the road. In some senses, this would have been more consistent with the film's reflective temperament as it would have visually captured fluctuations and shifts between social nearness and social casting-off.

5. For example, see Lawrence Bobo and Ryan Smith, *"From Jim Crow Racism to Laissez-Faire Racism."* In *Beyond Pluralism: The Conception of Groups and Group Identities in America*. Eds. Wendy F. Katkin, Ned Landsman & And Andrea Tyree (Urbana: University of Illinois Press. 1998).

6. Barbara Herman, *Moral Literacy* (Cambridge, MA: Harvard University Press, 2007), esp. ch. 5.

7. I want to caveat this argument, for I do not mean to say that intentionality is a necessary condition of immorality. It is an ongoing and interesting question as to how far the bounds of complicity extend and what exactly makes a person's hands dirty in the problem of dirty hands (i.e., soldiers ordered by commanders in a democratic regime to undertake morally dubious acts). However, I do want to make the following claim, though I cannot stop to defend it—there is a significant difference between the problem of dirty hands and implicit racism. One way of understanding that difference is that the beliefs comprising implicit racism reside within the agent's belief structure, whereas the act of following orders is exactly that—the agent has no or minimal ownership over his or her reasons for action.

8. Lisa Tessman, *Burdened Virtues: Virtue Ethics for Liberatory Struggles* (New York: Oxford University Press, 2005), 56.

9. On my reading of Tessman, the fundamental ordinary vice that prevents cultivating proper virtues is indifference, a notion that expresses close parallels to the propositions contained within white privilege. She writes, "Believing in one's own moral goodness regardless of its actual absence is facilitated by what I think of as a 'meta-vice,' namely, indifference or, more specifically, indifference to the (preventable and unjust) suffering of certain others" (ibid., 79).

10. This phrase is a flourish on the title of Barbara Herman's paper quoted below.

11. Barbara Herman, "Morality and Everyday Life," *Proceedings and Addresses of the American Philosophical Association* 74, no. 2 (2000): 29–45, 34 (emphasis in original).

12. Although I want to note that this is likely to be only one facet of the story. The life experiences that have led Tom to be the kind of person he is are likely to be varied and interconnected across a wide range of experiences.

13. Jeremy Kang, "Trojan Horses of Race," *Harvard Law Review* 118 (2005): 1489–1593.

14. Ibid., 1549–1550.

15. Miranda Fricker, "Powerlessness and Social Interpretation," *Episteme* 3 (2006): 96–108, 96. For an extended treatment of this theme, see Miranda Fricker, *Epistemic Injustice: Power and the Ethics of Knowing* (New York: Oxford University Press, 2009).

16. See Douglass S. Massey and Nancy A. Denton, *American Apartheid: Segregation and the Making of the American Underclass*. (Cambridge, MA: Harvard University Press, 1993).

17. Tommie Shelby, "Justice, Deviance, and the Dark Ghetto," *Philosophy and Public Affairs* 35, no. 2 (2007): 126–160.

18. Claudia Card, *The Unnatural Lottery: Character and Moral Luck* (Philadelphia: Temple University Press, 1996). For example: "I am skeptical of Kant's apparent assumption that the same basic character development is accessible to everyone. Even if his optimistic belief that everyone has opportunities to become good contains more truth than some would admit, I doubt that the opportunities are the same for everyone, that the level of difficulty is the same, and, consequently, that the goodness available to us is likely to take the same forms" (4). See also Iris Marion Young, *Responsibility for Justice* (New York: Oxford University Press, 2011).

19. Bernard Williams, *Moral Luck* (New York: Cambridge University Press, 1981); Thomas Nagel, "Moral Luck" in *Mortal Questions* (New York: Cambridge University Press, 1979), 24–38. In their respective works, Nagel and Williams take up the question whether various forms of luck either undermine or have the potential to radically amend typical kinds of moral judgment (i.e., if a drunk driver kills a young child on the way home, it could just be bad luck that the child walked into the street at that moment—30 seconds earlier and the driver would have made it home without incident). If so, the question that is thought to follow is: What worth do our moral judgments have if a lot of the outcomes in our lives could be explained by various kinds of luck, since it seems the driver is not actually guilty of a wrongdoing, just subject to bad luck?

20. Tessman, *Burdened Virtues*, 4.

21. Fricker, "Powerlessness and Social Interpretation," 96.

22. See Elijah Anderson, *Code of the Street: Decency, Violence, and the Moral Life of the Inner City* (New York: W. W. Norton, 2000), Kindle edition. In this work Anderson describes how notions like respect, while familiar to most persons, acquire a different valence for urban youths such that pursuing respect, given the conditions in which they find themselves often leads to confrontation, thus violence.

23. So far as I am aware, the debate that comes closest to making the issue of personal character relevant for justice comes out of G. A. Cohen's criticism of Rawls. See G. A. Cohen, "Where the Action Is: On the Site of Distributive Justice," *Philosophy & Public Affairs* 26, no. 1 (1997): 3–30. In his article Cohen believes that Rawls's ideal society is ultimately unjust. Cohen calls to account Rawls's insistence that a just society depends on persons acquiring the appropriate sense of justice. However, on Cohen's view, one of Rawls's main justifications for the difference principle (an economic distributive principle that redistributes wealth from the most well-off to the least advantaged but nonetheless allows for a great deal of inequality) is that inequality is necessary to provide material incentives such that while the wealthy will be much more wealthy than the less advantaged, this nevertheless helps to expand the total pool of goods available for distributive measures. Cohen argues that persons who genuinely affirm the principles of justice do not require the material incentives provided by Rawls's difference principle. Thus, one might surmise from his criticisms that a just society fundamentally depends on agents whose characters possess certain virtues, such as altruism, that deny the need for material inducements. Such a society will then be just not merely because more people have equal shares of primary goods but because that is how the typical citizen really believes people just ought to have equal shares of primary goods.

24. Aristotle, *Nicomachean Ethics*, trans. Martin Ostwald (Indianapolis: Liberal Arts Press, 1962), 33.

25. Joel J. Kupperman, "Virtues, Character, and Moral Dispositions," in *Virtue Ethics and Moral Education*, ed. David Carr and Jan Steutel (New York: Routledge, 1999), 202.

26. Ibid., 203.

27. Herman, *Moral Literacy*, vii.

28. Ibid., 1.

29. See Michael Dawson, "After The Deluge: Publics and Policy in Katrina's Wake" in *Du Bois Review* 3 no. 1 (2006), pp. 239–249.

30. See respectively Marianne Bertrand and Sendhil Mullainathan, "Are Emily and Brendan More Employable than Lakisha and Jamal? A Field Experiment on Labor Market Discrimination," *American Economic Review* 94, no. 4 (2004): 991–1013; and Mark Peffley and Jon Hurwitz,

"Persuasion and Resistance: Race and the Death Penalty in America," *American Journal of Political Science* 51, no. 4 (2007): 996–1012.

31. Herman, *Moral Literacy*, 99.

32. Ibid., 100.

CHAPTER 5

1. "Return of the King." *Boondocks*. Written: Aaron McGruder and Yamara Taylor. Cartoon Network. 15 January 2006.

2. This sentence is inspired by Richard H. Thaler and Cass R. Sunstein, *Nudge: Improving Decisions about Health, Wealth, and Happiness* (New York: Penguin Press, 2009).

3. In making a distinction between theoretical justification and what I have called political justification, I do not mean to make political consideration devoid of theoretical considerations. Indeed, on my own view, there is a great degree of mutual dependence. All I mean to do in making this distinction is draw our attention to a different kind of mutual dependence—that between methods of theory building and the contours of an empirical problem. In drawing our attention to political justification as distinct, I mean to indicate the ways our practices can appropriately contextualize our moral judgments.

4. Joseph Raz, *The Morality of Freedom* (Oxford: Clarendon Press, 1986).

5. Ibid., 140-141.

6. Ibid., 141.

7. Ibid., 371.

8. Thomas Hobbes, *Leviathan,* Revised Student Edition (New York: Cambridge University Press, 1996).

9. This view is present even in the work of deliberative democrats, who often do not invoke "thick" ethical concepts such as character or virtue. For example, Joshua Cohen writes: "The members of the association share…the view that the appropriate terms of association provide a framework for or are the results of their deliberation. They share, that is, a commitment to co-ordinating their activities within institutions that make deliberation possible and according to norms that they arrive at through their deliberation," in "Deliberative Democracy and Democratic Legitimacy," in *The Good Polity: Normative Analysis of the State*, ed. Alan Hamlin and Philip Pettit (Oxford: Blackwell, 1989), 17–34, 21.

10. Jeffrey Stout, *Democracy and Tradition*, New Forum Books (Princeton, NJ:: Princeton University Press, 2004), Kindle edition, 225.

11. Danielle Allen, *Talking to Strangers* (Chicago: University of Chicago Press, 2004), Kindle edition. She uses the term "epiphanic moment."

12. Ibid., 18.

13. Frederick Douglass, "What, to the Slave is the Fourth of July?" in *Great Speeches by African Americans*, ed. James Daley (Mineola, NY: Dover Publications, 2006), 18.

14. Ibid., 15.

15. Jason Frank, *"Staging Dissensus: Frederick Douglass and 'We, the People'"* in *Law and Agonistic Politics*, ed. Andrew Schaap (Farnham: Ashgate Publishing, 2009), 87–104, 92.

16. Douglass, "What, to the Slave," 21.

17. Ibid., 14 (emphasis added).

18. Ibid., 20.

19. Ibid., 29–30 (emphasis added).

20. Ibid., 30 (emphasis added).

21. Ibid., 26.

22. Ibid.

23. Ibid., 21.

24. Richard Arneson, "Shame, Stigma, and Disgust in the Decent Society," *Journal of Ethics* 11 (2007): 31–63, 32. Arneson offers his view to contest Martha Nussbaum's discomfort with "shame" language in *Hiding from Humanity: Disgust, Shame, and the Law* (Princeton, NJ: Princeton University Press, 2006).

25. Here, I do not mean to offer an endorsement of shame tactics for all crimes or for patronizing sex-workers in particular. Rather, I want to signal the nature of the considerations in play to in turn signal their appropriateness for racial inequality understood as the problem of social value.

26. See *Political Liberalism.* (New York: Columbia University Press, 1993).

27. Rawls writes: "The fact of a plurality of reasonable but incompatible comprehensive doctrines—the fact of reasonable pluralism—shows that, as used in *Theory*, the idea of well-ordered society of justice as fairness is unrealistic. This is because it is inconsistent with realizing its own principles under the best of foreseeable conditions" (*Political Liberalism*, xix).

28. See David McCabe, "Knowing about the Good: A Problem with Antiperfectionism," *Ethics* 110, no. 2 (2000): 311–338.

29. Corey Brettschneider, "The Value Theory of Democracy," *Politics, Philosophy & Economics* 5, no. 3 (2006): 259–278, 261.

30. Corey Brettschneider, "The Politics of the Personal: A Liberal Approach," *American Political Science Review* 101, no. 1 (2007): 19–31.

31. Ibid., 25.

32. The background argument implied here is something to the effect: institutions are already in the business of promoting racial values—why not turn them to the cause of promoting good ones? Susan Bickford offers a parallel argument for allowing institutions to take part in shaping identity: "The major reason *why* it is important to interact with and intervene in state processes is that current institutions of representation already shape citizen identity and its worldly manifestations." See "Reconfiguring Pluralism: Identity and Institutions in the Inegalitarian Polity," *American Journal of Political Science* 43, no. 1 (1999): 86–108, 95 (emphasis in original).

33. For instance, as found in Quine: "The interlocked conceptual scheme of physical objects, identity, and divided reference is part of the ship which, in Neurath's figure, we cannot remodel save as we stay afloat in it. The ontology of abstract objects is part of the ship too, if only a less fundamental part. The ship may owe its structure partly to blundering predecessors who missed scuttling it only by fool's luck. But we are not in a position to jettison any part of it, except as we have substitute devices ready to hand that will serve the same essential purposes" (*Word and Object*, (Cambridge, MA: MIT Press, 1960), 123–124).

34. The Nineteenth Amendment was passed in 1918.

35. Some fairly astonishing images can be seen here: http://www.youtube.com/watch?v=S38VioxnBaI.

36. Michael Janofsky, "Philadelphia Mandates Black History for Graduation," *New York Times*, June 25, 2005. http://www.nytimes.com/2005/06/25/education/25philly.html.

37. See Henry Louis Gates Jr.'s introduction in *Lincoln on Race and Slavery*, ed. Henry Louis Gates and Donald Yacovone (Princeton, NJ: Princeton University Press, 2011).

38. One possibility that is likely to come to the reader's mind is that of truth commissions: institutional mechanisms whereby past and recent past wrongs are not punished through punitive measures; rather, it is thought socially beneficial that the truth of the violations be publicly aired and admitted in a forum devoted to the pursuit of historical truth (i.e., which political figure gave the order to raze a village to which soldier, and so on). Here, the idea of truth is typically paired with "reconciliation" as it is thought that publicizing the truth of systematic wrongs facilitates forgiving one's former enemies, as well as vindicating the plight of victims at a very fundamental level—in the eyes of those with whom a social and political life is shared daily. Two facts about truth commissions are worth noting. First, they have typically been relied upon in countries where there were concentrated atrocities such as South Africa's attempt to come to terms with apartheid terror. Second, while racial inequality has been a serious feature of American society for over two hundred years, in the past fifty years, there has yet to be an event on the order of genocide to motivate the development of truth commissions, with the notable exception of the Greensboro commission. See Lisa Magarrell and Joya Wesley, *Learning from Greensboro* (Philadelphia: University of Pennsylvania Press, 2008). And there may be good reasons for this. The one I want to flag has to do with matching the structure of truth commissions to the structure of racial inequality as the problem of social value. While racial inequality is a moral problem that would in many instances justify the development of a truth commission due to the important moral, and sometimes nonmaterial questions in mind, it is striking that it is mostly unclear what any particular truth commission on racial inequality would endeavor to uncover that is already not statistically known. The problem here is consistent with that flagged in the introductory chapter: systemic racial inequality is problematic in large part because of its wide and deep reach into blacks' lives across so many spheres and life experiences. Now one may acknowledge that and insist that truth commissions might yet be useful for particular instances of, let's say, police abuse, but I am not sure we should follow that line of thinking. Another reason truth commissions are relied upon in cases like genocide is because the wrongdoing was so intense and grossly committed that the possibility of holding trials is unrealistic. However, in instances of police abuse or real estate steering or employment discrimination, it seems the possibility of holding a criminal trial is entirely plausible if not more morally appropriate. Additionally, because racial inequality is systemic and not typically motivated at such a broad level by particular orders or instructions given by political, social, or economic elites, it is unclear whom we would be bringing to account at a commission hearing, and without an agent to acknowledge responsibility for wrongful agency, it seems to me the potency of a truth commission begins to weaken. With respect to the moral grounds of truth commissions, see Amy Gutmann and Dennis Thompson, *"The Moral Foundations of Truth Commissions,"* in *Truth vs. Justice,* ed. Robert I. Rotberg and Dennis Thompson (Princeton, NJ: Princeton University Press, 2000).

39. The principle, as characterized, is sure to raise concerns over First Amendment rights, especially regarding freedom of speech. As stated, the principle sanctions the suppression of some expression while sharply regulating other forms of expression. The concern likely to arise will be something to the effect: Are justice and explicit curtailments of freedom of expression and speech compatible? In a word: yes. The easiest way to understand how so is by observing the many ways we already curtail freedom of expression. We allow pornography (though it remains controversial in some debates), but we outlaw child pornography. Why? Besides that it is intuitively repulsive, it leads to the harm of children. Moreover, it engages them in an activity requiring consent before they have reached an age where they could possibly understand what that kind of consent to

pornography entails. The primary principle here, though, revolves around harm: one's freedom reaches its limit at another's potential for harm. Now, the case of child pornography might seem too easy. The hard questions are cases where it is less clear that my freedom is harming you as compared to expressing a view you simply do not like. On this view, the fact that I am here willing to curtail the number of times blacks are perceived as drug dealers appears to fall into the latter category—I do not appreciate that portrayal so I would rather it be limited. But this conclusion is a mistake for reasons that have been indicated in a number of conversations leading to this point. As indicated by our reflections on institutional influences on our attitudes and the fact that blacks are portrayed in certain ways that comport with historical narratives of deviance and so on, it seems clear that persistently portraying blacks as criminals is more than a matter of artistic license. Such portrayals do not merely express the artistic vision of the director or writer but are conduits for long-standing and unfair characterizations of a whole population that then become a part of the public narrative about the nature of black morality and responsibility. This strikes me clearly as a harm, thus it seems to me that such measures are entirely justified in principle.

40. Other relevant concerns could be residential red-lining, discriminatory small loan practices, access to essential services like health care, as well as systematic poor quality of public schools in certain demographically distinct areas.

41. Reenah L. Kim, "Legitimizing Community Consent to Local Policing: The Need for Democratically Negotiated Community Representation on Civilian Advisory Councils," *Harvard Civil Rights–Civil Liberties Law Review* 36 (2001): 461–525, 477 n. 63.

42. See Michael E. Buerger, "The Limits of Community," in *The Challenge of Community Policing: Testing the Promises. Ed. Dennis P. Rosenblum* (New York: Sage, 1994), 270–271; 270–273.

EPILOGUE

1. http://vimeo.com/18413741.

2. Few phenomena capture this more powerfully than the intersection of democratic life and lynching. See Melvin Rogers, "Race and the Democratic Aesthetic: Jefferson, Whitman, and Holiday on the Hopeful and the Horrific," working paper.

3. Saigon, "The Invitation," *The Greatest Story Never Told* (Suburban Noize Records, 2011).

4. For example, see Michael Tonry, *Malign Neglect: Race, Crime, and Punishment in America* (New York: Oxford University Press, 1995).

5. Vesla M. Weaver, "Frontlash: Race and the Development of Punitive Crime Policy," *Studies in American Political Development* 21 (2007): 230–265, 236.

6. Ibid., 238.

7. Ibid., 238.

8. Michelle Alexander. *The New Jim Crow: Mass Incarceration in the Age of Colorblindness* (New York: New Press, 2012), Kindle edition, 6.

9. Ibid., 20.

10. Ibid., 120.

11. http://cnninsession.files.wordpress.com/2012/03/martinpolicreport.pdf.

12. http://www.thegrio.com/specials/trayvon-martin/whites-are-mostly-missing-at-trayvon-martin-rallies.php.

13. http://www.hiphopdx.com/index/news/id.19153/title.david-banner-speaks-about-the-lack-of-fear-and-respect-in-response-to-trayvon-martins-murder-and-his-2m1-movement.

14. Melvin L. Oliver and Thomas M. Shapiro, *Black Wealth/White Wealth: A New Perspective on Racial Inequality, 10th Anniversary Edition* (New York: Routledge, 2006).

15. Marianne Bertrand and Sendhil Mullainathan, "Are Emily and Brendan More Employable than Lakisha and Jamal? A Field Experiment on Labor Market Discrimination," *American Economic Review* 94, no. 4 (2004): 991–1013.

16. Tommie Shelby, "Justice, Deviance, and the Dark Ghetto," *Philosophy and Public Affairs* 35, no. 2 (2007): 126–160.

17. Ibid., 150.

ACKNOWLEDGMENTS

⌒───

WRITING A BOOK is curious mix of solitary effort and communal support. In the end, only the author can be held responsible for the quality and coherence of a book, but in important respects the author is not ultimately responsible for the book a reader holds in terms of the product it represents. Indeed, a book is a product of reflection, trial and error, consultation, imagination, ambition, and necessity. *The Color of Our Shame: Race and Justice in Our Time* almost did not see the light of day. It began life as an overly ambitious dissertation inelegantly titled. "Race, Power, History, and Justice in America." I am not ashamed to say that the dissertation did not pass the bar I had set for it, but it did provide me with a wealth of lessons learned—lessons that were honed, with the generous support of a group of scholars and friends, to present to you a product that is a very different thing than the nascent effort represented by my dissertation. The trail of gratitude begins with my dissertation committee who entertained my ambitions while trying to reel in the unfocused energy I committed to my project as a graduate student: Joshua Cohen, Sarah Song, Melissa Nobles, and Tommie Shelby. And additional gratitude to Tommie for serving as a kind and insightful mentor beyond the duty of advising my dissertation. Indeed, Tommie first began to take me under his wing while I was an undergraduate and had the opportunity to present a poster at a major conference; he remembered me from a fleeting earlier meeting at my undergraduate institution, and though it was late in the evening, he sat with me and discussed the process of applying and attending graduate school—I am deeply grateful for the time he took that evening and the continued faith he has shown in my abilities. During and after the completion of the Ph.D., there were those who were generous in sharing their time and thoughts with me even though they barely knew me: Jeff Spinner-Halev, Sharon Krause, Burke Hendrix, and Melissa Williams. While an assistant professor at the department of Politics at the University of Virginia I received support to host a manuscript workshop which came at a point in my process where I had taken the project as far as I could without external perspectives to prompt critical reflection; yet, the project was certainly far from "done." I called on a group of four exceptional scholars who answered that call with humbling generosity of heart and collegial spirit: Susan Bickford, Ian Ward, Melvin Rogers, and Rogers Smith. I would like to take the time to further express my gratitude to Rogers Smith—I reached out to Rogers as a third year graduate student who had little more than a lot of pages upon which were typed out a kind of philosophical manifesto, if it could even be called that. Rogers responded not by reading the work and sending me a kind but brief email as many would have; rather, he responded by making a phone appointment with me during which we spoke at length about what I had written. At that moment Rogers provided an exemplary model of what it means to extend a helping hand to junior scholars, and it is a model I hope to reproduce in my own habits. If we are lucky, we sometimes come across a colleague whose brilliance illuminates whatever room he or she enters. If we're very lucky, that colleague chooses to take an interest in our work, thus shedding some of that light on us and our efforts. And if we're extremely lucky, that person becomes a steadfast walking partner, ensuring that every step we take is well-considered and firmly planted. Melvin Rogers became that walking partner and I owe a great deal to him as he insisted that I be more true to my own vision of the book than I at times in fact was. He is not only an incredible colleague but a dear friend for whom I am deeply grateful. Clarissa Hayward and Corey Brettschneider served as something of a last line of defense against mediocrity by taking the time to provide quite extensive comments and suggestions in the book's final stages. Oxford University Press has been an incredible partner in the publishing process and I'd like to express a special sentiment of appreciation to my editor, Angela Chnapko, whose professionalism and support for the book have been more than I could have hoped for. This book's Epilogue was originally published by *Theory & Event* for their timely symposium reflecting on the shooting of Trayvon Martin (15, no. 3, 2012). While our professional colleagues do a great deal to help us reach our goals, family and friends are important. I almost didn't make it to graduate school—as with many minority students, my performance on the revered yet irrelevant GRE's were substandard for the programs I aspired to join. At the time, my personal financial situation—as with many aspiring minority students—was very insecure. Though I had been an excellent undergraduate student and had taken on high-level independent research projects, my initial GRE scores seemed a final impediment to my aspirations. At the time I lacked the money to take the exam again, but Sunil Maragh—my friend (my brother)—of more than twenty years wrote me a check without hesitation. I subsequently performed better on my second attempt and it is an open question whether I would have even been able to enter M.I.T. without that second attempt. I shall never forget that. My book, as you may have by now realized, is in some respects an exercise in rebellion and at times barely contained contempt for the injustices that plague American society. My parents, Frank Lebron and Minerva Rivera, are in many ways to thank for this—they never (and I mean, never) prevented me from being my own person, from seeking my own solutions to problems, from walking my own path even when they suspected I was walking in the wrong direction. Additionally, I learned the virtues of respect, courtesy, and compassion for others from both of them—these are virtues I certainly possess in an imperfect manner, but I am aware that they are virtues, thus to whatever extent those virtues display themselves in this book, they are to thank. I have been fortunate to have generous colleagues, steadfast friends, and remarkable parents. But my most relied upon and valued daily blessing during this book's genesis consists in having a life partner whose inspiration continuously motivates me to be my best. Vesla Weaver has been by my side since my early grad school days and had faith in me, my vision, and my abilities when many people didn't. But beyond her support, the remarkable brilliance of her mind represented in her own first-rate scholarship serves as a beacon for my aspirations and serves to keep me honest about the work required to realize the vision I set out for my research. Finally, I would like to thank my son, Lennox Grey Lebron-Weaver. He entered my life late in the project but at a time when I still had the opportunity to surrender to a kind of cynicism about people's capacity to be better. His inner beauty, perfection, and goodness are among the last and strongest influences on my hope that our society can achieve the goodness necessary to treat people decently.

C.J.L.

INDEX

Note: Page numbers followed by an italicized *n* indicate material found in Notes. Italicized names indicate fictional characters.

CPSIA information can be obtained
at www.ICGtesting.com
Printed in the USA
BVHW031423241118
533777BV00004B/18/P